The Logic of Delegation

American Politics and Political Economy Series
Edited by Benjamin I. Page

The Logic of Delegation

Congressional Parties and the Appropriations Process

D. Roderick Kiewiet and Mathew D. McCubbins

The University of Chicago Press   Chicago and London

D. RODERICK KIEWIET, professor of political science at the California Institute of Technology, is the the author of *Macroeconomics and Micropolitics: The Electoral Effects of Economic Issues*, published by the University of Chicago Press. MATHEW D. McCUBBINS is a professor of political science at the University of California at San Diego and is coeditor of *Congress: Structure and Policy.*

The University of Chicago Press, Chicago 60637
The University of Chicago Press, Ltd., London
©1991 by The University of Chicago
All rights reserved. Published 1991.
Printed in the United States of America

00 99 98 87 96 95 94 93 92 91   5 4 3 2 1

Library of Congress Cataloging-in-Publication Data

Kiewiet, D. Roderick.
    The logic of delegation: Congressional parties and the appropriations process / D. Roderick Kiewiet and Mathew D. McCubbins.
        p.   cm.—(American politics and political economy series)
    Includes bibliographical references and index.
    ISBN 0–226–43529–6 (cloth)—ISBN 0–226–43531–8 (pbk).
    1. United States. Congress—Committees. 2. United States.
Congress—Leadership. 3. Delegated legislation—United States.
4. Party discipline—United States. 5. Budget—Political aspects—United States. 6. United States—Appropriations and expenditures.
I. McCubbins, Mathew D. (Mathew Daniel), 1956–   . II. Title.
III. Series: American politics and political economy.
JK1029.K54   1991
328.73'0769—dc20   90-21019
                                                         CIP

To Jo Thielen and HungLay and Peggy Quon

Contents

Figures

Tables

Acknowledgments

We would like to thank the research assistants who have worked with us on this project: Scott Ainsworth, Marla Davison, Michael Greenberg, Sharyn O'Halloran, Bill Laury, David Moon, Suisheng Zhao, Brian Sala, Kenneth Williams, and especially David Falleck and Eric Claus, who collected much of the raw data. We thank Keith Poole for providing us with his data on congressional members' NOMINATE scores and Samuel Bookheimer for sending us his appropriations data. We would also like to thank George Pigman, Pamela Easley, Eloisa Imel, Tom Boyce, Debbie McGougan, Carol Pearson, Phyllis Pugh, Marty Hertzel, and Kathryn Kraynik for their assistance in preparing this book for publication.

We have benefited from the comments, criticisms, and advice provided by a large number of friends and colleagues, who are listed in alphabetical order: Joel Aberbach, Jim Alt, Stanley Bach, Kim Border, Tom Brock, Bruce Cain, Gary Cox, Lance Davis, Bob Erickson, Richard Fenno, John Ferejohn, Morris Fiorina, Gary Jacobson, Sam Kernell, Morgan Kousser, John Ledyard, Nick Masters, Gary Miller, Douglass North, Peter Ordeshook, H. L. Perry, Charles Plott, Keith Poole, David Rohde, Howard Rosenthal, Thomas Schwartz, Kenneth Shepsle, Steven Smith, Matt Spitzer, Charles Stewart, Barry Weingast, Joe White, Rick Wilson, and Chris Wlezian. We are particularly indebted to Roger Noll, who, after reading early drafts of some of the chapters, was able to tell us what this book is really about. That this book has been published now (as opposed to considerably later) is due largely to the efforts of our editor, John Tryneski.

Finally, we thank the California Institute of Technology, the University of Texas, the Business School at Washington University, and the University of California at San Diego for the support they provided us. Mr. McCubbins acknowledges the support of the National Science Foundation, grants SES–8421161 and SES–8811022.

CHAPTER ONE

Introduction

Congressional Parties and the Abdication Hypothesis

Few institutions have received as much disparaging comment from the political science community as the party organizations in the U.S. Congress. Indeed, the upshot of much scholarly criticism is that "organization" is too generous a term to use for such amorphous agglomerations of individuals. According to their detractors, congressional parties, unlike their parliamentary counterparts, cannot muster unified blocs of votes to enact policies espoused in the preceding election. In the absence of "responsible" parties in the Westminster mold, policy-making in Congress becomes subject to great uncertainty and instability. Majorities that coalesce to enact a piece of legislation are fleeting and ad hoc. Whatever stamp the majority party might put on legislation is further obscured by the tendency for winning coalitions to take the form of vast logrolls encompassing more than 90 percent of the members of both parties (Collie 1988).

Not surprisingly, those seeking to measure the influence of political parties upon national policy in this country have almost always premised their analyses upon which party controlled the presidency, and not upon the partisan balance on Capitol Hill (Hibbs 1977; Cameron 1978; Tufte 1978). The most influential formal analyses of legislative structures abstract away any policy-making role for parties. Weingast and Marshall's (1988) "industrial organization" model of Congress, for example, explicitly assumes that "parties place no constraints on the behavior of individual representatives" (p. 6). Dodd and Oppenheimer (1977) put it this way:

> Throughout most of the postwar years, political parties in Congress have been weak, ineffectual organizations. Power in Congress has rested in the committees or, increasingly, in the subcommittees ... Party leaders have existed primarily to assist in smoothing the flow of legislation and mediating conflict, not to provide policy leadership and coordination. The parties themselves—particularly the House Democratic party—have been loose coalitions of convenience, not programmatic, cohesive organizations dedicated to enacting a specified set of policies. In many ways, political parties in Congress during the postwar years, as one observer has written, have been "phantoms" of scholarly imagination that were perhaps best exorcised from attempts to explain congressional organization, behavior, and process. (p. 41)

Virtually all features of the American polity have been implicated as factors contributing to the shortcomings of congressional parties—federalism, the separation of powers, and single-member plurality districts, among others (Brady 1989, pp. 8–9). In much of the scholarly criticism, however, there is a sense that the shortcomings and limitations of congressional parties, especially those of the majority party, are largely self-imposed. The frustrating thing, as far as many are concerned, is that the majority party could be an effective policy-making force if only it would pull itself together and act like a majority. Instead, the dominant role in policy-making is habitually assigned to others—internally to standing committees and subcommittees within each chamber, externally to the president and to the bureaucracy (Lowi 1979).

Many congressional scholars attribute the willingness to engage in delegation primarily to electoral considerations. In the delegation of legislative authority to standing committees, the scholarly consensus is that members of Congress, keen on maximizing their reelection prospects, demand assignments to committees whose jurisdictions coincide with the interests of key groups in their districts; thus the more clout committees have, the better. Parties, in contrast, are "more useful for what they are not than for what they are" (Mayhew 1974, p. 97). According to Fiorina (1982), Congress's delegation of legislative functions to the president and to the bureaucracy also grows out of electoral motives. Here, however, delegation facilitates the avoidance of blame rather than the taking of credit. Aware that most policies entail both costs and benefits, and fearful that those bearing the costs will hold them responsible, members of Congress often find that the most attractive option is to let someone else make the tough calls. Shifting responsibility for policy-making to others creates some "political daylight between the legislators and those who feel the incidence of legislative actions" (Fiorina 1982, p. 19).

Others view congressional delegation to the president and to the bureaucracy as unavoidable (and even desirable) in light of basic structural flaws in the design of Congress. They argue that Congress, or any other representative assembly for that matter, is incapable of formulating policies that address the full complexity of problems plaguing the modern world (Huntington 1965). Another charge is that action on bills can be stymied at several junctures in the legislative process by small groups of strategically placed opponents. Predisposed to deadlock, the only decision Congress can often reach is to let somebody else decide what to do. But, regardless of what they see as the motives underlying the choice to delegate, congressional scholars are in general agreement with what we henceforth refer to as the abdication hypothesis: congressional parties have repeatedly forfeited the central policy-making role that they might otherwise have played by turning the job over to others. By this view, delegation leads inevitably to abdication—usually little by little, sometimes precipitously, but in any case quite completely.

The purpose of this book is to reexamine the unflattering image of congressional parties that pervades the literature. Doing so necessarily requires us to reassess the discouraging view of delegation upon which it is based. We recognize that the facts of delegation are incontrovertible. A great deal of policy-making authority has been delegated by congressional parties to their members serving on standing committees; Congress has in turn chosen to delegate major legislative tasks to the president and to the bureaucracy. But it is not these facts that we wish to challenge. Rather, our aim is to determine to what extent these delegations of authority, both internal and external, undermine the ability of the majority party in Congress to pursue its policy objectives. The alternative we pose to the abdication hypothesis is that it is possible to delegate authority to others and yet continue to achieve desired outcomes. Indeed, it is often the case that desired outcomes can be achieved *only* by delegating authority to others.

We analyze the key issues involving congressional parties and the delegation of policy-making authority in the context of the annual appropriations process. There are a number of reasons for this choice. First, appropriations decisions are expressed in straightforward, "dollars-and-cents" terms and are thus the clearest statements of policy that exist. Democratic and Republican politicians may spout similar rhetoric about attaining peace through strength or about building a kinder, gentler nation, but policy must ultimately be crystallized into decisions about how much to appropriate for aircraft procurement versus how much for housing subsidies. Second, the appropriations process is of great substantive importance. It is the mechanism through which hundreds of billions of dollars of federal programs and activities are funded annually.

Third, there is an extensive body of previous research upon which to build. In particular, Fenno's (1966) study of the appropriations process, *The Power of the Purse*, is one of the classic works of political science.

Obviously we would not be taking a fresh look at the abdication hypothesis unless we thought we might arrive at a more optimistic conclusion and, thus, a more favorable view of the policy-making capabilities of congressional parties. Before building our case against the hypothesis, however, we review the case that has been made for it. We proceed by briefly detailing the historical record of the three major forms of congressional delegation of policy-making authority: (1) from congressional parties to subsets of their membership serving on standing committees; (2) from Congress to the president; and (3) from Congress to nonelected officials in the federal bureaucracy.

Each form of delegation arises from a different set of considerations. Each involves a different relationship between principal and agent, and each entails a different set of problems. In no way, however, have decisions to delegate been premised on constitutionally derived principles of government. To the contrary, a common feature of all congressional delegation is that it runs directly counter to the ideals and expectations of those who organized Congress in the early, formative years of the institution.

Delegation and the Organization of Congress

One of the first casualties of the new American republic was the Jeffersonian vision of Congress as a "forum where every member was a peer and no man led" (Harlow 1917). Not that this ideal was rejected on philosophical grounds; rhetoric espousing an unstructured, egalitarian legislature persisted long after the institutional reality gave the lie to it. Rather, it was dissipated in a series of concessions to organizational and political imperatives. The Jeffersonians came to see that whatever the democratic virtues of the practice, working out the general principles of legislation on the floor before referring it to a "committee on detail" was an inefficient and ultimately unworkable way to proceed. It meant that members spent most of their time deliberating matters about which they knew little and cared less. Furthermore, without some internal division of labor the Congress would be devoid of an independent capacity for gathering and evaluating information. This would leave the legislative branch unable to challenge executive policy recommendations or to formulate alternatives—a troubling prospect when the presidency was held by the opposition party.

The corrective the Jeffersonians seized upon evolved into the defining structural characteristic of the U.S. Congress: the delegation of legislative authority to committees. The resultant division of labor not only expedited the flow of legislation, but also encouraged the development of policy expertise, institutional memory, and greater stability in policy-making. In arguing for the creation of a new committee, a member of the Ninth Congress invoked language reminiscent of Adam Smith's paean to the pin factory: "That the business of the House would, on this point, be greatly facilitated by the institution of a standing committee, whose decisions would be uniform, who would from long experience become more enlightened than a select committee, and who would be enabled to dispatch the business confided to them with great celerity" (quoted in Cooper 1970, p. 13).

Rules changes enacted by the 17th Congress (1821–23) ratified what had become standard practice: all bills would be initially taken up by the appropriate committee, and the committee would report legislation to the floor only if it chose to do so (Cooper and Young 1989). Although the Speaker typically saw to it that majority party members dominated committee rosters, it seemed natural that those assigned to a committee would have a keen interest, intellectual or otherwise, in the area of policy over which the committee had jurisdiction.[1]

Cooper's account reveals that members of the early House appreciated the tradeoffs involved in delegating to committees. Gains achieved in policy expertise and organizational efficiency came at the cost of great inequality in influence across policy domains. Committees could parlay superior information and other strategic advantages into disproportionately large amounts of influence over policy in their jurisdictions. Indeed, as Gilligan and Krehbiel (1987) recognize in a recent paper, members of Congress would not invest their time and energy in committee work if this were not the case.

Delegation, in short, entails side effects that are known, in the parlance of economic theory, as agency losses. There is almost always some conflict between the interests of those who delegate authority (principals) and the agents to whom they delegate it. Agents behave opportunistically, pursuing their own interests subject only to the constraints imposed by their relationship with the principal. The opportunism that generates agency losses is a ubiquitous feature of the human experience. It crops up whenever workers are hired, committees are appointed, property is rented, or money is loaned. The message that we are all feckless agents of a Divine Principal is at the very heart of Judeo-Christian theology.

From the point of view of nineteenth-century congressional parties and their leaders, agency losses that accrued from delegating legislative authority to standing committees seemed manageable enough. In the House, members were assigned to committees at the beginning of each Congress by the Speaker, who was himself an agent of the majority party.

This arrangement, characterized by Hasbrouck (1927) as the "foundation of party control," implied that "within limits set by the existing degree of cohesiveness, the key committees could therefore be staffed more consistently with an eye to the program desires of the most durable majority coalition in the House" (Cooper 1970, p. 62). The committee system thus matured in an era of full-fledged party government. In the last few decades of the century the majority party in the House pursued its policy agenda under the aegis of Speakers so hegemonic that the regime was known as Czar Rule.

Following the Revolt against the Speaker in 1910, however, the principle of seniority, which grants members the right to continued service and advancement on a committee, became firmly established. So too did the practice of accommodating members' desires for assignments to committees with jurisdiction over programs of vital concern to their constituents. Under these arrangements, policy-making in Congress became characterized by a pattern of cooperation and reciprocity in which non-committee members on the floor defer to committee proposals, in the expectation that their own committee will be similarly deferred to (Weingast and Marshall 1988). Dodd and Oppenheimer (1977) describe the Congress that emerged after the fall of Boss Cannon as a:

> system of committee government which dispersed power among a set of autonomous committees. Appointment to committees, particularly the major committees, came to be determined within parties largely by seniority in the House; selection to chair one's committee came to depend entirely on committee seniority among members of the majority party. Each committee was left to fashion public policy in its own jurisdiction; the fate of public policy came to depend largely on the composition of committees and thus, by indirection, on patterns of seniority within the House and within committees. (p. 22)

There is general agreement, then, that the delegation of legislative authority to committees is necessarily corrosive to party government: "... to the extent the committees decided policy, party leaders were limited" (Brady 1989, p. 10). Over the past few decades, approximately one hundred thirty subcommittees in the House have acquired many of the properties of committees themselves (Smith and Deering 1984). The ascendancy of subcommittee government would seem to scatter authority even more diffusely and to make policy-making even more fragmented and disjoint.

In the view of many observers, the pendulum has swung back a bit in recent years. The party caucuses (especially the House Democrats) have become more active and assertive, and some of the Speaker's prerogatives have been restored. Indeed, it is because of these and other innovations that Dodd and Oppenheimer felt that Congress—or at least what Shepsle (1988) characterizes as "the Textbook Congress"—should be reconsidered. But recent gains in the stature of congressional parties are impressive mainly in light of the low baseline from which they are measured (Sinclair 1983; Hook 1987). Compared to their counterparts in parliamentary regimes, party leaders in the U.S. Congress would still seem to have at least one hand tied behind their backs.

Delegation to the President

A second major element of Jeffersonian thought was that Congress, as the supreme branch of government, should be an independent body free of executive influence. It was permissible for executive branch officials to provide Congress with information only; they were not to offer opinions, recommendations, or legislative proposals. This, too, proved to be naïve. The Constitution itself posed insurmountable problems for any doctrine of legislative supremacy. Article II states that the president, in addition to providing information to Congress on the state of the union, shall "recommend to their consideration such measures as he shall judge necessary and expedient." More importantly, Article I confers upon the president the power to veto any bill passed by Congress. Contingent only upon being sustained by one-third of the members of either the House or the Senate, the veto means that any legislation must accommodate his preferences and effectively establishes the president as the "third branch of the legislature" (Wilson 1956, p. 52). Standing at the end of the legislative process, the veto casts a shadow over all prior stages of congressional action.

In addition to constitutional realities, it makes sense on purely practical grounds for Congress to rely upon the president and other executive branch officials for policy recommendations. In the first place, it is difficult to distinguish in practice between policy-relevant information and policy recommendations. Even if the distinction can be drawn, those responsible for implementing policy have the most information about its strengths and weaknesses, and so, presumably, the most insight into what can be done to improve it. Second, it is often advantageous to delegate the tasks of collecting, evaluating, and integrating information into a concrete policy proposal to a single agent who is plainly accountable, whether this person be the president, a department head, or some other executive officer.

The president is also the most prominent member of his party. With a common investment in the "brand name" associated with the party label, the president's fellow partisans in Congress have strong incentives to join with him in forging a common policy agenda. Not surprisingly, the Jeffersonian Democrats in Congress became markedly less reluctant to entertain executive policy recommendations after they took control of the White House:

> It became common during the years of Madison's presidency for Republican members to argue, on grounds of executive wisdom and knowledge, that proposals which the appropriate department heads did not think necessary or expedient should not be passed and even that the department heads should be the ones to suggest what was necessary and expedient in their various areas of concern. (Cooper 1970, p. 44)

As in the case of delegation to standing committees within Congress, party leaders in the early House did not think that delegation of legislative responsibilities to the president posed undue institutional risks. Even after the party caucuses in the House ceased making presidential nominations directly, they continued to play a leading role in naming their party's standard bearer. Indeed, Congress's hold on national policy-making in the decades following the Civil War was so secure that Sundquist (1981) describes this period as the Golden Age of Congressional Ascendancy (p. 25).

If the nineteenth century belonged to the Congress, however, the twentieth would seem to belong to the president. In the view of many political scientists, the expanding role of the federal government in domestic affairs and the transformation of the United States into a superpower relegated the notion of policy-making by Congress to a bygone era. According to a past president of the American Political Science Association, "Legislation has become much too complex politically to be effectively handled by a representative assembly" (Huntington 1965, p. 29). Sundquist (1981), similarly, identifies two "endemic weaknesses" of the legislative branch: an inability to act quickly and an inability to develop and coordinate comprehensive policies. Fortunately, in his view, at crucial junctures responsible members of Congress owned up to these liabilities and delegated to the president legislative tasks that the legislature itself could not accomplish:

> A legislative program for the country had to be assembled, coordinated, made internally consistent, fitted with available resources, and coherently presented, and within it priorities had to be assigned. As the size and scope of government grew in the twentieth century, the capacity of the Congress to perform those tasks itself did not keep pace, and the Congress turned outside itself for the leadership it needed—to the president. (pp. 152–53)

Political scientists who bemoan the role committees and subcommittees play in Congress often point to the deleterious consequences this has for the quality of legislation; lacking the integrative role that can only be provided by effective party organization and leadership, policy becomes disjointed, fragmentary, and inconsistent. It is possible, then, that in delegating so much legislative authority to committees inside Congress, the congressional parties necessitated a major legislative role for the president! On the other hand, Cooper (1970) argues that a major impetus for the committee system was to enhance internal specialization and policy expertise in order to ward off executive branch dominance of the legislative process. Whatever the relationship between internal and external delegation, the transfer of policy-making responsibility to the president would seem to be sufficient to undermine the ability of congressional parties to independently pursue a policy agenda. Today the legislative accomplishments of a particular Congress are interpreted in terms of how successful the president has been in winning support for "his" program. As Sundquist (1981) duly observes, however, it was Congress that was responsible for the president becoming the "Chief Legislator":

> The modern aggrandizement of the presidency was the product of considered legislative decisions, neither acts of impulse by the Congress nor presidential coups d'etat. The Congress had to consent, because it had to pass the laws. But more than that, much of the transfer of power was initiated by the legislative branch itself. (p. 35)

Delegation to the Bureacracy

The delegation of legislative initiative to the president is largely a matter of choice. It is unavoidable, however, that Congress delegate the task of implementing public policy to the nonelected employees of the federal government. In keeping with their ideal of legislative supremacy, the Jeffersonians insisted that these officials should be allowed the smallest possible room for discretion or interpretation in carrying out the laws of the land. To this end, it was imperative that Congress write statutes that were as concrete and specific as possible; allowing administrators wide latitude in interpreting the law was tantamount to allowing them to make the law. This doctrine opposing the delegation of legislative power to nonelected officials (*delegata potestas non potest delegari*) is deeply rooted in contractarian political theory, which holds that the consent of the governed—manifested in a popularly elected legislature—is "the only legitimate basis for the exercise of the coercive power of government" (Stewart 1975, p. 1672; see also Fisher 1985, p. 100). The Jeffersonians attached only minor importance to the role of post hoc oversight. As long as legislation was sufficiently explicit and detailed, any deviation from the letter of the law could be readily identified and the offending official impeached for breach of the public trust and brought to trial.[2]

The doctrine against delegation to nonelected officials unraveled in the same way as the other Jeffersonian principles regarding delegation. In the first place, the practical case for allowing administrative discretion is overwhelming. Legislation always concerns conduct and conditions in the future, which, at best, we see through a glass, darkly. There are always contingencies foreseen and unforeseen, both unanticipated disasters and fortuitous opportunities. Overly detailed laws, if followed to the letter, can result in great inefficiency and outright silliness. From the very beginning Congress relied upon executive branch officials to fill in the details of legislation at their discretion. To be sure, courts continued to give lip service to the doctrine forbidding delegation of legislative power well into the twentieth century; the 1928 *Hampton* decision held that "the legislature must promulgate rules, standards, goals, or some 'intelligible principle' to guide the exercise of administrative power" (Stewart 1975, p. 1672). But the right of Congress to grant nonelected officials the authority to take actions contingent upon facts that they themselves had ascertained was explicitly affirmed as early as the 1813 *Brig Aurora* case.

Like other forms of delegation, the delegation of authority to administrative officials appeared to present no serious problems for congressional party government until long after the precedent had been set. The federal government was simply too small in size and scope to make the prospect of a runaway bureaucracy particularly worrisome. At the beginning of this century total expenditures of the federal government amounted to less than three percent of GNP. More importantly, federal jobs were the spoils of electoral victory. The winning party brought into office with it thousands of loyal backers. After the Civil War, Congress succeeded in transforming what had originally been a presidential patronage system (over 90 percent of all federal employees lost their jobs following Lincoln's election in 1860) into a "fiefdom of Congress" (Dodd and Schott 1979, p. 22).

But times changed. Revulsion over Garfield's assassination at the hands of a disappointed office-seeker bolstered the advocates of reform, and passage of the Civil Service Act led to the gradual replacement of patronage armies by career bureaucrats. The federal government grew in size as well as in scope, as Congress established agencies to regulate the railroads and other major sectors of the economy. According to Lowi (1979), Congress actually got off to a good start in establishing regulatory agencies; language of the 1887 legislation that created the Interstate

Commerce Commission, "even where vague, had been 'freighted with meaning' by history." Thus the Commission was "relatively well shackled by clear standards of public policy" (p. 96). In subsequent years, however, Congress's proclivity to delegate policy-making tasks to nonelected administrators was surpassed only by the amount of discretion conveyed by the delegation. Agency charters became litanies of noble-sounding sentiments devoid of specific instructions, or even reliable signals, as to legislative intent. By the end of the New Deal a full-blown "administrative state" was firmly entrenched. As Schick (1976) puts it, "Inch by inch Congress gave ground until it no longer was a dominant participant in the conduct of administration" (p. 517).

According to many critical observers, these broad, sweeping delegations of policy-making authority to nonelected officials were the product of a colossal failure of institutional nerve. Facing public clamor to do something about pressing problems and unable to agree on precisely what to do, Congress had repeatedly passed the buck by establishing yet another agency and instructing *it* to solve the problem (Davis 1958).[3] Instead of preventing Congress from evading its responsibilities by enforcing the doctrine against delegation, the courts retreated to a much weaker position; as long as agencies followed correct procedures, treated evidence in an evenhanded manner, allowed for judicial review, and acted in a way that was not arbitrary and capricious, the courts studiously refrained from challenging administrative rulings and statutes (Lowi 1979; Stewart 1975).

In theory, Congress could always reclaim a portion of its legislative mandate by engaging in post hoc oversight of bureaucratic activity. According to Fisher (1985), however, the nature of the delegation itself makes this problematic: "How can Congress ... determine whether programs are being carried out effectively unless the original legislative goals are clearly stated? Unless statutory standards exist, how can courts judge whether agency actions are faithful to legislative intent?" (p. 102). Fiorina (1981a) points out another problem with oversight: because benefits derived from oversight are public goods, individual congressional members lack sufficient incentive to engage in it. Whether they blame collective action problems or not, scholars who have examined congressional oversight are in general agreement that very little of it gets done. According to Ogul (1976), the operations of the federal government have become so vast and far-flung that it is unrealistic to believe that it could ever be otherwise:

> No amount of congressional dedication and energy, no conceivable increase in the size of committee staffs, and no extraordinary boost in committee budgets will enable the Congress

to carry out its oversight obligations in a comprehensive and systematic manner. The job is too large for any combination of members and staff to master completely. (p. 5)

As before, then, delegation appears to have degenerated into abdication, producing, in Lowi's (1979) words, a regime of "policy without law" (p. 92). Dodd and Schott (1979) similarly describe the modern American bureaucratic state as a "prodigal child," but the image they have in mind is really one of Frankenstein's monster: "Although born of congressional intent, it [the federal bureaucracy] has taken on a life of its own and has matured to a point where its muscle and brawn can be turned against its creator" (p. 2).

The Appropriations Process

Nowhere is the logic of delegation more compelling than in the appropriation of funds for the myriad programs and activities of the federal government. But nowhere else is it more important for congressional parties to prevent their capacity to make policy from being lost to committees, to the president, or to bureaucrats. For it is in their spending priorities that parties tell the electorate most clearly what policies they favor and what groups they represent. It is ironic that one of the basic ground rules governing consideration of spending proposals in the House is the stricture against substantive legislation in appropriations bills. That Deschler (1977) devotes several hundred pages to stipulating what this means in practice only demonstrates that Congress has attempted to establish through a web of tradition and precedent a distinction that cannot be made in principle.[4] Spending *is* policy, and differences in spending priorities go a long way toward defining what it means to be a Republican or a Democrat.

Congressional delegation of authority over appropriations, however, faithfully recapitulates the basic pattern of congressional delegation in general. The Jeffersonians who dominated the early House realized that if Congress failed to develop an internal capacity for making spending decisions, the power of the purse, regardless of what the Constitution had to say about it, would lapse to their Federalist adversaries in the executive branch. Control of appropriations rested on mastery of the mundane details of building roads, outfitting ships, and staffing offices. The First Congress therefore established in the House a committee to oversee all legislation concerning revenue and expenditures. In 1802 this committee on Ways and Means became the first permanent, standing committee. Jurisdiction over spending devolved to a separate Committee on Appropriations at the end of the Civil War.

The resources, authority, and responsibility delegated to it make Appropriations a quintessential "power" committee. The chairmen of its subcommittees are referred to as the College of Cardinals. Members lucky enough to attain a seat on the committee rarely leave voluntarily. Compared to those on the outside, members on the committee enjoy tremendous advantages in the amount and quality of information to which they have access. Assessing what they knew about the contents of a pending $576 billion omnibus continuing resolution, a Republican leader ranked the committee chairman, ranking minority member, and non-committee members in the following order: "Jamie knows all. Sil knows some. The average member knows zip" (Wehr 1986). This asymmetry of information, in conjunction with the enormity of the committee's jurisdiction, immediately raises the key question of whether delegation is tantamount to abdication. Do congressional parties, in delegating legislative authority to their members serving on standing committees, thereby abdicate their capacity for shaping policy? More specifically, can congressional parties effectively pursue their spending priorities when so much authority over spending has been conveyed to the Appropriations Committee?

Previous research on the House Appropriations Committee weighs in heavily on the side of the abdication hypothesis. This is not to say that House Appropriations has been seen as a renegade committee wielding its enormous influence to further the parochial interests of its members— quite the contrary. The Appropriations Committee, by the prevailing view, provides the vital "institutional maintenance" role of guarding the U.S. Treasury from the relentless claims that are made upon it by members seeking to maximize the flow of federal benefits to their districts. The committee thus protects the House (and nation) as a whole from the actions of its own members. In light of the paramount importance of this mission, members of the committee, according to Fenno (1973), do not have the luxury of engaging in partisan sniping. New hands are instead quickly socialized into the virtues of hard work, subcommittee specialization, and the norm of "minimal partisanship." Most members Fenno interviewed concurred wholeheartedly with long-time Chairman Clarence Cannon's characterization of the committee's role: "constantly and courageously to protect the federal Treasury against the thousands of appeals and imperative demands for unnecessary, unwise, and excessive expenditures" (Fenno 1966, p. 99). Cannon and his alter ego, ranking Republican John Taber, were ever-vigilant for outbreaks of the "interest-sympathy-leniency" syndrome that rendered members insufficiently skeptical about claims on the budget.

Given House Appropriations' traditional "Guardian of the Treasury" role, the percentage of the total federal budget over which the committee has jurisdiction would seem to be a good indicator of congressional support for fiscal austerity. In the 1870s and 1880s authority to make appropriations in several areas was transferred from Appropriations to the relevant substantive committees (Brady and Morgan 1987). In order to pursue the restraint needed to manage the debt accumulated during World War I, its monopoly over annual appropriations legislation was restored in 1920. By this view, the committee's guardianship of the Treasury has subsequently been undercut by the growth of entitlement programs, permanent appropriations, and various forms of direct Treasury financing referred to as "backdoor spending" (LeLoup 1980; Cogan 1988).

When the congressional budget process and new Budget Committees were established in 1974, most congressional observers assumed that the policy-making role of the House Appropriations Committee would be eclipsed even further. Soon after, however, it appeared to many that the new constraints on backdoor spending and other features of the budget process actually meant that Appropriations was a net beneficiary of the reforms. Other innovations of the past several years—most notably the enactment of appropriations legislation in the form of giant, omnibus continuing resolutions—also seem to have enhanced the committee's stature within the House (White 1988). As David Obey (D, Wisconsin) observed:

> Most of the power appears to be in the Budget Committee. That is true only until September, when people realize we won't have anything in place for the new fiscal year. So we draw up a continuing resolution, and virtually all power passes to the Appropriations Committee. Members of the Budget and authorizing committees don't have much say. (quoted in Granat 1983a, p. 1215)

The delegation of authority within Congress to the House Appropriations Committee has been paralleled, according to proponents of the abdication hypothesis, by a wholesale delegation of budgetary responsibilities to the president. Throughout most of the nineteenth century, customs duties, excise taxes, and the proceeds from land sales yielded more revenue than was required for the modest purposes of the federal government. The unprecedented cost of waging World War I, however, brought this long age of budgetary innocence to an end. The federal government had new responsibilities, at home and abroad. Large deficits loomed unless the federal government managed to put its fiscal house in order. At the dawn of the modern budgetary age, Congress, according to Sundquist (1981), had two options:

> It could organize itself to seize the tiller and steer the ship,

retaining the exclusive responsibility for producing the comprehensive and unified budget, establish a consolidated process, and
equipping its committees with appropriate staff resources. Or it
could assign the responsibility for preparing the national budget
to the executive, reserving for itself a review capacity. (p. 40)

Congress opted to delegate. Under the Budget and Accounting Act of
1921 the president submits to Congress at the beginning of every session
a budget for the upcoming fiscal year. The legislation also created a new
agency, the Bureau of the Budget, to assist the president in carrying
out this task. Agency requests for appropriations would not come to
Congress until they had been filtered through the Budget Bureau.[5]

In the view of most students of American politics, this delegation of
budgetary authority was a watershed event in the history of executive-
legislative relations. As Sundquist (1981) puts it, "The modern presidency, judged in terms of institutional responsibilities, began on June 10,
1921, the day that President Harding signed the Budget and Accounting
Act" (p. 39). Surveying the state of appropriations politics fifty-one years
later in 1972, Al Ullman, at that time second-ranking Democrat on the
Ways and Means Committee, charged that for all intents and purposes
this delegation had shifted the locus of budgetary policy-making to the
executive branch: "The only place where a budget is put together is
in the Office of Management and Budget downtown. When they send
their recommendations to us we go through a few motions of raising or
lowering the spending requests, but we have lost the capacity to decide
our own priorities in this Nation of ours" (quoted by Sundquist 1981,
p. 210).

A large majority of his fellow members shared Ullman's frustration.
In an apparent reversal of the historical tendency to delegate away
all difficult policy-making responsibilities, in 1974 Congress passed the
Congressional Budget and Impoundment Control Act. This legislation
mandated that Congress adopt a joint resolution designating explicit
revenue, expenditure, and deficit targets before addressing appropriations or any other budget-relevant legislation. According to proponents
of the new budgetary order, mandating the adoption of binding budget
resolutions would force Congress finally to face the hard choices that had
to be made. By becoming a fiscally responsible body it could begin to
win back some of the decision-making capacity that had been abdicated
to the president. As Federal Reserve Chairman Arthur Burns put it in
testimony before the Joint Study Committee on Budget Control, "If
you can develop procedures that will enable members of Congress to
vote on an over-all fiscal policy that adequately reflects congressional
priorities, you will revitalize representative government in this country"

(quoted in *Congressional Quarterly Almanac*, 1973, p. 246). The 1974 legislation created a new Budget Committee in both the House and the Senate, as well as the Congressional Budget Office. Able to conduct its own legislative analysis and to generate its own budgetary forecasts, the CBO was designed to put Congress back on even informational footing with the president.

By most accounts, the congressional budget process has been less than a rousing success. In most years following passage of the Budget Act, Congress has voted to deactivate crucial enforcement provisions and, in some years, to waive the requirements of the act entirely. In virtually every session there are calls either to overhaul the process or to simply abolish it. Ironically, it appears that the only one to make effective use of the budget process was Ronald Reagan, who commandeered it en route to his widely heralded budget victories of 1981 and 1982.

The lesson for Congress in all of this seems to be that once authority has been delegated, it is not so easy to get it back. For better or for worse, the president would appear to remain the chief architect of the federal budget. In accounting for the unprecedented deficit spending of recent years, most fingers point directly toward the Oval Office:

> Congress seems to defer to the president on fiscal policy. If the president finds a way of keeping expenditures and revenues roughly in balance, Congress does little to disturb the equilibrium. But if the president insists on major new expenditures or significant tax reductions, Congress is also willing to acquiesce, even if this may mean budget deficits. (Peterson 1985, p. 396)

In considering the classic constitutional issues evoked by the delegation of legislative authority from Congress to the president, it is easy to forget that neither Congress nor the president actually write the checks. It is the other major recipients of congressionally delegated authority— nonelected officials in the federal bureaucracy—who actually disburse federal money. Congress can be as general or as specific as it wants in directing expenditures. Indeed, the scope of congressional delegation to the bureaucrats would seem to be plainly revealed by the lumpiness of appropriations line items. Appropriations acts for fiscal year 1982, for example, earmarked $29,000 for the Franklin Delano Roosevelt Memorial Commission, but $19.4 billion for "Operation and maintenance, Navy."

Debate in the early Congress over the proper nature of appropriations legislation revolved around precisely this issue. Consistent with their opposition to granting policy-making discretion to nonelected officials, the Jeffersonian Democrats advocated making appropriations as detailed as possible; legislation should designate "specific funds to every specific purpose susceptible of definition." The first Secretary of the Treasury,

Alexander Hamilton, rejected this notion as absurd; by depriving federal government officials of discretion and flexibility, such strictures would lead to great inefficiencies and quite possibly imperil national security. After some experience as president, Jefferson himself flipflopped. He observed that "too minute a specification has its evil as well as a too general one" and thought it better for Congress to "appropriate in gross while trusting in executive direction." Despite Jefferson's backsliding, early Congresses opted to err in the direction of too much detail rather than not enough (Fisher 1975, pp. 60–61).

Over time, however, without much notice or fanfare, appropriations became lumpier and lumpier. In the 1920s and again in the 1950s, Congress, inspired by the recommendations of public administration experts (most notably the 1949 Hoover Commission), voted to consolidate or eliminate hundreds of line items in the annual appropriations acts. How far things have gone can be sensed by comparing federal budgets across a century; the 1976 budget, despite being over a thousand times larger in nominal dollars and over one hundred times larger in real (constant dollar) terms, contained fewer line items than the budget for 1876 (Schick 1976).

In actuality, the level of aggregation in appropriations line items is a poor indicator of the amount of discretion allowed in making expenditures. Far more detailed directives are communicated in the hearings and reports of Appropriations subcommittees than in the text of the bills. Fisher's (1975) study points out several ways in which Congress makes expenditure directives more or less flexible. It can allocate appropriations to contingency funds for unforeseen opportunities or requirements. It can make the transfer of funds between accounts, or the reprogramming of funds within accounts, more or less difficult. It can set restrictions on the rate or timing of expenditures or on the carrying over of unexpended balances from one year to the next. Much of what falls under the oxymoronic rubric of "uncontrollable" federal spending is so designated because Congress has granted an agency permission either to commit or to borrow funds in advance of appropriations; Congress promises, through the requisite legislation, to liquidate the resultant borrowing or contract authority at some later date.

In making these choices Congress confronts a dilemma. Granting bureaucrats greater discretion and flexibility in committing to expenditures increases their ability to pursue congressional objectives, but it simultaneously increases their ability to evade legislative intent as well. In the field of foreign affairs, for example, policies that maximize the interests of the United States must constantly adapt to new conditions and new events that are largely uncontrollable and unforeseeable. Therefore Congress has usually allocated a large percentage of appropriations

for foreign assistance programs to a contingency fund. After reviewing the operation of the program, however, John Rhodes (R, Arizona)
concluded in 1961 that to some extent Congress had been snookered:
"Unfortunately, I think it is a matter of public knowledge that in many
instances this contingency fund has been used for one contingency only
and that contingency is that the House and Senate did not appropriate
as much money for the program as the people downtown would have
appropriated" (quoted in Fisher 1975, p. 67).

It is also the case that spending funds for purposes other than those
intended is only one of the ways that federal officials can exploit the
authority they have been granted to make expenditures. They can simply
fail to spend the money they have been appropriated. In the past this has
frequently occurred in response to a presidential directive to impound
appropriated funds, but this is not a necessary condition for funds to be
withheld. Nonelected officials in the bureaucracy can also take actions
which compel Congress to appropriate funds in the future. According to
Wilmerding (1943), of all the challenges to Congress's ability to direct
expenditures, the creation of "coercive deficiencies" was by far the most
serious.

As with congressional delegation to bureaucratic entities in general,
many of the sins of overdelegation in the realm of appropriations could
be redressed through vigorous and systematic post hoc oversight of
expenditure practices. A major theme of Wilmerding's classic study,
however, was that except for sporadic outcries of concern, Congress has
seldom paid much attention to how money was actually spent after they
had appropriated it. Throughout most of the nineteenth century, it was
extremely difficult for members of Congresss to even obtain the relevant
information. To state that in the nineteenth century the federal government did not conform to generally accepted accounting principles is
putting it mildly. The federal government did not even operate on a fiscal
year basis until 1843. After Congress began appropriating by fiscal year,
many agencies sought to evade even this mild control by carrying over
balances from year to year that were often larger than the amounts they
were annually appropriated. This and other laxities in accounting and
expenditure practices made it virtually impossible to relate expenditures
to appropriations. As Wilmerding puts it: "One central fact emerges.
From 1843 or thereabouts to the period of the first World War Congress
completely ignored its duty rigorously to examine into the application
of appropriated moneys. I use the word 'ignored' in its primary sense; it
was not so much that Congress neglected or repudiated its duty as that
it knew not what its duty was" (Wilmerding 1943, p. 248).

The ability of Congress to determine whether or not expenditures were
consistent with appropriations was ostensibly enhanced by creation of

the General Accounting Office in 1921. The response of Congress to delegation problems, in other words, was to delegate responsibility for addressing these problems to another agency. Wilmerding, however, calls the GAO a "pseudo-solution": the new agency was given no capabilities that those formerly in charge of overseeing expenditures—the auditors in the Department of the Treasury—had not already possessed.

But even if creation of the GAO and other reforms have eliminated the most blatant abuses, there are some who believe that congressional over-delegation to the bureaucracy has had consequences that are far more serious than the shenanigans described by Wilmerding. Many schol-ars, especially those in the public choice school, argue that agency bu-reaucrats enjoy such a strategic advantage over the legislature that they are able to extract large and ever-increasing budgets from them (Niskanen 1971). The main engines of government growth, by this view, are bureaucratic (Buchanan 1977).

Overview

The abdication hypothesis is not spun from straw. The arguments made for it are persuasive, and it seems to be broadly in accord with the histor-ical record. Why, then, have we come to question the received wisdom? To a large extent, our thinking has been influenced by the basic texts of business management (Drucker 1973) as well as by the "new economics of organization" and the "new accounting" (Moe 1984; Demski and Kreps 1982). In these literatures delegation is not necessarily a dirty word; the effectiveness of a manager, or the performance of the organization he or she manages, is determined not by how much authority is delegated, but rather by how well it is delegated.

Our doubts about the abdication hypothesis also grow out of a sense that political scientists have been preoccupied with what congressional parties are not, and with what they are unable to do. They have been particularly fixated on the inability of congressional party leaders to impose sanctions on recalcitrant members. Conceding that their capa-bilities are limited and often tightly constrained, we nevertheless want to explore more fully what parties and their leaders *can* do. There are many mechanisms other than the imposition of sanctions that can be employed to influence behavior. In general, sanctions are more expensive and less effective than more subtle, less obtrusive methods.

Political scientists, finally, are also inclined to infer far too much from the appearance of power. It is not surprising that this is the case; delineating the distribution of power in a political system is one of the traditional concerns of the discipline. This is completely unrelated, how-ever, to our concern over whether or not the internal and external delegation of legislative authority undercuts the ability of congressional parties to pursue their policy objectives. Congressional parties could be highly successful in their delegation to committees, for example, and yet appear to be very weak in comparison to them.

In order to reject the abdication hypothesis we do not need to accept in its place the notion that the majority party in Congress is able to achieve whatever policy outcomes it desires. Given the presence of the the president, the courts, and subnational governments, this is obviously out of the question. That the House and Senate are sometimes controlled by different parties complicate things even further. It should also be kept in mind that our interest in the annual appropriations process lies in what it reveals about the efficacy of congressional delegation. This is not a book about budgeting or the appropriations process per se. For that reason we do not address many of the central concerns of budgetary studies, such as whether budgeting is or should be "top down" versus "bottom up," or the extent to which budgeting is "incremental." It is possible that our analyses will shed some new light on these issues, but this is not our primary concern.

The outline of the book is as follows. In chapter 2 we explore the basic theoretical issues involved in delegation. We argue that certain dilemmas must be overcome if a community is to undertake collective action. One prominent solution is for the community to delegate authority to a central agent. Doing so, however, necessarily generates additional problems in the form of agency losses. These losses must be successfully contained if the benefits of collective action are to be realized. In chapter 3 we use this framework to examine the community which is of concern here— the congressional party caucus—and its delegation of authority to its leaders.

In the next two chapters we analyze mechanisms that the majority party in the House has employed to minimize agency losses resulting from the delegation of tasks and authority to the House Appropriations Committee. The same analyses could be applied to the Senate, but the paramount importance played by the House committee in the appropriations process leads us to confine our attention to the lower chamber. As indicated earlier, the House Appropriations Committee has long been seen as an agent of the parent chamber, protecting the collective interests of the institution from the demands of individual member of Congress for more and more spending. As a corollary, congressional scholars have seen important changes in the role of House Appropriations, especially the reassignment of appropriations legislation to other committees in 1885, primarily as sanctions imposed against the committee by the parent chamber. In chapter 4 we argue that members of the committee should instead be seen as agents of their respective party caucuses and that conventional interpretations of the 1885 divestiture and of other reforms fail to appreciate the degree to which these innovations were made by the majority party in order to further its policy objectives. In chapter 5 we focus on assignments to the House Appropriations Committee. Even though it involves a minimum of time and effort, filling vacancies on the committee at the beginning of each Congress is one of the most effective means available for shaping committee decisions.

Chapter 6 investigates floor action on appropriations bills in both the House and Senate since the end of World War II. One of our major objectives in this chapter is to determine the extent to which the Appropriations Committees in both chambers are able to exploit strategic features of House-Senate conference procedures. This is a difficult task, in that it is often impossible to infer from observed behavior (on amendment activity, for instance) the structure of the relationship that gave rise to it. Congressional researchers have been insufficiently attuned to this problem and, as a result, have often fallen prey to a number of inferential traps.

In chapter 7 we move from delegation problems within Congress to those encountered by Congress in delegating authority to other institutions. We focus specifically upon the ongoing efforts of the majority party in Congress to manage the inherently problematic agency relationship that exists with the Office of Management and Budget. In chapter 8 we turn our attention to the bottom line and estimate the impact of the partisan composition of Congress upon appropriations awarded to seventy federal programs and agencies in the postwar era. In chapter 9 we investigate the extent to which delegation problems crop up in the administrative actions that turn appropriations into expenditures. In the final chapter we summarize our major findings and offer some closing comments and observations.

CHAPTER TWO

Delegation and Agency Problems

Collective Action and Delegation

Congress makes policy in an ever-growing number of issue domains. The federal budget it oversees has grown from less than one million dollars in 1789 to over one trillion dollars today. The organizational problems that confront members of the 101st Congress, however, are much the same as those that confronted members of the First. Little can be accomplished in Congress without collective action. But as revealed in the extensive literature on social choice—or by a cursory glance at the human condition—collective action is fraught with difficulties.

The most familiar collective action problem is the prisoner's dilemma. It takes its name from the simple two-person game, but the social contexts in which most human interaction takes place tend to make n-person prisoners' dilemmas the more pervasive phenomenon. The crux of the dilemma is that individuals, in seeking to maximize their self-interest, have incentives to behave in ways that are inimical to the interests of the community as a whole (Hardin 1968). A good example of the dilemma is that of public goods (Olson 1965). The community would on net benefit from such a good, but those who do not contribute to its provision cannot be excluded from enjoying it. Everyone therefore has an incentive to free ride on the contributions of others. Even though the community may unanimously favor acquisition of the public good, little or no effort is expended to supply it. Rational individual choices produce irrational collective outcomes.

Collective action may also be stymied by a lack of coordination (Farrell and Saloner 1985, 1987; Crawford and Haller 1988). In contrast to the prisoner's dilemma, where dominant strategies yield an inefficient equilibrium, other situations confront the community with multiple efficient equilibria. Members of the community are uncertain as to which strategies other members will pursue, and coordination may never be achieved. A simple coordination problem occurs when two cars enter an intersection simultaneously. Neither driver cares particularly who goes first; both are far more concerned about avoiding a collision. What frequently occurs, however, is a nerve-wracking *pas de deux* of false starts and sudden stops as the drivers make their way through the crossing. Even if everyone in the community would benefit from all alternatives under consideration, problems of coordination are exacerbated when different alternatives benefit some members relative to others.

Another obstacle to collective action is social choice instability (Arrow 1951). The decisions of a community to undertake collective action might cycle from one choice to another, for example, from choosing to build a park, a road, a library, and back to a park again. The community might devote resources to one alternative, then to another, but never accomplish any of its objectives. An important implication of social choice instability is that one or more members of the community can, by acting strategically, manipulate the decision-making process to their advantage (Satterthwaite 1975; Levine and Plott 1977; Riker 1986). Voters can theoretically defend themselves from agenda manipulation by behaving strategically themselves, but the actual voting procedures used in Congress and most other legislatures allow for agenda manipulation even under strategic voting (Ordeshook and Schwartz 1987). Agenda manipulation can yield choices that advantage a small minority of the membership at the expense of the majority. This not only leads to the collapse of collective action, but may also threaten the continued existence of the community itself.

According to property rights theorists, the best response to collective action problems is to minimize their occurrence, something that is accomplished by relegating as much human activity as possible to the realm of the marketplace. Adam Smith argued long ago that the well-being of a community is better realized through individual market transactions than through the schemes of even the most benevolent planner. Much social benefit can also be derived from simple patterns of reciprocity (Axelrod 1984). But there are limits to what can be achieved through voluntary trade and cooperation; uncoordinated, unorganized activity will get a community only so far. In most cases, the benefits of collective action are realized through organizations. It is in the context of organizations that collective action is most effectively coordinated, that prisoners' dilemmas are most readily overcome, and that stable social decisions are most likely to be reached.

The organizational bases of collective action are many—firms, bureaucracies, associations, committees, leagues, representative assemblies, to
name a few. What the most prominent forms of organization have in
common, however, is the delegation of authority to take action from
the individual or individuals to whom it was originally endowed—the
principal—to one or more agents (Mirrlees 1976; Holmström 1979; Grossman and Hart 1983).[1] One major organizational theorist, in fact, defines
organizations as "networks of overlapping or nested principal/agent relationships" (Tirole 1986, p. 181). Delegation from principals to agents
is the key to the division of labor and development of specialization;
tremendous gains accrue if tasks are delegated to those with the talent,
training, and inclination to do them. This, when all is said and done,
is what allows firms to profit, economies to grow, and governments to
govern.

The underlings in an organization are obviously agents of their supe-
riors, but the heads of organizations, such as coaches, firm managers,
party leaders, are agents, too (Fama 1980). Indeed, it is the delegation
of authority to a central agent to lead or manage the organization that
is the key to overcoming problems of collective action. Agents performing as leaders or managers must be endowed with the resources they
need to discharge their duties effectively. In the case of congressional
parties, leaders can exploit the prominence of their position to identify
a focal point, thus solving problems of coordination by rallying support
around one of possibly many acceptable alternatives. Their ability to
structure the voting agenda, moreover, can overcome social choice instability (Aldrich 1988). As Calvert (1987) explains in his analysis of
legislative leadership, any power or influence a party leader has is a
consequence of delegation from the membership: "The leader can only
'influence' members who want to be influenced, and exercises 'power'
only as long as he uses it to provide them with what they want" (p. 47).

In such a relationship the agent seeks to maximize his or her return
subject to the constraints and incentives offered by the principal. The
principal, conversely, seeks to structure the relationship with the agent
so that the outcomes produced through the agent's efforts are the best
the principal can achieve, given the choice to delegate in the first place.
There is, then, a natural conflict of interest between the two. In economic
settings this conflict is often over the amount of effort expended by the
agent. In political settings it is more likely to be over the course of action
the agent is to pursue. The policy agenda of agency bureaucrats, for example, can be quite at odds with the preferences of the elected officials
who oversee them (Pertschuk 1982). As a consequence of this conflict
of interest, the principal always experiences some reduction in welfare.
First, he suffers agency losses that result from the agent behaving in

ways other than those that best serve his interests. Second, the principal incurs agency costs in undertaking efforts to mitigate agency losses. Agency problems may be so great that they exceed the benefits to be derived from collection action, in which case the delegation should not occur.

The opportunistic behavior that is at the root of agency problems is by no means confined to principal/agent relationships. Individuals involved in market transactions have similar incentives to behave in a less than noble manner (Kintner 1978). Certain conditions that are generally present in principal/agent relationships, however, make it a particularly congenial environment for opportunism. These are the conditions of hidden action, hidden information, and a form of strategic vulnerability on the part of the principal that we refer to as Madison's dilemma.

Hidden Action and Hidden Information

In a wide variety of agency relationships, the agent possesses or acquires information that is either unavailable to the principal or prohibitively costly to obtain. The agent has incentives to use this information strategically or to simply keep it hidden—a situation referred to variously as the problem of truthful revelation or incentive incompatibility. In a firm, workers have information that is not available to management, such as how fast the assembly line can run before quality is compromised. They would prefer not to reveal this information, however, because they would rather not work at a breakneck pace. Another type of information that agents often have and principals do not is the agent's type (for example, knowledge of whether the agent is hardworking or lazy, talented or untalented, risk-averse or risk-acceptant). This variation on the hidden information problem is referred to as adverse selection.[2]

Situations in which agents acquire information that is unavailable to the principal pervade public policy-making. The basis of Niskanen's (1971) argument as to how bureaus maximize the size of their budgets is that bureaucrats are privy to information about service delivery costs that is not available to elected politicians. Through their investigations, congressional committees uncover information that is not available to other members of the chamber. Individual members, similarly, have better information than do congressional party leaders as to whether or not supporting the party's position might cause them trouble back home (Sinclair 1983).

The second problem, that of hidden action, manifests itself in a variety of situations. Stockholders cannot observe whether the actions that firm managers take are in their best interest. Voters cannot observe whether the actions of elected representatives—their agents—are in their best interest. Hidden action is especially problematic when the agent's actions only partially determine outcomes, as in the case of team production or committee decisions, or when outcomes are partially determined by chance. In such cases, the principal is unable to infer the appropriateness of the agent's actions even from observed results.

Madison's Dilemma

Arguing for the separation of powers specified under the new Constitution, Madison wrote in *Federalist 51*, "In framing a government to be administered by men over men, the great difficulty lies in this: you must first enable the government to control the governed; and in the next place oblige it to control itself." Whatever their views about the document that was ultimately produced, members of the Constitutional Convention were keenly appreciative of Madison's observation. They had seen that under the Articles of Confederation the federal government had not been delegated enough authority to accomplish much of anything. Yet they feared that a government powerful enough to govern effectively would necessarily be powerful enough to oppress them.

In addition to problems of hidden action and hidden information, this third problem, one we call Madison's dilemma, is a potential pitfall in all institutions that rely upon delegation. The essence of the problem is that resources or authority granted to an agent for the purpose of advancing the interests of the principal can be turned against the principal. Although the problem is a general one of agency, it has long been recognized in liberal political theory as being of paramount importance when the agents involved are those in a position of leadership. Madison's dilemma is not a consequence of agents taking hidden action or acquiring hidden information, although these conditions can certainly make matters worse. Rather, it arises from agents exploiting the favorable strategic situation in which they have been placed.

In seeking to solve collective action problems, members of the community must be prescient in their delegation of authority to a central agent. If not, they may find that that they would have been better off continuing to endure their problems than they are living with the solution their agent has achieved.

Collective Principals and Collective Agents

Problems of hidden action, hidden information, and Madison's dilemma are endemic to all agency relationships. There are additional hazards to delegation, however, when either collective principals or collective agents are involved. Specifically, the very same collective action problems that delegation is intended to overcome—prisoners' dilemmas, lack of coordination, and social choice instability—can reemerge to afflict either the collective agent or a collective principal. A collective principal may be unable to announce a single preference over its agent's actions or to offer a single contract governing compensation for the agent. A subset of the membership may strategically manipulate the decision-making process of the collective principal. Similarly, agents who are delegated management or leadership roles may use their agenda powers to do the same thing, thus leaving the collective principal vulnerable to a form of Madison's dilemma. A related consideration is that in appointing a new individual to a collective agent, such as a production team or a committee, that person's abilities and preferences cannot be evaluated in isolation. The principal must consider instead how the new agent will interact with existing members of the team or committee.

Distinct from the problems of collective principals and agents are problems specific to multiple principals and agents. An agent attempting to serve multiple principals often finds that any action he or she might take to benefit one principal injures another. As Moe (1984) observes, federal agencies are buffeted by conflicting pressures from their departments, the president, the courts, their interest group clients, as well as several congressional committees and subcommittees. Second, when there are multiple agents it is possible that they will collude against the principal (Tirole 1986). This can occur in a number of ways. Workers who break the curve, for example, are likely to be castigated by their fellow workers. The essence of "iron triangle" or "subgovernment" theories of public policy formation is that collusion between two sets of agents—federal agencies and the congressional committees that ostensibly oversee them—serves to undermine the welfare of the general public (their ultimate principal) rather than to promote it.

Overcoming Agency Problems

Agency losses can be contained, but only by undertaking measures that are themselves costly. There are are four major classes of such measures: (1) contract design, (2) screening and selection mechanisms, (3) monitoring and reporting requirements, and (4) institutional checks.

Contract Design

Any contract between a principal and agent must satisfy the participation constraint. The agent's compensation must be at least as great as his or her opportunity costs, but less than the marginal benefit the principal derives from the actions of the agent. If this condition is not met, one side or the other will not be made better off by entering into the relationship and will decline to do so. Assuming that the participation constraint is satisfied, the principal's goal is to delegate tasks and responsibilities and to specify a corresponding schedule of compensation in such a way that the agent is motivated to best serve the principal's interests. Such contracts may specify negative rewards, or sanctions, particularly when the agent is capable of taking actions that are very harmful to the principal. In some situations, particularly when noncompliance with the principal's directives is hard to detect, the sanctions required to effect compliance are far greater in magnitude than the benefits that the principal derives from compliance (Holmström 1979).

Under conditions that usually exist in principal/agent relationships—hidden information and hidden action—designing compensation schedules is a tricky business. Examples abound of compensation schemes that create incentives for agent behavior other than that intended by the principal. If not otherwise constrained, brokers receiving a commission on trades churn through their clients' portfolios. Ford factory managers, no less creative than their celebrated Soviet counterparts, often met their quotas by surreptitiously building large numbers of automobiles prior to the official start of the production run (Halberstam 1986). Governmental agencies have an especially difficult time designing appropriate compensation schedules. Medicare administrators, for example, came to realize that simply reimbursing hospitals for all "reasonable" costs incurred in treating patients contributed to rapidly escalating claims. In 1982 they won congressional approval for a new system under which hospitals receive a fixed fee for treatment based upon the diagnosis related group (DRG) to which the patient has been assigned. In short order the system began to experience "DRG creep"; elderly Americans were succumbing to increasingly expensive diseases that often could be diagnosed only with the most advanced (and expensive) medical technology.[3]

The problem of inappropriate incentives in compensation schemes can be mitigated by giving agents a residual claim on output. The compensation received by corporate executives, for example, is often in the form of profit sharing or other bonuses linked to the performance of the firm. Another example of this arrangement is sharecropping. Instead of charging a fixed rent, the landlord leases land to a tenant in return for a percentage of the crop. Compensation contracts of this form can be used in the public sector as well. In previous centuries, the king of France and other European monarchs garnered much of their revenue from "tax farmers," that is, individuals who were given the right to collect taxes in a particular geographic area so long as they surrendered an agreed-upon amount of the proceeds to the crown. The state of Ohio actually implemented this method for garnering revenue at the end of the Civil War; counties and cities were permitted to engage "tax inquisitors" who were empowered to find concealed taxable holdings (usually stocks and bank deposits) in return for a percentage of the proceeds.

Although such profit-sharing arrangements can help mitigate agency losses, they are hardly a panacea. They can be very expensive to the principal and do not necessarily remove all inappropriate incentives.[4] In the realm of public policy, awarding agents a residual claim on output can have particularly obnoxious consequences; the interested student should be able to surmise why the institution of tax farming fell out of favor.[5] Even if it were desirable to motivate public servants with a piece of the action, most important policy outputs are impossible to measure. How, for example, could the military establishment be awarded an incentive bonus that hinged upon whether or not they had had a good year?

Given the difficulties involved in designing optimal contracts prior to the establishment of an agency relationship, an alternative strategy for the principal may be to simply offer a compensation contract and, conditioned on the agent accepting it, to see how well he or she works out. There is, after all, no better information about how well an agent performs than his or her actual performance. Most employment contracts specify an initial probationary period (ranging from three or four days for waiters to three or four years for professors) and provide for periodic reviews after that. The principal can minimize the risk associated with this strategy by initially assigning an agent a modest set of tasks and responsibilities at a modest level of compensation. Those who perform well are rewarded by increasing the range of their authority and responsibility and, concomitantly, the level of their compensation.[6] Agents who perform poorly will not similarly advance, or may even be demoted or dismissed. Like other strategies available to the principal, this one works best when agents can be induced to compete with each other. One of the major rationales for hierarchy in organizations is that it means there are more people seeking promotion to the next level than there are opportunities available.

Screening and Selection Mechanisms

A policy of hiring first and adjusting compensation later does nothing to address the problem of adverse selection discussed earlier; the offer of a given level of compensation attracts only those applicants whose opportunity costs are lower than the offer. This is not a damaging critique, however, because there is little that can be done about adverse selection simply by altering the terms of the compensation contract.[7] The more telling problem is that information revealed by the agent's on-the-job performance, as valuable as it is, can be exceedingly expensive to obtain. Spence (1974) details several reasons why it can be so costly to sort out

good agents from bad after they have been hired and why it pays both
principals and agents to invest time and effort into avoiding bad matches
in the first place:

> One might ask why the employer would not simply hire the
> person, determine his productivity, and then either fire him or
> adjust his wage or salary accordingly. There are several reasons
> why he will not do this. Frequently, he cannot. It may take
> time (even a long time) for the individual's real capabilities to
> become apparent. There may be a specific training required be-
> fore the individual can handle certain kinds of jobs. There may
> be a contract and a contract period within which the individual
> cannot be fired and his salary cannot be adjusted. All of these
> factors tend to make the hiring decision an investment decision
> for the employer. Certain costs incurred in hiring and in the
> early period of employment are sunk and cannot be recovered if
> the investment turns out badly. (p. 14)

To the extent they share in the benefits of minimizing agency losses
and agency costs, both sides are better off if principals are able to identify those individuals who possess the appropriate talents, skills, and
other personal characteristics prior to the establishment of the princi-
pal/agent relationship. The greater the investment entailed in the hiring
decision, the more critical screening and selection mechanisms become.
Thus Spence's arguments apply with even more force in the public sector
than in the private. Congressional members appointed to committees do
not serve a probationary period to see how well they work out. Civil
Service employees, for all practical purposes, cannot be fired. And as
incumbent presidents typically point out when running for reelection,
the Oval Office is no place for on-the-job training.

But how are principals and agents able to find suitable matches when
they lack the requisite information? Principals cannot observe agents'
actual performance until after the commitment to hire them has been
made. Potential agents, similarly, cannot know exactly what the job
is like until they start doing it. This problem is compounded by the
fact that both potential principals and potential agents frequently have
an incentive to misrepresent their abilities and preferences. According
to Spence, this informational gap is bridged by observing properties of
each other that are reliable signals of the underlying qualities of interest.
Many signals that employers attend to in the labor market are beyond
the applicants' control, such as race, age, or gender, and for that reason
can be illegitimate sources of discrimination. Other signals, however, the
applicant has at least partial control over, such as appearing on time for
the job interview, presenting a neat personal appearance, and expressing
enthusiasm for the job.[8]

Signaling is an important phenomenon in the political world as well. Congressional candidates who have served in an elected office before are far more likely to get elected than those who have not. A major reason for this is that their previous success signals to potential contributors that they are high-quality candidates (Jacobson and Kernell 1981). Congressional parties also tend not to name freshmen to the House Appropriations Committee. According to Fenno (1966), this is because freshmen have not been around long enough to demonstrate that they are the type of *homme sérieux* who has traditionally served on the committee—hardworking, respectful, and, whatever their ideological predilections, responsive to the needs of the party.

Monitoring and Reporting Requirements

Once a principal and agent have entered into a relationship, the most straightforward way to eliminate the conditions of hidden action and information would seem to be to institute procedures requiring agents to report whatever relevant information they have obtained and whatever actions they have taken. After all, hidden information is no longer hidden if you make the agent reveal it. On the basis of information provided by the agent, the principal can presumably tie the agent's compensation more directly to his or her actual conduct. As before, to the extent both sides share in a reduction in agency losses and agency costs, both principal and agent can be made better off.

In fact, reporting requirements are ubiquitous in both the private and public sectors. Employees fill out weekly progress reports for their supervisors, who in turn report to their supervisors on the status of their operations. Every year congressional committees, regulatory agencies, and executive departments report millions of pages of material on their hearings, investigations, and policy recommendations.

There are, however, costs entailed both in the agent's provision and in the principal's consumption of information (Williamson 1975). If nothing else, the transfer of information deflects time and attention away from tasks that they would otherwise be performing. Rather than require agents to report all relevant information, their reports should be at an optimal level of "coarsification" (Demski and Sappington 1987). Unfortunately, this is difficult to modulate; a principal can either be starving for information or, more often, drowning in a sea of it. That hundreds of millions of dollars are invested annually in the design of management information systems attests to the difficulty of this problem.

The more serious drawback to reporting requirements, however, has already been broached, and that is the problem of truthful revelation or incentive incompatibility. The agent has incentives to shade things, to make reports that reflect favorably upon himself, or to reveal information in some other strategic manner. Employees may discover that energy, skill, and creativity applied to their weekly progress reports pays off much more handsomely than actually doing the job. Even if agents can somehow be constrained to be truthful in their reports, the principal will still not know what they are not reporting. For that reason principals typically supplement these requirements with what McCubbins and Schwartz (1984) have dubbed "police patrol" oversight—audits, investigations, and other direct methods of monitoring. To be effective, monitoring policies should be applied stochastically so as to preserve the element of surprise (Kanodia 1985). Direct monitoring can cost the principal a great deal of time and effort. Anyone who has ever worked on a factory floor can attest to the fact that constant supervision is also demeaning and corrosive to the morale of both supervisor and supervisee.

Frequently an agent's actions affect individuals who are not a party to the original principal/agent contract. These individuals may be the intended beneficiaries of the agent's actions, as when an employee supplies a service to a customer on behalf of the firm's owners, or when bureaucrats deliver benefits to constituents on behalf of members of Congress or the president. Because affected third parties have an incentive to observe and to influence the actions of the agent, opportunities arise for oversight that is potentially less costly and more reliable than "police patrols." Instead of examining a sample of the agent's activities (or, more typically, the agent's reports about his or her activities), looking for inappropriate actions or improper use of information, the principal instead obtains information from the affected third parties. This McCubbins and Schwartz refer to as "fire alarm" oversight.

Fire alarm oversight offers several advantages. First, it allows the principal to gather information at lower cost; even when it is as costly as police patrol oversight, much of the cost is borne by the affected third parties. Second, it can yield better information. Under a realistic police patrol policy the principal examines only a small sample of the agent's actions and is therefore likely to miss violations. Under a well-designed fire alarm system, third parties can bring to the principal's attention any serious violation by the agent. More important, the affected third parties have incentives that are in accord with the principal's interests and not, as in the case of the agent, in conflict with them. Third, it is usually difficult to specify a priori a contract with the agent that unambiguously covers all contingencies, and consequently it is hard to tell whether an agent has violated the contract. In this situation, complaints by the affected third parties give principals the opportunity to spell out their goals more clearly.

Often it is no easier for affected third parties to oversee the agent's actions than it is for the principal. In such cases the principal can provide third parties with the means and the incentive to gather information and to report it to him. One common example is that of companies who post on the rear of their trucks an 800 number that motorists can call to report reckless driving by the vehicle's operator. Until 1874 the federal government awarded 25 percent of the fines and forfeiture collected to those who informed on fraudulent valuations by customs officers (Studenski and Krooss 1952, p. 170). Today several agencies of the federal government, including the Department of Defense, the Internal Revenue Service, and the Security and Exchange Commission, have taken similar measures by setting up fraud "hotlines" and advertising rewards for whistle-blowers. Although such programs have a number of operational problems, their deterrent effect may be substantial.[9]

Alternatively, principals can set up a fire alarm system by requiring agents to notify third parties of any actions that affect them. According to McCubbins, Noll, and Weingast (1987), this requirement is a key feature of the Administrative Procedures Act of 1946. To comply with this legislation, an administrative agency must announce its intention to consider an issue well in advance of any decision. It must solicit comments and allow all interested parties to communicate their views. The agency must explicitly address any and all evidence presented and provide a rationalizable link between the evidence and its decisions. Such procedures, of course, do not necessarily remove inherent biases in agency decision making.[10] But the mandated sequence of notice, comment, collection of evidence, and deliberation affords numerous opportunities for members of Congress to respond when an agency seeks to move in a direction that a key constituency group finds objectionable. This makes it very difficult for agencies to strategically manipulate congressional decisions by presenting a fait accompli, that is, a new policy with already mobilized supporters.

Institutional Checks

Most applications of the principal/agent framework in economics characterize the principal's problem as one of seeking to induce the agent to expend more effort. The assumption is that the harder they work, the more they produce. But agents are often in a position to do more harm to the principal than to simply withhold effort; embezzlement, insider trading, official corruption, abuse of authority, and coups d'etat are all testaments to this fact. Whenever an agent can take actions that might seriously jeopardize the principal's interests, the principal needs to thwart the agent's ability to pursue such courses of action unilaterally.

We refer to various countermeasures the principal may take in this regard as institutional checks. Operationally, institutional checks require that when authority has been delegated to an agent, there is at least one other agent with the authority to veto or to block the actions of that agent. The framers of the Constitution established many interlocking checks with the intention of constraining the more powerful central government they had created. Most firms also employ systems of checks. Large expenditures, for example, typically require the approval of both management and the comptroller. Some of the most check-laden institutions are universities. Granting tenure usually requires an overwhelmingly favorable vote in the department, the approval of the dean, the acquiescence of a university-wide ad hoc committee, and ratification by the trustees.

As Madison observed, ambition is best checked by ambition—agents positioned against each other should have countervailing interests. This is most readily accomplished by making the agents' compensation contingent on different standards, such as rewarding managers for increasing production but rewarding comptrollers for cutting costs. Checks can also be applied in information acquisition. Rather than striving for an unbiased source of information, a principal may do better obtaining biased reports from different agents who have conflicting incentives. The view that legal proceedings should be adversarial rather than administrative is based on the same logic. Conversely, checks are disabled when agents' incentives cease to be in conflict.

Checks are equivalent to what social choice theorists refer to as the presence of veto subgroups. The major theoretical results concerning the effects of veto subgroups are generally intuitive. First, the more veto subgroups (checks) there are, the harder it is to change the status quo. The status quo also becomes more difficult to change as preferences within veto subgroups become more homogeneous and as preferences between veto subgroups become more diverse (Cox and McKelvey 1984). Checks, then, inhibit the ability of agents to take actions that the principal considers undesirable, but necessarily retard agents from taking desirable actions as well; security comes at the price of flexibility. The desirability of imposing checks on delegated authority thus increases with the utility the principal derives from the status quo and with the amount of danger posed by inappropriate agency actions.[11]

Principal/Agent Relationships and Inherited Instability

Why are some methods for containing agency losses chosen and others not? In many instances it is a matter of feasibility; certain features of a situation simply preclude alternative methods. Once a professor has been granted tenure, a judge appointed to the bench, or a member of

Congress assigned to a committee, it is very difficult to remove them
or to otherwise change their compensation contract. In these cases the
principals involved rely heavily upon screening and selection procedures.
Fire alarm oversight is an option only when there are affected third
parties with the incentive and wherewithal to report actions they find
unsatisfactory. Second, the costliness of agency control measures implies
that they should be adopted only when justified by a large enough reduction in agency losses. In particular, the opportunity costs associated with
institutional checks dictate that they should be instituted only when the
potential losses of inappropriate agency action are great. When the costs
of agency control mechanisms are too high, the principal should forego
delegation altogether.

We also believe that innovations in delegation and in agency control
measures occur in response to learning and adaptation. Agents seek
out loopholes in their contracts. Principals counter by altering existing arrangements or by designing new ones. The classic statement of
this point of view is Alchian's (1950). He argues that because of uncertainty and costly information, institutional arrangements (such as
agency control measures) can be designed only imperfectly. They evolve
through a process of trial and error. Observed uniformity among surviving institutional arrangements, such as hierarchy in firms, cost and
output sharing in land rentals, or committees in legislatures, is thus the
product of an "evolutionary, adoptive, competitive system employing a
criterion of survival" (p. 31).[12] In economic settings the criterion for
survival is market fitness. Innovations that capture important economic
gains, such as economies of scale, a transfer of risk to those willing to
bear it, or a reduction in transactions costs (of which agency losses are
a major component), will survive and be imitated (Davis and North
1971).

In the legislative arena, however, Alchian's argument would seem
problematic. Instead of the selection of efficient forms of organization
through market competition, there is instead the instability and unpredictability of social choice. In any realistic choice setting, the core
of majority rule voting or any other social decision-making procedure is
empty; any alternative chosen can be defeated by some other alternative.
If stable equilibrium choices are to emerge, they must be "induced" by
restrictions on the ways in which alternatives are posed against each
other (Shepsle 1979). But if the decision makers themselves choose these
arrangements—which they do in democratic, majority-rule legislatures
such as the U.S. Congress—and they are cognizant of what policy choices
a particular arrangement will generate, then the choice over institutional
arrangements will "inherit" the instability present in the choice over
outcomes (Riker 1980). Take, for example, a situation in which there

are three alternatives, A, B, and C, and a simple voting cycle exists:
A defeats B, B defeats C, but C defeats A. The legislature, however,
initially selects from three alternative voting procedures: procedure I
pits A against B; procedure II pits B against C; procedure III pits C
against A. Obviously a prior vote on which procedure to use would cycle
in the same way as would voting on the alternatives themselves.

Despite the problem of inheritability, many political scientists have
nevertheless constructed legislative models that assume a particular institutional arrangement, such as a system of committees with orthog-
onal, mutually exclusive jurisdictions, as a given (for a thorough review of this literature see Krehbiel 1988). This mimics the strategy of
economic analysis, which has long differentiated the "short-run," where
technology, markets, firms, and the like are assumed to be fixed, from the
"long-run," where these features are themselves variables. The problem
is that in a legislature there are no physical sources of "stickiness," such
as an existing assembly line or distribution system.

The types of delegation and agency control mechanisms we have discussed in this chapter are simply different forms of institutional arrangements. In delegating policy-making authority to one agent as opposed
to another, or in selecting one configuration of agency control mechanisms instead of another, Congress would presumably alter the nature
of the policies that ultimately emerged. Choices over delegation or over
agency control mechanisms, then, would seem to inherit the instability
properties of social choice in general.

We are sympathetic to Riker's argument. As we shall see in succeeding
chapters, Congress frequently alters agency control mechanisms, whether
internally with respect to its committees or externally with respect to
the agencies and bureaus of the federal government. Occasionally the
reforms or innovations made are substantial. But there are crucial considerations that generate preferences for patterns of delegation, agency
control mechanisms, and other institutional arrangements that are distinct from and far more stable than preferences over the next set of
outcomes that will emerge from those arrangements. First, members of
Congress, in their creation of agency control mechanisms, are in pursuit
of objectives that are much more far-reaching than that of getting the
next few votes to come out right. These arrangements are not meant to
assure the choice of a particular policy, but rather to prevent policy from
being blunted and dissipated by agency losses. Much of the structure of
the committee system and of executive departments can be analyzed
and understood as resulting from efforts to mitigate a variety of agency
problems. Another source of stability in preferences over institutional
arrangements is the fact that most members of Congress have invested a
substantial amount of time and energy in the institution as it is presently

configured. They have a personal stake in a particular arrangement, for example, seniority, or the selection of the Speaker by the majority party, that is little fazed by how the next vote turns out. Such investment by participants in an institution often fosters far more support for its continuation than would otherwise make sense. This is true of even the most ridiculous of institutions. Participants in a Ponzi scheme, even if they are completely aware of what is going on, have tremendous incentive to keep it going.[13] Unfortunately, this is also true of the most coercive and pathological regimes in history.

Finally, in most organizations, including congressional parties, those who have been delegated leadership positions are able to use the resources available to them to protect their positions. They are also in a favorable strategic position relative to those who would upset the status quo. As Calvert (1987) argues:

> It is easy to see why one member, acting individually, has the incentive to cooperate. Going against the leader's wishes, on matters in which most members are inclined to follow the leader, requires organized action by a coalition of members in order for rebellious followers to achieve any better outcome. Such a rebellion faces the usual problem of collective action, exacerbated by the opposition of the leader and faithful followers. (p. 48)

There are, in short, a number of sources of "stickiness" in preferences over agency control mechanisms and other institutional arrangements. As a consequence, institutional rigidity is at least as troubling a prospect as institutional instability.

Delegation and the Abdication Hypothesis

According to the literature reviewed in the previous chapter, congressional decisions to delegate appear to have been motivated primarily by a desire to shed policy-making tasks that were too onerous, too likely to provoke controversy, or that were simply beyond the limited capabilities of either the congressional parties or the legislative branch as a whole. As this theoretical overview has shown, however, the delegation of authority and responsibility from principals to agents is crucial to the division of labor and development of specialization; tremendous efficiency gains accrue to principals and agents alike if tasks are delegated to those with a comparative advantage in performing them. We thus find it inconceivable that congressional parties or any other large organization could achieve their collective aims without engaging in prodigious amounts of delegation.

Certainly, the benefits derived from delegation come at a price. The principal suffers welfare losses caused by opportunistic behavior on the part of his or her agents. Even under the best of circumstances, agency losses cannot be eliminated. There is available to the principal, however, a large repertoire of mechanisms for reducing agency losses—screening and selection procedures, contract design (including both compensation schedules and sanctions for malfeasance), monitoring and reporting requirements, and institutional checks. These mechanisms are themselves costly to invoke, but the principal can choose the mix of mechanisms that is most effective and least costly. Under favorable circumstances, principals can transfer some of these costs to third parties. The most effective mechanisms for reducing agency losses are typically the least obtrusive. The degree to which the principal's strategies are effective should therefore never be inferred from the amount of time, energy, and attention the principal devotes to them.

CHAPTER THREE

Congressional Party Leadership

Party Labels and the Electoral Connection

Is it possible for congressional parties to effectively pursue their policy objectives when they delegate so much of their policy-making authority to members serving on standing committees? Before considering this question, it is necessary to ask the prior question of whether the idea of congressional parties having policy objectives even makes sense. Given the fundamental difficulties involved in aggregating individual preferences, modeling a collectivity as if it were a single entity with stable goals and preferences requires considerable justification.

Congressional parties have existed for nearly as long as Congress. Despite their many critics, no one suggests that they are in any danger of disappearing. But party organizations are not mandated by the Constitution or by anything else; like any other institutional arrangement in Congress, they exist because members choose to organize themselves in this fashion. It is thus safe to infer that congressional party organizations are present and persist because members find them electorally beneficial (Mayhew 1974). In our view, the key rationale congressional members have for organizing as parties is the common investment they have made in the informational content (and thus electoral value) of the party label. Voters decide between candidates according to their expectations about how they will perform in office. Although individual characteristics of candidates weigh heavily in the formation of these expectations, so too do the positions they adopt on important issues of national policy. A party label thus serves members in the same way as does a "brand name" for a multiproduct firm. The firm's reputation, as conveyed through its brand name, spills over across the whole product line. As firms with well-known brand names expand into new product lines, consumers can infer the characteristics of new products on the basis of their experience with the company's other products. The more homogeneous the products are in style, price, and quality, the higher the informational value of the label. The same is true for parties. Greater consistency in positions across issues increases the informational value of the label. Ideally, the party label conveys a simple, low-cost signal to "rationally ignorant" voters as to the policies a candidate would pursue in office and the constituencies he or she would seek to benefit (Downs 1957; Fiorina 1981b).

This line of reasoning would appear to be at odds with several areas of previous research. First of all, claims about the informational content of party labels might seem reasonable enough if we were talking about the British House of Commons or the Swedish Riksdag. Most accounts of roll call voting in the U.S. Congress, however, emphasize the extent to which individual incumbents can tailor their voting records to suit the preferences of voters in their districts. Indeed, congressional party leaders are usually seen as willing accomplices, actually encouraging their members to "vote the district first." We agree that congressional party caucuses tolerate more diversity in the voting records of their members than do parties in parliamentary regimes. We also agree that the highly individualistic nature of congressional campaigns allows candidates, especially those who raise large amounts of money, considerable flexibility in creating and projecting a particular sort of personal image. Nevertheless, party labels are a concise and efficient source of information about the policies favored by Democratic and Republican candidates. Even though it may be possible to do so, it is difficult and expensive for members to stake out a great deal of distance between the policies they espouse and those associated with their party. A candidate faces an uphill battle, for example, in seeking to convey the message that despite being a Republican, he is actually against cutting the capital gains tax, in favor of more environmental regulation, and opposed to new weapons systems. The ability of candidates to offer a policy mix that varies much from that associated with their party is further constrained by the requirement of initially winning their party's nomination.

But what about southern Democrats? If party labels are such reliable signals about candidates' policy preferences, how is it that segregationists from the South continued to be elected as Democrats even as northern Democrats called for sweeping civil rights legislation? We concede that the southern Democrats' "heresy" on civil rights was on a large enough scale that their ability to maintain an identity separate from the rest of the party might have persisted if black voters in the South had remained disfranchised. Soon after passage of the Voting Rights Act, however, the participation of blacks in Democratic primaries made the position of white segregationist Democrats untenable. In the following years the GOP contested and won more and more elections throughout the South, as southern whites, who had rejected Democratic presidential candidates since 1948, increasingly voted for Republican congressional candidates as well. By the mid-1970s, the pattern of party preferences and voting behavior in the South was virtually identical to that of the national electorate.[1] Southern Democrats have continued to be quite successful in winning election to Congress, but this is because their support among blacks is so overwhelming that Republicans must take over two-thirds of the white vote in most southern states if they are to win (Petrocik 1987).

Another place where we would seem to run into trouble with the literature on congressional elections is in asserting that party labels are an indispensable asset to congressional candidates. Most accounts tend to characterize party as more of a hindrance than anything else. "Party" and "constituency" are presented as alternative sources of influence upon members, with "constituency" generally winning out. There is no doubt that members often fail to support their party's position because it is at odds with the interests of their districts. It should be stressed, however, that for most members, party and constituency pressures coincide more often than they conflict. If congressional districts represented by Democrats often resemble other districts that are represented by Republicans, the *reelection* constituencies of Democratic and Republican members do reliably differ (Fiorina 1974; Fenno 1978; Poole and Rosenthal 1984). Given the strong incentives that exist in state legislatures to produce "bipartisan gerrymanders," most members represent districts that are safely in their party's fold (Cain 1984). Common electoral origins are thus the source of substantial commonality in the policy preferences of congressional candidates and incumbent members of the same party (Schneider 1979; Shaffer 1980; Erikson and Wright 1985; Poole and Rosenthal 1985).

Finally, making the electoral value of party labels the key rationale for the existence of congressional parties might seem dubious given that American voters appear to rely far less upon party cues than they used to. Survey researchers, pointing to increases in split-ticket voting, to trends in responses to the standard party identification measure, and to their analyses of the open-ended party "likes" and "dislikes" questions, conclude that the average level of partisanship in the electorate has declined over the past several years (e.g., Wattenberg 1984). To be sure, some recent findings run in the opposite direction; Stanga and Sheffield (1987), for instance, report that their discriminant analysis of several

party-related survey items reveals a resurgence of partisanship in the
1970s and 1980s, following a modest decline in the 1960s.

In evaluating these findings, however, it is important to keep in mind
that our argument depends not upon the amount of affection or loyalty
that voters feel for the parties, but rather on how much information is
embodied in the party label.[2] Some evidence that most American voters
can associate each party label with the general thrust of the policies that
party espouses is presented in table 3.1, taken from Erikson, Luttbeg,
and Tedin (1991). These data, which reflect the average self-placement
and perceived party positions on eight issue measures included in the
1988 National Election Study, indicate that most voters place themselves
and both major parties in a coherent order along a liberal-conservative
ideological dimension. Democrats see themselves as either to the left of
both parties or in between them. Republican identifiers see themselves
as either to the right of both parties or in between them. We are thus
confident that a candidate's party affiliation continues to provide cheap,
reliable information as to his or her policy preferences, and it is because
of this that the party label remains the best single predictor of voting
behavior in congressional elections (Jacobson 1987; Brady and Alford
1988).

Table 3.1   Voter Perceptions of Their Policy Positions Relative to
            the Two Major Parties (in percentages)

Respondents' Perceived Position	Respondents' Party Identification				
	Strong Dem.	Weak Dem.	Ind.	Weak Rep.	Strong Rep.
Left of Both Parties	53	38	26	5	6
In Between*	44	50	50	67	46
Right of Both Parties	3	12	21	28	49
n	183	141	276	144	200

*Includes respondents who see self at same location as one party but
not the other (11%).

Source: 1988 NES Election Data. Based on respondent (voters only)
perceptions on eight issues. Includes only voters who (on average) saw
Democrats to the left of Republicans.

Congressional Parties and the Role of Party Leaders

Congressional members share a common investment in the electoral value of the party label. But maintaining and enhancing the collective reputation of the party is no small task; its value declines if there are too many frequent and dramatic changes in the party's policy positions or if defections from the party's position by individual members are so widespread that they undermine the connection between party and policy. Even though the policy preferences of typical congressional Democrats are reliably different from those of typical congressional Republicans, party caucuses face the same problems of collective action, coordination, and social choice instability that all organizations face.

A fundamental approach to managing these problems is to delegate responsibility for coordinating the actions of party members to a central agent—in this case the party leadership (Shepsle and Humes 1984; Calvert 1987). A theme that dominates the literature, however, is that congressional members, at least since the Revolt against the Speaker in 1910, "stubbornly resist being led" (Davidson 1985, p. 250). The collegial nature of the Senate is thought to imply that the authority delegated to party leaders in the Senate is even less than that delegated to the Speaker of the House (Huitt 1961; Davidson 1985). Congressional parties, it seems, fail to endow their leaders with the resources they need to do their job effectively. In particular, party leaders lack the ability to dispense valuable rewards for loyalty and meaningful sanctions for disloyalty.[3] Party leaders refrain from disciplining the recalcitrant, even, as in the early 1980s, when most members of the caucus want them to do so (Sinclair 1983). But how can party leaders truly lead if they cannot punish those who will not follow? How can they maintain the informational content of the party label if members of the caucus can defect with impunity from the party's position on major roll call votes?[4] As Brady (1988) puts it: "throughout most of the House's history, party leaders have been able only to persuade, not to force, members to vote 'correctly.' Party leadership without even the threat of sanctions is likely to be unsuccessful in building consistent partisan majorities" (p. 9).

We agree with much of this literature. Party leaders in the modern Congress cannot threaten the hold that individual members have on their seat in the same way that their counterparts in parliamentary regimes can. There are not the same tight limits on individual campaign expenditures and staff resources, nor the threat of dissolution if a major vote is lost (Beloff and Peele 1980; Cox 1987). National party organizations in this country have little to do with the selection of congressional candidates and are usually not a major source of campaign funds (Salmore and Salmore 1987; Jacobson 1987). In Sorauf's (1976) terminology, "party as

organization" does not support the programmatic operations of "party
in government." These inducements to the maintenance of highly cohe-
sive voting blocs are negated by provisions of the U.S. Constitution—
separation of powers, regular elections, and protection of free speech—or
by other institutions, such as primary elections, that were specifically
designed to loosen the parties' hold over individual candidates.

It is going too far, however, to assert that congressional party leaders are totally without the ability to provide incentives for cooperative
behavior. In addition to whatever leverage they can exert through the
committee assignment process, the many favors they choose to grant or
not to grant can significantly affect a member's quality of life (Davidson
1985). It is also erroneous to infer that sanctions are ineffective in the
context of the U.S. Congress because they are invoked so infrequently.
Indeed, if sanctions are completely effective, the objectionable behavior
they are meant to deter never occurs and they are never invoked. The
events of 1975, for example, when the Democratic caucus removed three
committee chairmen and threatened to oust others, need not be replayed
over and over again for members to get the point.

Even if we accept the premise that congressional party leaders are
generally unable or unwilling to impose sanctions on members of their
caucus, this is not necessarily the fatal liability that the literature would
lead us to believe. There are many other mechanisms that can be employed to influence individual behavior and thus the collective course
of events; imposing sanctions is usually more expensive and less effective than other, less obtrusive methods. In the particular context of the
U.S. Congress, sanctions are an even less attractive option than usual.
Truly meaningful sanctions would likely be electorally damaging to the
member and could thus do the party more harm than good. As Sinclair
(1983) observes, punishing a conservative Democrat for failing to support
the party's position might result in his replacement by an even more
conservative Republican. These considerations apply at a more general
level as well. Sanctioning a bloc of members for supporting heterodox
policies might well provoke them into bolting the party, either to form
a third party or to join the opposition. Sanctions can stifle dissent and
induce conformity or, in the terminology of Hirschman (1970), eliminate
"voice." They cannot guarantee loyalty, however, if "exit" remains an
option.

It is unwise, furthermore, to become preoccupied with what party
leaders cannot do, especially given that there are so many things they can
do to shape the content of major legislative proposals and to assemble
the majorities needed to enact them. Although the importance of it is
often underestimated, party leaders can exploit the sheer prominence of
their position to stake out a highly visible focal point on key issues, thus

encouraging support to coalesce around one of possibly many acceptable alternatives (Calvert 1987). The leadership structures of congressional parties further coordinate the actions of their members by gathering and disseminating vital information on members' preferences (Ripley 1967, 1969; Sinclair 1983).

Other resources accrue to the majority party leadership simply because theirs is the majority party. The most tangible of these is the ability to manage the flow of legislation—referring bills to committee, scheduling floor consideration of bills coming out of committee, and overseeing the process of resolving differences with the other chamber. In the House, the reception bills encounter on the floor is very much the product of the protection, if any, they have been afforded by the Rules Committee. The majority party typically maintains a majority on Rules that is larger than their majority in the chamber as a whole. In recent years Rules has facilitated the Democratic policy agenda on the House floor by adroitly fashioning restrictions on the number, source, order, and degree of amendments that may be offered against committee proposals (Smith and Bach 1988; Smith 1989). In the Senate, party leaders manage floor activity by brokering unanimous consent agreements, which are the procedural arrangements under which the upper chamber usually conducts its business (Oleszek 1984; Ainsworth and Flathman 1990).

Virtually any case study of the legislative process in Congress attests to the pivotal role the majority party leadership plays in building coalitions, holding them together, and choreographing what Wilson (1956) so aptly describes as the "dance of legislation" (see, among others, Redman 1973; Barton 1976; Reid 1980). Sinclair's (1983) account of the Speaker's role in budget legislation provides an especially vivid example of what party leaders can accomplish with a repertoire of tools that does not include sanctions. During Tip O'Neill's tenure as Speaker, many House Democrats insisted that they had to demonstrate a commitment to budget cuts. In 1979, the Speaker and others in the leadership were able to persuade those who felt they would not support the Democratic resolution to vote against the Republican substitute as well. The next year, when the Republicans offered two substitutes, those members were persuaded to vote for neither substitute or, for one substitute only, but not for both. As long as these members divided their votes between the two alternatives evenly—and the leadership saw to it that they did— both of them would fail, which is exactly what happened. Similarly, members who defected on one vote often helped provide the margin of victory on the next one. As party leaders from Rayburn to Wright have observed, there is always another day and another bill.

As these episodes clearly illustrate, the simple count of how many members supported the party position and how many did not often

obscures the full extent of the role played by the majority party leadership in directing the course of legislation. Moreover, what doesn't happen
in Congress is often as important as what does happen. As Sinclair
(1983), Smith and Deering (1984), and many other scholars point out,
effective party leaders in Congress pursue policy victory in those areas
in which the caucus is in broad agreement, but submerge legislative
initiatives that would be divisive to the party. In the 1950s, according
to Sundquist (1968), the greatest service that Democratic leaders in
the House and Senate rendered to their respective caucuses was to keep
intraparty disagreements over civil rights from spilling onto the chamber
floor:

> Speaker Rayburn faced the same problems that Lyndon Johnson
> faced in leading a divided party, and he adopted the same tac-
> tics. Like Johnson, he avoided party caucuses where program
> issues that divided the party might be discussed. Like John-
> son, he avoided setting forth a program, preferring to wait for
> Eisenhower proposals and then to seek an opposition posture
> around which a degree of Democratic unity could be achieved.
> He concentrated, wrote Neil MacNeil, on "minimizing" the "di-
> visiveness" of his party. "The avoidance of open conflict is his
> genius," said Representative Lee Metcalf of Montana. (p. 403)

Although the Speaker's ability to schedule debate and floor votes (or,
more accurately, to not schedule them) is the source of substantial "gatekeeping" authority, the Rules Committee has long served as the majority
party's instrument of choice for stifling conflictual issues. Although the
committee won considerable notoriety for its scuttling of liberal policy
initiatives in the late 1950s, it also spared liberals in the 1980s the grief
of casting roll call votes on nettlesome issues they preferred to finesse.
In both chambers the Judiciary Committee has also served the Democratic majority (as well as some Republicans) by failing to report bills on
abortion, busing, school prayer, and budget balancing schemes (Cohodas
1982). The Senate, of course, has no scarcity of veto gates; every member
can potentially hold up legislation by objecting to unanimous consent
agreements, filibustering, offering a long series of dilatory amendments,
or by simply threatening any of the above tactics. Party leaders need
only refrain from undertaking the often arduous task of engineering the
compromises required to move legislation forward.

When a committee does become the graveyard for a bill, its proponents often charge that it would pass if only it could get to the floor,
but that it is being obstructed by a small minority of opponents who
just happen to be on the committee. Liberal Democrats, for example,
hurled this charge against the Rules Committee in the 1950s, when it

blocked floor action on civil rights, federal aid to education, and other items on their agenda. Jones (1968) and other scholars dispute these claims and point out that when the partisan composition of the House shifted in the early 1960s, Speakers Rayburn and McCormack led a series of successful attempts to discharge such legislation from the Rules Committee, to make the Committee more representative of the floor, and to substantially undercut its gatekeeping ability.

In our view, neither Jones nor the congressional liberals of the time quite appreciate what the Rules Committee was doing and why it was allowed to do so. The liberals were certainly accurate in perceiving Rules Chairman Judge Smith to be a preference outlier—he made no secret about that. They may have also been right in asserting that the bills they favored would have passed if they had made it to the floor. Jones, on the other hand, is correct in noting that the Rules Committee had far more support on the floor than the liberals let on. What neither recognize, however, is that the alternative preferred by the majority leadership at the time, as well as by many members on both sides of the issues involved, was to not vote on them at all—especially if the bills were going to die anyway in the Senate.[5]

Party Leaders and Madison's Dilemma

The authority that congressional parties have delegated to their leaders allows them to effectively address the coordination and other collective action problems that the parties confront. But this delegation in turn gives rise to a problem of agency that we have defined as Madison's dilemma. Agents who are placed in a position of leadership, or any other favorable strategic situation, can be expected to exploit it—to use the authority they have been granted to advance their own interests instead of (or even at the expense of) the interests of the principal. In analyzing the evolution of the Speakership in the House of Representatives, Cooper (1970) clearly recognizes the potential for this type of agency problem and the importance of avoiding it:

> ... power must be distributed with an eye both to allowing the leaders of the most stable and cohesive majority present, i.e., the majority party leadership, sufficient leverage to pass their programs when they can in fact mobilize majority support, and denying them the kind of leverage that would allow them to ram their programs through the House or obstruct other bills on the basis of personal distaste. (p. 123)

What can the party caucus do to prevent agency losses that arise from Madison's dilemma? As indicated in the previous chapter, there are four major classes of mechanisms that principals may employ to minimize agency costs: (1) optimal design of contracts; (2) screening and selection procedures; (3) monitoring and reporting requirements; (4) institutional checks. The first mechanism, contract design, has already been discussed in great detail. Congressional scholars generally stress the inability of modern party leaders to impose sanctions on their members, and making only limited, provisional delegations of authority is obviously one way to limit the extent of Madison's dilemma. We, of course, are skeptical that this is much of a limitation and also see the optimal delegation of authority to party leaders as something that is very difficult to achieve; small changes in delegation can transform effective leadership into ineffective leadership, and equally small differences separate an effective leader from someone you call Boss. Reporting requirements are also problematic in this context, in that they could seriously undercut the leaders' ability to carry out the tasks that the caucus has delegated to them. Enacting legislation requires making deals, and few deals would stay struck if party leaders were required to tell everybody precisely what they had promised to whom in exchange for what.

The two remaining classes of mechanisms—screening and selection procedures and institutional checks—are more workable and have been relied upon by the congressional parties in managing the delegation of authority to their leaders. Close attention to the qualities of those chosen to be leaders is important because the investment in the hiring decision is so substantial. Although it is always possible to remove leaders who perform unsatisfactorily, doing so always entails some cost to the party's reputation and to its legislative agenda. The other mechanism, the creation of institutional checks, was championed by Madison himself as the most efficacious way of avoiding the dilemma we have named after him. As indicated in chapter 2, checks inhibit the ability of agents to take actions that the principal considers undesirable, but necessarily retard agents from taking desirable actions as well.

Selection of Party Leaders

To the extent party leaders are able to move legislative outcomes closer to their own ideal points, potential agency losses are greatest when leaders' preferences are extreme or idiosyncratic. In order to minimize such losses, congressional members should select leaders whose preferences are as representative as possible of the caucus as a whole. Assuming that location along a liberal-conservative continuum is a reliable indicator of preferences across a wide range of policies, this implies selection of the median individual. This is hardly a novel hypothesis. Nor need selection of the median be motivated by the desire to minimize agency losses, as the same predictions follow from Black's (1958) theorem.[6] In his classic study of congressional parties, however, Truman (1959) surmised that as far as party leaders are concerned, the likelihood of getting elected and of performing effectively as an agent of the party both hinged on being a "middleman":

> One would expect that a Leader who accepted any degree of responsibility for the substantive actions of the party would almost certainly be a middleman, not only in the sense of a negotiator but also in a literal structural sense. One would not expect that he could attract the support necessary for election unless his voting record placed him somewhere near the center in an evenly divided party, and one would not expect him to be effective in his role unless he continued to avoid identification with one of the extreme groups within his nominal following. (p. 106)

In order to determine whether or not party leaders tend to be drawn from the ideological middle of their respective caucuses, we examine the NOMINATE scores of Democratic and Republican floor leaders in the House and Senate from the 80th Congress (1947–48) through the 99th (1983–84).[7] These scores, derived from scaling almost all roll call votes taken during a session of Congress with Poole and Rosenthal's (1985) Nominal Three-step Estimation (NOMINATE) procedure, reveal a member's location along a liberal-conservative dimension.[8] NOMINATE consistently identifies two or more dimensions in the roll call data, but the first dimension accounts for most of the variance. Using NOMINATE scores, though, does not require us to assume that all issues facing Congress can be projected neatly onto a single dimension. This could never be possible. No leader ever has the "right" preferences on all known dimensions. Issues arising in the future may cut along dimensions that cannot be foreseen. In light of these constraints, it makes sense for members to select leaders on the basis of the overall liberal or conservative drift of their voting record. The NOMINATE scores are thus highly suitable for the purpose of determining how well the members' leadership selection criteria conform to our hypotheses.

Table 3.2, which displays NOMINATE scores from 1984 for a select sample of prominent U.S. Senators, reveals the high correlation between NOMINATE scores and those assigned by the Americans for Democratic Action. Poole (1988) reports that ADA and most other interest group ratings are all correlated at about the .9 level with NOMINATE scores. One might wonder why we do not base our analysis on the commonly used ADA ratings. In fact, our original plan was to do just that, but the NOMINATE scores are preferable for a number of reasons. First, in the earlier years of the series, ADA scores are based upon as few as six roll

Table 3.2   NOMINATE and ADA Scores of a Select Sample of U.S.
             Senators, 1984

Name	State	Party	NOMINATE Score	ADA Rating
Barry Goldwater	Arizona	Republican	.997	5
Strom Thurmond	S. Carolina	Republican	.894	0
Paul Laxalt	Nevada	Republican	.805	5
Richard Lugar	Indiana	Republican	.680	10
Alan Simpson	Wyoming	Republican	.610	20
John Warner	Virginia	Republican	.492	10
John C. Danforth	Missouri	Republican	.382	35
Paula Hawkins	Florida	Republican	.295	25
David Durenberger	Minnesota	Republican	.186	50
Howell Heflin	Alabama	Democrat	.078	20
Arlen Specter	Pennsylvania	Republican	−.024	50
Sam Nunn	Georgia	Democrat	−.111	35
Charles Mathias	Maryland	Republican	−.217	65
Mark Hatfield	Oregon	Republican	−.330	75
Lowell Weicker	Connecticut	Republican	−.429	90
Lloyd Bentsen	Texas	Democrat	−.485	55
Walter Huddleston	Kentucky	Democrat	−.629	60
Jennings Randolph	W. Virginia	Democrat	−.727	70
Daniel Moynihan	New York	Democrat	−.805	85
Dale Bumpers	Arkansas	Democrat	−.922	75
Daniel Inouye	Hawaii	Democrat	−.984	85
Thomas Eagleton	Missouri	Democrat	−1.090	90
Patrick Leahy	Vermont	Democrat	−1.235	95
Christopher Dodd	Connecticut	Democrat	−1.345	100
Gary Hart	Colorado	Democrat	−1.432	60
Edward Kennedy	Massachusetts	Democrat	−1.508	85
Paul Sarbanes	Maryland	Democrat	−1.578	100

calls. They are thus very lumpy. Of the twelve members of the Rules Committee in 1960, for example, four scored 100, two scored 67, three scored 11, and the remaining three scored 0 (Cummings and Peabody 1963). NOMINATE scores, because they are derived from hundreds of roll call votes, constitute a very fine-grained measure. Second, the ADA, like other groups who rate members of Congress, selects votes for the purpose of identifying friends and exposing enemies (Fowler 1982). The selection bias this entails is problematic in and of itself. Such a procedure also skews the distribution of scores toward the extremes, thereby reducing further the discriminatory power of data that are coarse enough to begin with. A problem the NOMINATE scores share with ADA ratings is the arbitrary nature of the underlying scale. We cannot say, for instance, that the .602 difference between Richard Lugar and Howell Heflin is slightly greater than the .586 difference between Edward Kennedy and Dale Bumpers. Our analyses, however, require only ordinal rankings, which are easily derived by converting the raw scores into percentiles. According to Poole and Spear (1989), such ordinal rankings are extremely robust to specification error and to unequal error variances.

There are other matters to consider before turning to the data. First, party caucuses in the Senate are much smaller than in the House, and the pool of individuals who possess the knowledge and experience needed to be an effective floor leader is correspondingly smaller as well. These considerations lead us to expect that party leaders in the upper chamber tend to display more ideological deviation from their caucus medians than do their lower chamber counterparts. Similar expectations derive from the fact that the prerogatives individual Senators possess (most notably the option of objecting to unanimous consent agreements) make the selection of an ideologically atypical leader a far less threatening prospect than it would be in the House. Second, during the period covered by this study, the Republicans have almost always been the minority in both chambers. Because of their inferior status, one might also expect that the Republicans tolerate more ideological diversity in their leaders.

Tables 3.3 and 3.4 report the average percentile rank in their caucus of House members and senators during the years in which they served as the party floor leader in the House and Senate, respectively. Percentile rankings are ascending in conservatism, so 0 is the extreme liberal position, 100 the conservative extremum, and 50 the median. Looking first at the data on House leaders, we see that the Democrats have had some moderately liberal leaders in McCormack and O'Neill and that Charles Halleck was noticeably more conservative than the median House Republican of his time. Most leaders of both parties, however, have clearly tended toward the caucus median. Indeed, in 1979, then majority leader Jim Wright's NOMINATE score indicated that he was *the* median Democrat in the House of Representatives! In contrast, many floor leaders in the Senate have been remarkably atypical of their membership, especially in the early years of the series. Among Democratic leaders, Alben Barkley and Scott Lucas were substantially more liberal than the caucus as a whole, while Taft and Knowland were markedly more conservative than the median Republican. Truman's (1959) analyses of roll call data also place Knowland in the conservative wing of his party, but he seems to have undergone something of a transformation in this regard; located

Table 3.3 Percentile Rankings of House Party Leaders, 1947–84

Leader	Years	Average Percentile
Democrats:		
Sam Rayburn	1947–48	30.4
John McCormack	1949–52	33.6
Sam Rayburn	1953–54	54.1
John McCormack	1955–62	28.3
Carl Albert	1963–70	48.8
Hale Boggs	1971–72	53.3
Tip O'Neill	1973–76	36.3
Jim Wright	1977–84	54.5
Republicans:		
Charles Halleck	1947–48	62.0
Joseph Martin	1949–52	45.9
Charles Halleck	1953–54	70.0
Joseph Martin	1955–58	37.4
Charles Halleck	1959–64	43.8
Gerald Ford	1965–74	44.5
John Rhodes	1975–80	42.3
Robert Michel	1981–84	57.6

in the 83d percentile on average during the three Congresses he led
the Senate Republicans, Knowland had averaged a percentile rank of
43 (slightly liberal) during the three Congresses prior to becoming floor
leader. Truman characterizes Taft, on the other hand, as much more of
a centrist than his NOMINATE scores would indicate.

The truly remarkable entry in table 3.4 is that of Kenneth Wherry,
who was firmly ensconced in the extreme right wing of the caucus. In
seeking to explain why the Republicans had selected someone so at
odds with his "middleman" hypothesis, Truman speculated that during
Wherry's tenure "the demands upon the Senate Republicans and the
opportunities available to them, as the minority both in the legislature
and in the executive, may have been so slight as to make an extreme
Floor Leader an inexpensive luxury" (p. 110). This is consistent with our
expectation that the minority party might tolerate more ideologically
diverse leadership.

There are a couple of other factors that help account for why the
median selection hypothesis fares so poorly in the early postwar Senate.

Table 3.4 Percentile Rankings of Senate Party Leaders, 1947–84

Leader	Years	Average Percentile
Democrats:		
Alben Barkley	1947–48	23.9
Scott Lucas	1949–50	29.8
Ernest McFarland	1951–52	37.3
Lyndon Johnson	1953–60	50.3
Mike Mansfield	1961–76	42.3
Robert Byrd	1977–84	55.0
Republicans:		
Wallace White	1947–48	56.9
Kenneth Wherry	1949–51	95.5
Styles Bridges	1952	63.8
Robert Taft	1953	79.2
William Knowland	1954–58	82.7
Everett Dirksen	1959–69	62.7
Hugh Scott	1970–76	31.3
Howard Baker	1977–84	50.3

Truman notes that in contrast to the Democrats during this period, Senate Republicans assigned the offices of Floor Leader, Chairman of the Conference, Chairman of the Policy Committee, and Chairman of the Committee on Committees to four different individuals. This allowed each major faction in the party to hold at least one leadership post (p. 101). Truman, Davidson (1985), and others also observe that in the early 1950s the position of Senate floor leader was not all that coveted a position. Certainly it appeared to be more of an electoral liability than an asset, as a number of senators were defeated soon after taking on the job. In the years following the early 1950s, however, the data on Senate leaders conforms to the median selection hypothesis as nicely as does the data on party leaders in the House. Those who are credited with transforming the position of party leader into a pivotal, prestigious post—Lyndon Johnson and Everett Dirksen—were located close to their respective caucus medians. Senate party leaders since then have either been remarkably close to the median (Byrd, Baker), or at most moderately left of center (Mansfield, Scott).

Institutional Checks on Party Leadership

Another important mechanism for ameliorating agency losses is the placement of institutional checks—or veto gates, as they are sometimes called—which allow one agent to block the actions of another. When political scientists describe authority within an organization as being divided or fragmented, they are pointing to the existence of many (often mutual) checks.

Historically there has been substantial variation in the extensiveness of the checks that congressional party caucuses have built into their leadership structures. Under Czar Rule, the Speaker made all committee assignments and, working in concert with his minions on the Rules Committee, directed the agenda of legislative business taken up on the House floor. The Revolt against the Speaker in 1910 shattered this tight, interlocking directorate of party leadership by making the Rules Committee independent of the Speaker and by devolving control over committee assignments to the Democratic contingent on the Ways and Means Committee. In recent years the majority House Democrats have reconsolidated the authority of the Speaker by allowing him to select the members of the Democratic contingent on the Rules Committee, thereby transforming it once again into an "arm of the leadership" (Oppenheimer 1977). In 1974 the Democrats also turned over responsibility for making committee assignments to the Steering and Policy Committee, whose membership includes most of the leadership and several others appointed by the Speaker. According to Shepsle's (1988) characterization of the present House, "party leaders have not had so many institutional tools and resources since the days of Boss Cannon" (p. 46).

The key determinant of the desirability of checks within the structure of party leadership is the degree of homogeneity in the policy preferences of the membership. When preferences are sufficiently homogeneous, the fragmentation of authority among the party's various agents only impedes broadly favored policy initiatives (Cooper 1970; Shepsle 1988). Conversely, when the party caucus is riven by serious policy disputes, there is more support for checks. Without them, one faction, upon gaining control of the machinery of leadership, might pursue policies that are anathema to another faction, thereby weakening or even splintering the party.

The reconsolidation of the Speakership thus reflects increased homogeneity in the policy preferences of congressional Democrats. In the years following World War II, southern and border state members constituted about half of the Democratic caucus. In this situation the party leadership's central task was to keep sharp disagreements over civil rights and other issues from spilling onto the House floor. When they failed to do so, southern Democrats often sided with Republicans to thwart liberal Democratic policy initiatives (Sundquist 1968; Manley 1977; Shelley 1983). By the mid-1960s, after two decades of small, tenuous majorities and a couple of Congresses in the minority, the Democrats' margin of seats over the Republicans had grown large and stable. The share of seats held by southerners had fallen to its present level of about one-third of the Democratic caucus. Moreover, several major developments— urbanization, industrialization, economic growth, and migration—were transforming the political character of the South. As indicated earlier, the Voting Rights Act and follow-up legislation enfranchised millions of black voters. As the constituencies of southern Democrats came to increasingly resemble those of their northern counterparts, so too did their votes in Congress (Rohde 1986, 1988). The Conservative Coalition still wins some important legislative battles. But it has become easier to put together legislative packages which enjoy the support of all major segments of the Democratic party (Gettinger 1984). The removal of checks from the structure of the House Democrats' leadership thus facilitates the increased legislative capacity made possible by the homogenization of preferences.

Summary

Like all institutional arrangements in Congress, party organizations are rooted in the electoral connection. Members organize as parties in order to maintain and to enhance the informational content of their party's label. To overcome the problems of collective action, coordination, and social choice instability that they face, party caucuses delegate agenda-setting authority to their leaders. The coherence their actions impart to legislative activity is substantial enough to allow us to proceed with the premise that congressional parties have stable, identifiable goals in broad areas of public policy. If the congressional party is to effectively pursue its objectives, however, it must successfully manage the delegation of legislative authority to members serving on standing committees. Gauging exactly how successful this delegation has been in the case of the House Appropriations Committee is the subject of the next several chapters.

CHAPTER FOUR

Congressional Parties and the House Appropriations Committee

The House Appropriations Committee and the Abdication Hypothesis

As most congressional scholars see it, spending decisions confront Congress with a collective dilemma. In the belief that federally funded projects and programs benefit their constituents and thus contribute to their reelection prospects, members of Congress seek to direct as much federal spending to their districts as possible. Because tax costs are spread across all districts, they have little incentive to restrain expenditures in their own. Nor are they much troubled about the impact of their demands upon the size of the total budget; forfeiting the benefits that the expenditures would bring to their district would yield a proportionally far smaller amount (i.e., the district's share) of tax savings. Furthermore, proponents of spending on one activity, for example, urban mass transit, have an incentive to support spending on another, such as commodity subsidies, so long as that support is reciprocated. As is so often the case, individually rational behavior can yield lousy social outcomes. As Mayhew (1974) puts it, "There is a primal danger here that any taxing and spending body has to come to grips with" (p. 145).[1]

It is generally accepted that the system of standing committees in Congress exacerbates this dilemma. Through an assignment process driven by self-selection, members come to serve on those committees with jurisdiction over the programs that benefit their constituents, resulting in committee rosters that are dominated by policy (and spending) advocates (Shepsle 1978). The agenda powers that committees possess induce noncommittee members to "defer" to their proposals when they come to the floor for a vote (Shepsle and Weingast 1987a). The committee system thus serves as a crucial mechanism for the construction and defense of the now implicit vote trades that produce an expenditures logroll (Ferejohn 1985).

The Appropriations Committee, according to the prevailing view, has been the House's primary mechanism for preventing expenditure logrolls from getting out of hand. As Fenno (1966) puts it, proponents of the committee have long seen it as "a means of holding down as far as possible the appropriation of money in the face of the increasingly strenuous demands being pressed upon them" (p. 8). Many members of House Appropriations described the committee to Fenno as a sort of legislative butchershop, where, through line-by-line scrutiny of agency budgets, "fat," "grease," and "pork" was "chopped," "sliced," "shaved," and "whacked" from expenditure requests (p. 105). The committee's commitment to guarding the Treasury manifests itself in four important and interrelated ways. First, there is the cult of hard work. Members have long claimed that service on the committee demanded endless toil and largely unappreciated sacrifice. Eulogizing his predecessors in a 1941 address to the House, former Chairman Edward Taylor (1937–41) averred that guarding the Treasury was a cause to which these men had given the last full measure of devotion:

> All of the six chairmen immediately preceding me undermined their health by the terrifically hard, complicated, exacting, constant, and never-ending detailed work of the chairman. They prematurely exhausted their vitality on the altar of public service and duty. Two of them died in the service and the four others passed away not long after retiring. They literally wore themselves out fighting to hold down appropriations. (p. 14)

Second, there is the norm of "minimal partisanship" (Fenno 1973, p. 88). Under all but exceptional circumstances, Republican and Democratic members alike are expected to set aside partisan differences and join together in the pursuit of budgetary restraint. Third, new members undergo a period of apprenticeship; regardless of which side of the aisle they had come from, they are schooled to immerse themselves in the intimate details of agency budgets and to learn from their elders the best techniques for detecting waste and identifying superfluity. Finally, the very logic of the committee's organizational structure—its system of stable, highly distinct subcommittees—incorporates the commitment to guardianship:

> A restricted scope of decision making helps members obtain the kind of intimate, detailed knowledge of an agency which facilitates budget cutting ... assignments are patterned so as to hedge against this [interest-sympathy-leniency] syndrome by

assigning some members to subcommittees in which they have
no personal experience and their constituency has no interest.
And the apprenticeship period is used by elders to socialize the
newcomers in the perceptual and logical underpinnings of budget cutting. On the evidence, they have a good deal of success;
but if they fail, the very compartmentalization of the Committee
keeps any spending virus isolated. (Fenno 1973, p. 97)

The Appropriations Committee, then, has been seen as an agent of the
parent chamber, protecting it from the actions of its individual members. It is a mechanism that enables members to just say no. This is
not to say that the committee's efforts are always successful or that
they are always appreciated. The 1885 vote to divest the committee
of several appropriations bills and, more recently, the resort to alternative funding channels known as "backdoor spending" are interpreted
as congressional unwillingness to abide by the committee's stern fiscal
discipline. The committee's loss of turf resulting from these circumven-
tions is in turn blamed as a major factor contributing to large federal
deficits.

The Guardian of the Treasury model of the House Appropriations
Committee is thus entirely in keeping with the abdication hypothesis,
but in an ironic sort of way. Unlike members on other committees, those
on House Appropriations are not seen to exploit the authority they have
been granted to pursue their own parochial interests. The consensus is
rather that the committee acts to constrain the striving for constituency
benefits. Its mission is vital to the well-being of the House as a whole
and therefore transcends mere partisan politics.

Problems with the Guardian of the Treasury Model

Our questioning of the abdication hypothesis begins with our misgivings
about seeing the Appropriations Committee as an agent of the collective
membership of the House. In our view, there are several problems with
this portrayal of the committee. First, there is the problem of motivation.
It is not obvious that individual congressmen have much stake in the
interests or reputation of the House per se. They have little difficulty
avoiding responsibility for things that happen on Capitol Hill and run
for Congress by running against Congress. Voters often view Congress
as the "broken branch," but they do not blame their own representative
for the institution's failures (Fenno 1975). Second, it is difficult to define
exactly what "the House" is. Defining it as the 435 current incumbents
is formally correct but not very useful, in that it is hard to attribute
common goals and purposes to such a disparate group of individuals.
Fenno (1966) explicitly recognizes this problem in discussing sanctions

that "the House" from time to time has invoked against the Appropriations Committee: "The precise composition of 'the House' will vary with the type of conflict and the type of sanctions being applied. 'The House' which selects Committee members is not the same as 'the House' which implements backdoor spending. And neither is exactly the same as 'the House' which has extended annual authorization" (p. 77). Fenno goes on to note that "the House" often requires the intervention of outsiders, particularly the Senate and the president, to rein in Appropriations. "The House" thus becomes a catchall category for any and all sources of constraint on the committee's sphere of decision making.

A third problem with this depiction is that it is necessary to believe that members of Congress, an institution whose very structure allegedly promotes expenditure logrolls, could somehow commit themselves to a mechanism for restraining expenditures. What is it about the process that makes the cooperative solution, namely, economy in spending, binding? If the Appropriations Committee calls for funding levels below those that the House would otherwise agree to, what is to prevent the House from increasing spending above the committee's recommendations? Similarly, if the House encounters an n-prisoners' dilemma in passing spending legislation, why does the Senate not confront the same problem? The members of the Senate Appropriations Committee, by all accounts, act nothing like their penny-pinching brethren in the House. One might argue that the Senate Committee, and the entire Senate as well, free rides on the services provided by the House Committee. But if the House Committee must always play "bad cop" while the Senate Committee plays "good cop," why would the House Committee put up with this arrangement?

Because the "institutional maintenance" function of restraining expenditure logrolls is a public good, there need to exist selective incentives for its provision. This requirement identifies another major problem in viewing the Appropriations Committee as an agent of the collective membership of the House: the collective membership of the House is not the source of any important selective incentives! True, the House can censure members, or even unseat them for behavior that is either criminal or in especially bad taste. Ordinarily, however, members advance along a path that is party-specific. This is true not only for those with a position in the hierarchy of the party leadership, but for all members. It is their party, not the House as a whole, to which they direct their requests for committee assignments. It is their party, not the House as a whole, which grants them the right to continued committee service and advancement through seniority.

The conventional view of the House Appropriations Committee is thus flawed in a subtle but important way. The true principal here is

the congressional party caucus, not the House as a whole. Because of
differences in their core constituencies, the parties differ on how much
they want the federal government to spend and on what they want to
spend it on. Democrats favor higher levels of domestic spending. Relative to Republicans, they want more federal money spent on public
health, social welfare programs, housing, and, over the past few decades,
on environmental programs. Republicans favor relatively more military
spending, but desire lower taxes and less spending overall. The majority
party in the House appoints a majority to the committee. The bills the
committee reports to the floor consequently reflect the majority party's
spending priorities.

An immediate objection to our line of argument is that it is contra-
dicted by how members themselves describe the committee. As indicated
earlier, those Fenno interviewed insisted that partisanship stopped at
the door of the subcommittee hearing room; they certainly did not see
themselves as agents of their party and were confident that ideology
had little or nothing to do with their being assigned to the committee.[2]
In reply, we would first point out that it is a mistake to characterize
Fenno's account of the committee as a record of unremitting bipartisanship. He reports that during the late 1940s and early 1950s, a period
in which the parties alternated control of the House, Appropriations
subcommittees were the scene of fierce conflict between majority and
minority party members. If some minority party members were grateful
for the respectful treatment their subcommittee chairman afforded them,
others expressed frustration and a sense of powerlessness. Fenno's analyses also indicate that appropriations decisions were strongly affected
by changes in the configuration of party control. During the Republican
80th Congress (1947–48) the committee cut deeply into funding requests
submitted by the Truman administration. Controlled by the Democrats
during most of the Eisenhower administration, House Appropriations
cut much less from Budget Bureau estimates and often recommended
more than had been requested.

We also respond to this objection by maintaining that it is often unwise to infer much about the nature and function of an organization from
what members of that organization have to say about it. Employees of
a firm, for example, are far more likely to describe the jobs they do as
the quid pro quo for the compensation they receive and not as their
contributions to the firm's profits. Nevertheless, economists have long
taken as given the proposition that firms are profit maximizers, and
there are good reasons for maintaining this view; for one thing, firms
that are not profit maximizers tend to lose ground in competition with
those that are. Similarly, the primary motivation that members have
for signing on with the committee is most likely not a desire to serve

their party, but rather the compensation they receive. This compensation takes many forms—prestige, influence, the authority to monitor and to intervene in the policy-making activities of the agencies within their subcommittee's jurisdiction, perhaps even the utility they receive from guarding the Treasury. The Democratic and Republican contingents on the House Appropriations Committee can effectively serve the interests of their respective caucuses without this being the primary motivation of individual committee members.

In interpreting what members of Appropriations have related to Fenno and other scholars, it also helps to put their remarks into context. Democratic and Republican members who spend years together on the same subcommittee ("repeat play" conditions) are likely to achieve some degree of comity, and it is thus perfectly reasonable for them to describe the prevailing atmosphere as one of minimal partisanship. Similarly, the reason why Democrats and Republicans on the committee so often feel that they are working together to achieve economy is probably because the witnesses in subcommittee hearings, whether from the affected interest group, agency, or authorizing committee, are usually program advocates. *Any* concerns that committee members might express about program costs thus stand out against a background of nearly ubiquitous striving for larger budgets. It should also be kept in mind, though, that members of the majority party can achieve their objectives without constantly haranguing minority members. Conversely, it makes little sense for minority party members on the committee to make partisan appeals; if you are one of four Republicans on an eleven-member subcommittee, an argument invoking the traditional principles of the GOP is not likely to carry the day. Finally, Longley and Oleszek (1989) identify an entirely practical reason why committee Democrats would bargain in good faith with committee Republicans: it is advantageous to have them "on board" when going to conference to negotiate with members from the other chamber—especially when the Senate is under Republican control.

One might also object that we have created a straw man by misconstruing what committee members mean by "guarding the Treasury" or "pursuing economy"; what they are referring to is not budget cutting per se, but rather the elimination of waste, fraud, abuse, and overlap in government programs. Bipartisanship prevails, in other words, because members of both parties can agree that whatever the federal government spends money on, it should be spent as efficiently as possible. We concede that this point has some validity. We hasten to add, though, that while both liberal Democrats and conservative Republicans deplore waste, fraud, and abuse, they harbor very different views as to where the worst drains on the taxpayers' money are located. Democrats tend to be more upset by Pentagon procurement practices than by the illicit market in food stamps. For most Republicans the reverse is true.

A third objection to our line of argument is that the model we are seeking to supplant has already been supplanted by the passage of time. As dozens of scholars have observed, so much has changed since the days of the Textbook Congress; although accurate at the time of Fenno's study, the Guardian of the Treasury model is no longer accepted by scholars, members of Congress, or even by committee members. Not only have we created a straw man, in other words, but an old one at that. Or, more charitably, one might conclude that the Guardian of the Treasury model was an accurate portrayal of the committee in the 1950s and 1960s, but following the reforms of the 1970s and the revitalization of congressional party leadership, current conditions now favor our view of committee members as agents of their respective parties.

Lest there be any mistake about it, the point of our argument is *not* that the Guardian of the Treasury model used to be valid, while our model of committee members as agents of their respective parties is now a more accurate depiction. What we want to show is that ours provides a better explanation for the structure and behavior of the committee throughout its entire history. Still, as in the case of the other objections we have discussed, we are willing to accept that there is merit to the point that the image of the committee has changed. This would seem inevitable, if for no other reason than that the world around the committee has changed so dramatically. There are also strong suggestions in Fenno's account (which is now twenty-five years old) that the departure of Clarence Cannon, John Taber, and others of the Old Guard presaged dramatic changes in the committee's way of doing business. In particular, Cannon's successor, George Mahon, professed to be far more willing to accommodate the preferences of fellow Democrats for spending increases. Along these same lines, Schick (1980) argues that the congressional budget process instituted in 1974 created incentives for the committee to behave as a claimant on the Treasury instead of as its guardian.

After reviewing the recent literature on the committee, however, we are struck by how much staying power the traditional model has. According to Maass (1983), reports concerning the demise of guardianship are greatly exaggerated. He asserts that data on appropriations decisions over the past several years reveal no change in the committee's behavior and that the things members of Appropriations say about themselves hasn't changed much either: "Public statements of committee members, especially the chairman, give little support to the view that the committee has abandoned or substantially altered its concern for economy" (p. 133). In contrast to Maass, White (1989) reports that by the 1980s budget-cutting was no longer the "dominant expressed purpose" of the committee (p. 9). Despite this change in its public persona, however, White concludes that key elements of the Guardian of the Treasury model—subcommittee specialization, the socialization of new members, the commitment to budgetary values—live on inside the committee.

Positing that members of the House Appropriations Committee are agents of their respective parties leads to a very different view of the committee and of the legislation it produces. Its mission is not to constrain the size of an expenditure logroll composed of spending proposals that other committees have managed to get approved by the House. It never actually confronts a legislative package of this nature. The committee instead acts upon funding requests submitted to it by executive agencies, proposals that since 1921 have been incorporated into the president's budget. True, these proposals reflect previously enacted program authorizations and to some extent are premised on what the authorizing committees are going to do in the future. Ultimately, however, the president's budget embodies his own policy preferences and spending priorities. The changes that the committee makes in the president's proposals in turn reflect the preferences and priorities of the House majority.

Our party-based interpretation of congressional spending decisions also leads to radically different accounts of major changes in the appropriations process—the 1885 divestiture of the House Appropriations Committee and the 1974 Congressional Budget and Impoundment Control Act. As indicated above, most congressional scholars characterize the 1885 measure as a decision of the parent chamber to reduce the jurisdiction of a committee that had been too zealous in its guardianship. Conversely, the creation of the congressional budget process nearly a century later is viewed as a response to growing federal deficits, that are attributed, at least in part, to the inability of the committee to stem the growth of spending in areas outside its jurisdiction. Common to standard treatments of both the 1885 and 1974 reforms, then, is the faulty Guardian of the Treasury model and the mistaken view that Congress can commit itself, through structure or procedure, to binding constraints on spending. A fuller and more cogent understanding of both reforms requires that they be seen instead as innovations adopted by the majority party to further its own policy objectives.[3]

The Divestiture of 1885

As part of a reorganization plan that transferred much of Ways and Means' jurisdiction to other committees, in 1865 the House created the Appropriations Committee and assigned it the task of drawing up all annual funding bills. Those who favored the reform argued that Ways and

Means held sway over virtually all important legislation passing through the House. Supporters of the new committee also felt that the resultant division of labor would facilitate the reduction of expenditures—a goal subscribed to by almost everyone at the time, given the large debt that the federal government had accumulated during the Civil War. Some members worried that the innovation would actually be counterproductive, in that it would seem to uncouple decisions about expenditure from those concerning revenue; in a metaphor attributed to Lord Welby, they reasoned that "those who were charged with maintaining a certain head of water in the reservoir should have some control over the outflow from the sluices" (Wilmerding 1943, p. 143). Whatever the case, the intention that lay behind the creation of House Appropriations was to hold down expenditures by assigning responsibility for guarding the Treasury to a single entity within the House (Marvick 1952).

In 1877 the House voted to allow the Commerce Committee to transmit its funding recommendations for rivers and harbors improvements directly to the floor instead of to the Appropriations Committee. Responsibility for that bill was subsequently transferred to a newly created Committee on Rivers and Harbors in 1883. House Appropriations experienced another setback in 1880, when the House transferred jurisdiction over the Department of Agriculture's appropriations to the Agriculture and Forestry Committee. The major assault on the committee occurred in 1885, when the 49th Congress voted to transfer half of the remaining bills in its jurisdiction—Consular and Diplomatic Service, Military Academy, Army, Navy, Post Office and Post Roads, and Indian Affairs— to the relevant substantive committees.

There is a virtual consensus in the scholarly literature that the divestiture of Appropriations was intended to sanction and to emasculate a tightfisted, hegemonic committee that, in the view of most members, had rejected legitimate demands for more spending. There is also general agreement that the major consequence of divestiture was a significant increase in spending that eventually put the federal government in the red (Selko 1940; Wilmerding 1943; Harris 1964; Fenno 1966; Brady and Morgan 1987; Cogan 1988). Even if opponents of the committee had not desired increased expenditures, in Cogan's view a structural change of this nature made a surge in spending inevitable:

> Broadening spending authority undoubtedly served as a mechanism to facilitate an increase in expenditures. But it also created what is known as a common resource problem (Demsetz 1967; Hardin 1968). The common resource is general fund revenue. The problem is that when many Congressional committees have authority to spend general fund revenue, no single committee has any incentive to restrain its spending commitments since

the total level of spending is beyond any committee's responsibility. In fact, the opposite of restraint occurs. Competition develops between committees. The result is an accelerating rate of expenditures relative to general revenues until the available revenue pool is exhausted and deficit financing is relied upon. This common resource problem occurs regardless of the original reasons spending authority was broadened. (p. 4)

A post-1885 increase in spending is certainly evident in the data. Elimination of the income tax and steady reduction in internal taxes after the Civil War led to a decline in revenue from $558 million in 1866 to $258 million in 1878. Expenditures fell just as sharply, from $521 million to $237 million.[4] At that point tariff revenues began rising again, but spending remained flat for several more years. In contrast, in the ten years following divestiture of the Appropriations Committee total spending rose from $268 million to $352 million, and by 1894 the federal budget was in deficit. There is also no disputing the fact that in the decade prior to 1885 the House Appropriations Committee had been committed to restraining expenditures. In the debate over divestiture and other proposed reforms, members of the committee and their allies pointed with pride to its guardianship of the Treasury. They warned sternly that distributing appropriations bills to other committees would lead to a ruinous increase in spending. Samuel Randall, chairman of the committee, made virtually the same argument as Cogan:

A particular Department or bureau may prefer to have its special committee, with which it has intimate and cordial relations, to make the appropriations for its use rather than to undergo the scrutiny of an appropriations committee having control of the appropriations for all the Departments and having attachment no more to one than to another. But it is the part of wisdom to adhere to the precedents of the past, which have proved so efficacious heretofore in promoting economy and good government. If the proposition shall prevail, and the work of the Appropriations Committee be divided among other committees and added to their present duties, the extinction of the Appropriations Committee is not far distant; and when appropriations shall be withdrawn from the consideration and control of one committee, and no longer kept within due order and subordination to each other, and to the burdens of taxation imposed upon the people, and those several committees are launched out into unrestrained freedom of appropriations, each striving to surpass the other in greater recognition and larger appropriations for its special charge, it will not be difficult to prophesy the day of wasteful extravagance and all its attendant corruptions is near at hand. (*Congressional Record,* 14 December 1885, p. 171)

According to Fenno, members who favored divestiture were also re-
acting against "Appropriations Committee imperialism" (1966, p. 44).
This too is borne out by the transcript of the debate. Detractors charged
that the committee had repeatedly obstructed other committees' bills
by moving consideration of its own, which, according to the rules, were
privileged and therefore took precedence over other orders of business
(*Congressional Record*, 15 December 1885, p. 202). They complained
that the committee had frequently delayed reporting its bills until the
last few days of a session and then brought them up under suspension
of the rules in order to preclude amendments. Another grievance was
that the practice of sending two members of Appropriations and one
from the relevant substantive committee to House-Senate conferences on
appropriations bills had been abandoned in favor of sending only members of Appropriations. But this was not all. A provision in House rules
made it in order for the Appropriations Committee to attach legislative
riders (amendments) to its bills so long as such changes in existing law
served to reduce expenditures (Marvick 1952; Stewart 1989). Named
after the Indiana Democrat who had authored it, the Holman rule effectively erased the boundary between the jurisdiction of Appropriations
and that of other House committees. According to one member who
favored divestiture, the Appropriations Committee could invoke the rule
to completely rewrite substantive legislation, the only condition being
that "some plausible phraseology is adopted which gives the measure
the semblance of reducing expenditures" (*Congressional Record*, 17 December 1885, p. 284).

Cognizant of how strongly sentiment was running against the committee, its backers urged that rather than divest it of half its jurisdiction,
the House simply remove existing members and replace them with individuals who were more to their liking. Indeed, six of the seven new
members who were subsequently added to the committee in the 49th
Congress voted for divestiture, as opposed to only one of the eight returning members. This rear guard action was to no avail, however, as the
divestiture proposal passed, 232–73. Members of all other major House
committees strongly supported the measure, as did the many members
of the committees to whom the appropriations bills would be assigned.
More importantly, the vote for divestiture appeared to have nothing to
do with party politics. Noting that 75 percent of the Democrats and
72 percent of the Republicans voted against the committee, Fenno surmised that "the conflict cannot be understood in partisan terms. On the
other hand, most evidence does support an analysis in terms of House-
Committee or system-subsystem conflict" (1966, p. 44). The House also
voted to scrap the Holman rule by a similar margin, but a number of
other reform proposals did not pass. These measures would have given

privileged status to legislation reported by several other committees, packed the Appropriations Committee by assigning to it members drawn from each of several other authorizing committees, and divested it of the sundry civil bill as well.

The regime of 1885 endured until 1920, when the House, in order to reduce spending and thus pare down the unprecedented debt resulting from wartime expenditures, restored the Appropriations Committee's jurisdiction over all annual funding bills. With the House Appropriations Committee reinstated in its traditional role, expenditures quickly fell back into line with receipts (Harris 1964; Fenno 1966; Cogan 1988). This account of the rise and fall (and rise again) of the House Appropriations Committee is thus a key element of the Guardian of the Treasury model. The 1885 divestiture represents the House's sanction of a committee that had been too zealous in its pursuit of economy. The 1921 restoration occurred because fiscal exigencies again necessitated an institutional mechanism to hold the line on spending.

Viewing the 1885 reforms through the lens of the Guardian of the Treasury model thus does no violence to the basic facts of the matter. There is, however, a *post hoc ergo propter hoc* quality to this line of reasoning; if spending grew faster after 1885 than before, it must be because of the reforms enacted that year. That appropriations bills require approval by the full House, the Senate, as well as the president obviously makes it problematic to attribute the entire post-1885 increase in spending to the divestiture of House Appropriations. It also weakens the analogy that Cogan makes between the post-divestiture arrangement of several committees writing appropriations legislation and the tragedy of the commons. The n-person prisoners' dilemma that creates such problems exists because individuals do not need anyone else's approval to exploit a common resource. Another problem with the analogy is that the committee's jurisdiction over all annual appropriations bills was a monopoly in only a formal, legalistic sense. As is the case today, in many instances the funding levels recommended by Appropriations merely ratified decisions that the committee had played little or no role in making. The Post Office bill, for instance, was extremely detailed in the categories to which it appropriated money, but the amount drawn from the Treasury each year was solely a function of the difference between expenditures and receipts. The committee thus routinely specified that if the revenue of the Post Office Department was not sufficient to cover expenses, whatever sum was required to cover the department's shortfall would be appropriated. Another case in point is that of pensions for ex-soldiers and their survivors. As Stewart (1989) notes in his comprehensive study of congressional budgetary reforms, for all intents and purposes pensions were an early form of entitlement program; although

the Pension Bureau was funded through annual appropriations acts, the
Appropriations Committee had no choice but to recommend funding
needed to underwrite legislatively mandated expenditures:

> The annual appropriations bill merely replenished the fund out
> of which pensions had been paid the previous year and ensured
> that the fund would be sufficient the following year. It was the
> pension committees that had jurisdiction over pension rates and
> private pension bills. The job of Ways and Means [Appropria-
> tions after 1865] was not really independent decisionmaking, but
> technical prediction of how much the pension bills would cost
> that year. (p. 146)

Another problem with this account of the divestiture of Appropriations is that this reform was hardly the only thing that happened
during the latter part of the nineteenth century that might have affected federal spending. Among other things, between 1870 and 1900
the manufacturing output of the United States quadrupled. Population
and per capita income nearly doubled. When the Democrats charged
in 1891 that appropriations approved in the previous two sessions had
made the Republican-controlled 51st the first Billion-Dollar Congress,
GOP propogandists, pointing to the increase in population and wealth,
replied that the United States had become a Billion-Dollar Country
(Morgan 1969). Nor was the divestiture the only important change the
House made in rules governing the appropriations process. Indeed, given
the simultaneous decision to dispense with the Holman rule, it may not
even have been the most important rules change made in 1885.

These analytical problems notwithstanding, the most serious shortcoming in the conventional account is its failure to consider the role
of the committee, the divestiture, and changes in actual appropriations
in light of the partisan politics of the time. As a result, the essential
causes and consequences of the 1885 reforms have been obscured. It is
important to understand, first of all, that the commitment of the House
Appropriations Committee to guarding the Treasury was a commitment
to the policy agenda of the Democratic party. Economy in government
was accepted doctrine by both parties, but as Keller (1977) and Brady
and Morgan (1987) note, post–Civil War Democrats remained especially
faithful to the ideals of minimalist government. Grover Cleveland, the
only Democratic president of the era, was so adamant in his opposition
to federal spending that he vetoed a bill appropriating $10,000 for seed
grain to be sent to drought-stricken counties in Texas.

In the debate over divestiture, Democratic supporters of the committee argued that their party had campaigned against Republican extravagance, that their commitment to restraining spending was the key to

past and future electoral success, and that the House Appropriations Committee had been instrumental in carrying out this mandate (*Congressional Record*, 17 December 1885, p. 281). To be sure, there were calls for more spending in a number of areas. Some members bemoaned how little the federal government was spending on agriculture and internal improvements; they could not and did not blame the Appropriations Committee, however, as jurisdiction over these bills had years earlier been transferred to other committees. There were also pleas that more be spent on coastal fortifications, and one member urged that the Army be given more money to chase down Geronimo. The main thrust of the prodivestiture argument, however, was not an attack on the committee for holding down spending. It was instead that divestiture would bring about a more equitable division of the legislative workload and that, contrary to the ominous warnings of committee supporters, it would not lead to fiscal extravagance. As Charles B. Lore (R, Delaware) put it:

> Nor am I afraid of the phantom that our friend from Indiana [Mr. Holman] has with great and masterly, I may say with consummate, skill held up before other Congresses and this Congress. Like the terrific ghost of Banquo, it will not down, but is ever by his side. Increase of expenditures has been the argument that has been used again and again. It is the one argument upon which opposition to the amendment of the rules rests. (*Congressional Record*, 17 December 1885, pp. 285–86)

In response to the claim of divestiture opponents that spending on agriculture and rivers and harbors had increased after those bills had been transferred to the substantive committees, advocates of the reform asserted that members of Appropriations had overwhelmingly supported the bills when they came to the floor, that the House bills called for less spending than those passed by the Republican-controlled Senate, and that whatever growth there had been was modest in light of the rapidly expanding population of the country.

It is also important to realize that the Appropriations Committee was imperialistic because House Democrats had designed it to be imperialistic! In 1874, after the states of the Confederacy had been readmitted to the Union, the Democrats won a majority in the House for the first time since the Civil War. The White House remained under Republican control, though, as did the Senate. House Democrats responded to their situation by making the Appropriations Committee the vanguard of their policy agenda. They adopted the Holman rule and the other rules that gave the Appropriations Committee so many strategic advantages by a virtually straight party-line vote. As noted above, the most

important consequence of these provisions was to allow the committee
to imbed substantive legislation into "must pass" appropriations bills.
The Democrats' rationale for bundling legislation in this manner was
to induce Republican presidents to accept policy measures that they
would veto if allowed to consider separately. It was under the aegis
of the Holman rule that the Democrats attacked Reconstruction and
sought to abolish patronage positions created in the previous decade by
Republican administrations. As Stewart (1989) notes, the Holman rule
was "generally seen by both parties as a Democratic weapon for use
against Republican presidents" (p. 87).

In 1885, with a Democrat in the White House, the justification for the
Holman rule disappeared. So, too, did the willingness of non-Committee
Democrats in the House to tolerate an arrangement that allowed Appropriations to encroach so freely upon the jurisdiction of virtually every
other committee. A clear majority of Democrats voted to jettison the
rule, as did all but one House Republican. This was not the end of the
Holman rule, though; in the years following 1885, according to Stewart,
it was usually reenacted whenever the requisite condition of divided
control reoccurred: "...the chances of the rule being enacted increased
substantially when a Democratic House faced a Republican president;
the rule was typically repealed [as in 1885] when the two institutions
were controlled by the same party" (p. 86).

But why did House Democrats not stop there? Why did they also
choose to transfer policy jurisdiction away from a committee that was
so closely identified with the party's commitment to fiscal restraint?
According to both historians and the *dramatis personae* themselves, the
divestiture of appropriations bills served the Democratic majority in a
crucial way. As indicated earlier, in the decades following the Civil War
the federal government ran a long series of budget surpluses. Managing
the deposits that piled up presented serious problems for the U.S. Treasury, and there was widespread agreement that the annual surpluses
should be reduced. The issue was over how to do it. What gradually
emerged within the Democratic party as the preferred way to reduce
the surplus was to reduce the tariff, which at that time was the largest
source of government revenue. This was anathema to the Republicans,
who were virtually unanimous in their support for protectionism. In this
era, the Republicans usually controlled either the Senate or the White
House and were thus able to thwart any attempt at tariff reduction
by House Democrats. But the Democrats were also stymied by a small
faction of protectionists within the party led by Samuel Randall of Pennsylvania. In 1884, forty-one Democrats (Randall and the Forty Thieves)
joined a united Republican minority to defeat the celebrated Morison
horizontal tariff reduction bill by four votes. Protectionist Democrats

also thwarted adoption of a reductionist plank in the 1884 Convention platform.

The chairman of the House Appropriations Committee at the time divestiture was proposed was none other than Samuel Randall. His hostility toward government spending had made him a leading force in the Democratic party. Elected Speaker of the House in 1877, Randall was a contender for the presidential nomination in 1880. As reductionist sentiment in the Democratic party grew, however, his support for the tariff proved to be "the kiss of death" (Morgan 1969, p. 82). In 1883 he lost the Speakership to reductionist John Carlisle of Kentucky, and by the time the 49th Congress convened in 1885 there was considerable pressure within the Democratic caucus to strip Randall of the Appropriations Committee chairmanship. Carlisle and other Democratic leaders feared that a vote on Randall would be another contentious vote on the tariff, but they knew that the vast majority of members, reductionists and protectionists alike, would favor divestiture of the committee and a more egalitarian division of policy-making labor.[5] The purpose of the assault on the committee ("not much disguised at the time," according to Joseph Cannon in 1919) was thus to undercut Randall still further. In an era when the Chairmen of Ways and Means and Appropriations were the second- and third-ranking members of their party respectively, the divestiture of Appropriations was much more a devaluation of the protectionists' "portfolio" within the Democratic party than a sanction imposed by a dissatisfied parent chamber.

The strategy of diminishing the presence of the protectionists by diminishing the presence of the Appropriations Committee succeeded nicely; only at the tail end of debate was the tariff issue even broached. Appealing to his Republican colleagues who were united in their support for protectionism, McKinley of Ohio said this of Randall: "We were glad to have him help defeat the Morison tariff bill. Is that the reason that gentlemen occupy the position they do on this side of the House? Is that to be the meaning of this vote? If it is, then let us vote down this proposition to distribute the bills" (*Congressional Record*, 18 December 1885, p. 319).

Randall and the Appropriations Committee did receive disproportionately more support among protectionists; 39 percent of the Democrats in the 49th Congress who subsequently voted against a tariff reduction bill also voted against divestiture, compared with only 23 percent of those who voted for tariff reduction. Presumably the Republican votes that were cast against divestiture were also in support of their protectionist ally across the aisle. The bottom line here, though, is that even a large majority of protectionist Democrats voted for divestiture. Carlisle, in other words, had managed to pull off what Riker (1986) would call a

nice piece of "heristhetics": the political art of achieving an outcome
on one dimension—the rebuff of Randall and the the protectionists—by
voting on another.

Downsizing the committee Randall chaired represented a clear signal
to protectionists that there was no room for them in the Democratic
party, thus serving to clarify the meaning of the party label. After
Cleveland's speech calling for tariff reduction in 1887, the party divisions were clear: "Thereafter national politics frequently pivoted on the
clash between Republican protectionism and Democratic reductionism"
(Keller 1977, p. 378).

But wasn't this a Pyrrhic victory, coming only at the cost of wrecking
a committee that had effectively pursued the party's policy agenda and
a resultant spending surge that ran counter to the party's fundamental
principles? If the divestiture of the House Appropriations Committee
was not responsible for the increase in expenditures that occurred, then
what was?

Probably the best way to understand the post-1885 upward trend in
spending is to first consider that one of the most serious fiscal problems
of the post–Civil War era, as indicated earlier, was the accumulation of
large annual surpluses. As shown in table 4.1, the federal government ran
a surplus in every fiscal year between 1870 and 1893. The persistence of
these surpluses was due not to any shortage of ideas as to how to dispose
of them, but to the fact that each of the many schemes offered was unable
to surmount political opposition of one form or another. Thwarted in
their efforts at tariff reduction, many Democrats also favored reducing
revenue by cutting excise taxes, which fell heavily on liquor and tobacco. These proposals foundered in the face of strong prohibitionist
sentiment. Many members favored increasing expenditures on public
works, but were stymied by the executive branch; even though federal
spending on local improvements was rarely considered unconstitutional
after the Grant administration, presidents of both parties—Arthur in
1882, Cleveland in 1887—vetoed Rivers and Harbors funding bills they
deemed extravagant. Some advocated massive expenditures on coastal
fortifications, but concern over the Chilean naval threat faded before
much money was appropriated for such purposes. Other ideas included
spending the surplus on public education or to divide it up among the
states. There was even a seemingly crackpot notion to spend hundreds
of millions of dollars to construct a canal across the Isthmus of Panama.
With revenue cuts or spending increases not forthcoming, the Treasury
had little choice but to retire the federal debt at a much faster rate than
that called for by the sinking-fund law.[6] Between fiscal years 1886 and
1890 the interest-bearing debt fell from $1.2 billion to a little over $800
million.

There was one area, however, in which significant expenditure growth was politically viable in the post–Civil War era: compensation for war veterans and their survivors. There was certainly strong demand for such expenditures; guidebooks for obtaining pensions and other war-related benefits appeared soon after Appomattox (e.g., Raff 1866). Keller (1977) reports that in the years following the war, "an extensive infrastructure of pension and claim agents, pension attorneys (an estimated 60,000 by 1898), medical boards, and 4,000 examining surgeons served this first large-scale federal welfare system" (p. 311). It is also the case that the veterans were well organized; the Grand Army of the Republic was perhaps as potent a force politically as it had been militarily. Republicans were especially supportive of pensions for Union Army veterans (this category of recipients included very few individuals from the solidly Democratic South), but the importance of the veterans' vote also made it difficult for most northern Democrats to oppose increases in pension expenditures.[7]

In the decades following the Civil War, Congress voted repeatedly to increase pension benefits and to ease eligibility requirements. Legislation passed in 1871 dropped the requirement for veterans of the War of 1812 that disabilities had to be service-related to warrant benefits. In 1878 the same provision was dropped for their widows who had not remarried. In 1879 a coalition of Republicans and northern Democrats voted to make benefits accrue to eligible veterans from the time of their discharge from active duty and not, as previously provided, from the date they had filed their claim with the Pension Bureau.[8] Lump-sum payments mandated by this bill, known as the Pension Arrears Act, averaged about $1,000 per recipient—enough in 1879 to buy a house or small farm. Within a year of its passage the number of pension recipients increased from 26,000 to 138,000, and outlays jumped from an average of $28 million in the five years prior to 1879 to $60 million in the five years after 1879 (Studenski and Krooss 1952, p. 164). An 1886 act increased widows' pensions to $12 a month, and in 1887 all veterans of the Mexican-American War who were over sixty-two years of age became eligible for pensions. In most sessions of Congress during this era, Friday evening was "pension night," reserved for consideration of special acts granting pensions to those whose claims had been rejected by the Pension Bureau. Such acts account for roughly half the bills passed by Congress in the 1880s. It was in rejecting hundreds of such bills that Grover Cleveland accumulated a veto total surpassed only by Franklin Roosevelt.

No previous piece of legislation, however, increased pension expenditures as much as the Dependent Pensions Act of 1890, which made virtually all Union veterans and their dependents eligible for pensions. In the 1888 campaign Benjamin Harrison castigated Cleveland for having

Table 4.1   Trends in Federal Expenditures, FY1870–1900
(Millions of Dollars)

Fiscal Year	Rivers Harbors	Agri-culture	Navy	War	Military Academy
1870	3.7	0.15	21.8	54.2	0.09
1871	4.8	0.18	19.4	31.4	0.18
1872	5.4	0.21	21.2	30.4	0.09
1873	6.3	0.22	23.5	40.0	0.07
1874	5.5	0.23	30.9	36.6	0.12
1875	6.4	0.29	21.5	34.7	0.09
1876	5.4	0.24	19.0	32.4	0.13
1877	4.1	0.12	15.0	32.4	0.06
1878	3.7	0.10	17.4	28.4	0.06
1879	8.2	0.12	15.1	32.1	0.08
1880	8.0	0.13	13.5	30.0	0.11
1881	8.5	0.22	15.7	31.4	0.09
1882	11.4	0.25	15.0	32.0	0.10
1883	13.6	0.30	15.3	35.3	0.14
1884	8.2	0.43	17.3	31.2	0.09
1885	10.5	0.53	16.0	32.2	0.30
1886	4.1	0.49	13.9	30.2	0.30
1887	7.8	0.64	15.1	30.8	0.28
1888	7.0	1.41	16.9	31.5	0.10
1889	11.2	1.04	21.4	33.2	0.08
1890	11.7	1.61	22.0	32.9	0.23
1891	12.2	1.80	26.1	36.4	0.24
1892	13.0	2.20	29.2	33.9	0.32
1893	14.8	2.23	30.1	34.8	0.23
1894	19.9	1.88	31.7	34.7	0.36
1895	19.9	1.89	28.8	31.9	0.40
1896	18.1	1.98	27.1	32.7	0.18
1897	13.7	2.18	34.6	35.3	0.23
1898	20.8	2.35	58.8	71.2	0.28
1899	16.1	2.45	63.9	213.7	0.16
1900	18.7	2.64	56.4	119.0	0.20

Foreign Inter.	Postal Def.	Indian Affairs	Pensions	Interest	Total	Surplus
1.49	2.8	3.4	28.3	129.2	309.7	101.6
1.60	3.7	7.4	34.4	125.6	292.2	91.1
1.84	3.6	7.1	28.5	117.4	277.5	96.6
1.57	4.8	8.0	29.4	104.8	290.3	43.4
1.51	4.2	6.7	29.0	107.1	302.6	2.3
1.26	6.6	8.4	29.5	103.1	274.6	13.4
1.41	4.5	6.0	28.3	100.2	265.1	29.0
1.23	5.7	5.3	28.0	97.1	241.3	40.1
1.23	5.7	4.6	27.1	102.5	237.0	20.8
1.33	5.3	5.2	35.1	105.3	266.9	6.9
1.21	3.1	5.9	56.8	95.8	267.6	65.9
1.09	3.9	6.5	50.1	82.5	260.7	100.1
1.31	0.1	9.7	61.3	71.1	258.0	145.5
2.42	0.1	7.4	66.0	59.2	265.4	132.9
1.26	0.0	6.5	55.4	54.6	244.1	104.4
1.92	4.5	6.6	56.1	51.4	260.2	63.5
1.33	8.2	6.1	63.4	50.6	242.5	94.0
1.36	6.5	6.2	75.0	47.7	267.9	103.5
1.59	3.1	6.2	80.3	44.7	267.9	111.3
1.90	3.9	6.9	87.6	41.0	299.3	87.8
1.64	6.9	6.7	106.9	36.1	318.0	85.0
2.03	4.7	8.5	124.4	37.5	365.8	26.8
1.74	4.0	11.2	134.6	23.4	345.0	9.9
1.98	5.9	13.3	159.4	27.3	383.5	2.3
1.70	8.2	10.3	141.2	27.8	367.5	−61.2
1.70	11.0	9.9	141.4	31.0	356.2	−31.5
1.60	9.3	12.2	139.4	35.4	352.2	−14.0
2.08	11.1	13.0	141.1	37.8	365.8	−18.1
2.49	10.5	11.0	147.5	37.6	443.4	−38.0
2.62	8.2	12.8	139.4	39.9	605.1	−89.1
3.21	7.2	10.2	140.9	40.2	520.8	46.4

vetoed similar legislation and promised the American people that he would not weigh "the claims of old soldiers with apothecary's scales" (Studenski and Krooss 1952, p. 214). That the Republicans gained control of both chambers of Congress as well as the White House assured the bill's enactment, but a major increase in expenditures would have occurred even without it. This is because Harrison had appointed James Tanner, chief lobbyist for the Grand Army of the Republic, to be Commissioner of the Pension Bureau. Corporal Tanner had made his intentions clear, having proclaimed "God save the surplus," as well as a promise to "drive a six-mule team through the Treasury" (Morgan 1969, p. 331). Under his direction the Pension Bureau accepted virtually every claim filed, so, in a sense, the 1890 Act simply ratified this policy.

As shown in table 4.1, expenditures on pensions clearly responded to the legislation discussed above. Spending remained flat throughout the 1870s, as the increase in benefits awarded veterans of the war with Mexico and previous conflicts was counterbalanced by the mortality rate in the recipient pool. Passage of the Pension Arrears Act produced the spending surge that occurred in fiscal year 1880, and expenditures jumped again in the early 1890s in response to enactment of the Dependent Pensions Act. By fiscal year 1893 pension benefits totalled $159 million and accounted for 42 percent of the federal budget.[9]

Table 4.1 also displays expenditures covered by the bills that were transferred away from the House Appropriations Committee.[10] The data bear out Brady and Morgan's (1987) finding that expenditures on rivers and harbors and on agriculture rose in the years following transfer of the bills in 1877 and 1880, respectively. There were also postdivestiture increases (i.e., in the period after FY1887) in expenditures on the Navy, on deficiencies of the Post Office, and on Indian Affairs. It is difficult, however, to attribute much of the spending increase in these areas to the release of "pent-up demand" created by the tightfistedness of the House Appropriations Committee. Spending on rivers and harbors did rise soon after 1877 (i.e., FY1879), but then fell off dramatically in the first Cleveland administration (FY1886–89). Even though it rose again in subsequent years, it never exceeded more than about two percent of the federal budget. Second, as Stewart (1989) notes, much of the increase in the Department of Agriculture's budget (which never exceeded more than trace amounts of total spending during this period) occurred when the Weather Bureau was transferred to it in 1891. Third, funds allocated to Indian Affairs and to meeting postal deficiencies did not increase until many years after divestiture. Finally, the data reveal no consistent increase in expenditures on the Military Academy or on Foreign Intercourse (covered under the Diplomatic and Consular Affairs bill). Expenditures on the Army and Navy jumped dramatically in fiscal years 1898 and 1899, but this was of course due to the war with Spain.

In short, the big story in late-nineteenth-century budgetary trends was not the divestiture of the House Appropriations Committee. It was pensions. In the ten years following the 1885 reforms, total government spending rose by $109.7 million, from $242.5 million to $352.2 million. Pension expenditures accounted for $75 million, or nearly 70 percent of the total increase. In conjunction with the McKinley Tariff, the growth of pension expenditures means that it was the Republican solution to the problem of the surplus that ultimately carried the day.[11]

The Congressional Budget Act of 1974

During the 1972 campaign, Richard Nixon repeatedly attacked Congress for increasing federal spending above the levels he had recommended, thus producing large federal deficits and promoting inflation. The problem, as Nixon saw it, was not so much the spendthrift ways of individual members, although few of them seemed terribly concerned about how new and bigger programs would be financed. It was, rather, the fragmented, piecemeal way in which Congress made spending decisions:

> ... the Congress suffers from institutional faults when it comes to Federal spending ... Congress not only does not consider the total financial picture when it votes on a particular spending bill, it does not even contain a mechanism to do so if it wished ... The Congress, thus, has no sure way of knowing whether or when its many separate decisions are contributions to higher prices, or possibly to higher taxes. (quoted in Schick 1980, p. 44)

Nixon even went as far as to justify his unprecedented use of impoundments on "the failure of Congress to develop legislative mechanisms that would review the overall fiscal situation and take appropriate action in advance of clearing specific appropriations" (Glass 1973).

Nixon's charges against Congress were leveled in the midst of a highly partisan reelection battle and late in a period of inter-branch strife so rancorous that Schick characterizes it as the Seven-Year Budget War. Nevertheless, there was widespread agreement among both liberals and conservatives on Capitol Hill that the annual appropriations process was no match for modern budgetary realities. Congress responded to Nixon's indictment by creating the Joint Study Committee on Budget Control. Composed primarily of senior members of both chambers' appropriations and revenue committees, the JSC was instructed to recommend new procedures and new arrangements that would correct major shortcomings in the way Congress made decisions about spending and revenues.

In its April 1973 Report, the JSC noted that deficit spending had occurred almost continuously over several decades and in recent years had grown worse. In their view, the source of this unsound fiscal practice was not the Appropriations Committee, which they felt had struggled mightily to resist spending pressures. The problem was rather that there were many doors to the Treasury, and the Appropriations Committee stood guard at only one of them. Since restoration of the committee's monopoly over annual appropriations in 1921, the rise of "uncontrollable" permanent appropriations, trust funds, and various forms of direct Treasury financing had resulted in its de facto loss of jurisdiction over more than half of all federal spending. Although the JSC Report regrettably lacked the rhetorical flourishes of the speech Samuel Randall had made against the divestiture of his committee nearly ninety years earlier, the logic was identical:

> The present institutional arrangements in many cases appear to make it impossible to decide between competing priorities with the result that spending is made available for many programs where the preference might have been to make choices among the programs rather than providing for spending in all cases.
>
> The fact that no committee has the responsibility to decide whether or not total outlays are appropriate in view of the current situation appears to be responsible for much of the problem. Perhaps still more critical for the process is the distribution of jurisdictions over components of the budget among several different congressional committees. As a result, each spending bill tends to be considered by Congress as a separate entity, and any assessment of relative priorities among spending programs for the most part is made solely within the context of the bill before Congress. (p. 1)

Later in its report the JSC again observed that "the splintering of spending authority from the Appropriations Committee has been a substantial factor in Congress' loss of overall budgetary control" (p. 10). The committee had faithfully carried out its role as Guardian of the Treasury, but their guardianship was no longer enough. Fisher's (1982) analysis of budgetary trends during this period strongly bears out the JSC's allegations. He reports that between fiscal years 1969 and 1973, appropriations bills authored by the committee cut $30.8 billion from presidential budget requests, but increases in entitlements and other forms of direct Treasury financing simultaneously added $30.4 billion.

Although conceivably they could have recommended that jurisdiction over all spending decisions be returned to Appropriations once again, the JSC instead called for Congress to adopt a comprehensive new budget process overseen by new committees. Congress acted upon the JSC's recommendations the following year, with overwhelming majorities in both the House and Senate approving the Congressional Budget and Impoundment Control Act. The legislation requires Congress to annually adopt joint resolutions that designate projected revenue, ceilings for about twenty major categories of expenditures, and explicit deficit figures for the upcoming fiscal year. Ceiling targets would be specified in an initial resolution due by 15 April, followed by a binding resolution to be approved before 15 September. (Congress has chosen to adopt only one budget resolution per year since 1982.) Both chambers created a new Budget Committee to draft these resolutions, and the Congressional Budget Office was established to provide Congress with economic forecasts, spending and revenue projections, and other relevant information. To be sure, much of the Democrats' enthusiasm for the 1974 act arose from the fact that for all intents and purposes it outlawed presidential impoundment of appropriated funds. Members on both sides of the aisle, however, were persuaded that deficits would come down. Surely no one would vote for a budget resolution that explicitly called for a deficit as large as the $25 billion shortfalls that had occurred in the previous couple of years. No longer could Congress obscure hard budgetary choices in a jumble of piecemeal annual spending bills, bobbing in the sea of permanent appropriations disingenuously referred to as "uncontrollable" spending.

Many members soon became disenchanted with the 1974 reforms. In their view, the new process infused the consideration of budgetary decisions with needless complication, acrimony, and delay. Indeed, in many sessions Congress has wrangled over budget resolutions months after their deadline for adoption and has approached adjournment with action pending on most appropriations bills. Perhaps these side effects would have been more tolerable if deficits had come down as anticipated, but no progress on this front was forthcoming. In the first several years after the process was instituted, the size of the deficits at least remained stable, averaging $64 billion during the Ford administration and $63 billion during the Carter years. In the first Reagan administration, however, the size of the deficits nearly trebled to an average $183 billion. The congressional budget process was blamed for either having done no good at all or for actually having made things worse; as Schick (1986) puts it, "The growth in deficit spending is widely regarded as the most conspicuous failure of the budget process" (p. 26).

If there was any beneficiary of congressional disaffection with the budget process, it was, according to many congressional scholars, the House Appropriations Committee. A budget process functioning the way it was supposed to would seem to remove much of the *raison d'être* of the House Appropriations Committee; with another committee setting binding spending levels, Appropriations becomes a "subdued guardian," or, even worse in light of its traditional mission, just another claimant on the the Treasury.[12] But with the budget process in disarray and the Budget Committees increasingly discredited, the House Appropriations Committee came back strong:

> When the budget process was threatened with paralysis in 1983 and 1984, the House Appropriations Committee came forward with its bills without waiting for adoption of the budget resolution. Seeing an opportunity to demonstrate that it could handle the budget without the overlay and frictions of the budget process, the committee reclaimed its role as guardian of the purse by playing the incremental role in which it had long excelled. (Schick 1984, p. 110)

The severity of the criticism leveled against the congressional budget process is probably due to the fact that expectations for what it would accomplish had run so high. Whatever its many shortcomings, however, it is erroneous to blame it for the large deficits the federal government has incurred since 1974. Those who do fall prey to the same *post hoc ergo propter hoc* fallacy that has led so many scholars to attribute the increase in federal expenditures after 1885 to the divestiture of House Appropriations. For one thing, the severe recession of 1981 to 1983 made larger deficits inevitable, and in the view of most macroeconomists, desirable. Most other advanced industrialized nations suffered some sort of economic downturn at this time, and most ran deficits that were comparable in size to that of the United States. More importantly, though, the belief that Congress could use the budget process to hold down deficits is based on the faulty premise that members of Congress can commit either themselves or future Congresses to binding levels of revenues, spending, or deficits. In a majority-rule institution like Congress, any spending proposal can be amended upward, and any limitation on expenditures that is adopted one day can be overturned the next.

But if Congress truly cannot commit itself to a ceiling on expenditures, why is the belief that it can so persistent?[13] As indicated earlier, the Guardian of the Treasury model possesses tremendous staying power. Similarly, in virtually every session of Congress over the past twenty-five years, one or more senators or House members have proposed new budgetary reforms designed to put the brakes on spending. This is all the more remarkable in light of the fact that the 1974 Budget Act was only one in a series of unsuccessful attempts to set binding limits. Congress had approved expenditure caps in both 1969 and 1970, but in both years voted to raise them to accommodate subsequent spending increases. In 1972 the House adopted Nixon's proposed $250 billion ceiling, but the measure died in the Senate and spending surged past that figure. The two chambers passed different ceilings in 1974, but actual spending exceeded both of them.

It may be that the many proposals for procedural constraints on spending that have been offered and adopted over the years grow out of a profound naïveté. Maybe they are merely the utterances of politicians making a cynical play to voters who are worried about deficits. Perhaps, but we are prepared to give them (the politicians and the voters) more credit than this. Even though such proposals are usually couched in terms of imposing binding constraints on spending, politicians do not necessarily mean the same thing by this as do lawyers or economists. We think that the congressional budget process and other expenditure limitation procedures are instead based upon the following, interrelated set of premises: (1) most voters dislike large deficits; (2) most members therefore find it embarrassing to vote for large deficits; and (3) once a spending ceiling has been adopted, most members find it embarrassing to vote for expenditures that exceed it. (For members of Congress, an embarrassing vote is one that can be used against them by their opponent in the next election.) Procedures for constraining expenditures, then, are another form of heristhetic—parliamentary stratagems that seek to change the outcomes of congressional decisions by changing perceptions about what they mean.

To properly evaluate the impact of the congressional budget process upon the overall level of spending and the size of federal deficits we must therefore do more than simply note the continued existence of spending increases and large deficits. We need to gauge the extent to which the budget process has transformed what would have been votes to fund popular programs into votes on the overall level of spending and the size of the deficit. This is certainly the sort of "spin" that members who favor less spending strive to impart to things during the annual struggle over passage of the budget resolution. On a couple of occasions they have achieved some degree of success. By most accounts, the budget resolutions adopted for fiscal years 1982 and 1983 were tantamount to a rejection of continued public sector growth. In both years a coalition of Republicans and conservative Democrats in the House joined with the Republican Senate to adopt budget resolutions that incorporated many of the spending cuts favored by the Reagan administration. Stockman (1986) and others argue that subsequent backsliding by Congress made the cuts that actually resulted far more modest than what the budget resolutions called for. More important, though, voting for budget resolutions that specify very large deficits has apparently not been as embarrassing as expected. As shown in table 4.2, in the first year the process was implemented, Congress passed a budget resolution calling

Table 4.2   Projected and Actual Federal Deficits, FY1976–89

Fiscal Year	President's Budget	CBR	CBR,$_{FY+1}$	CBR,$_{FY+2}$	Actual
1976	51.9	74.1	—	—	73.7
1977	43.0	50.6	—	—	53.6
1978	57.8	61.2	—	—	59.2
1979	60.6	38.8	—	—	40.2
1980	29.0	29.8	—	—	73.8
1981	15.8	27.4	11.7	+28.7	78.9
1982	45.0	37.7	19.1	1.0	127.9
1983	91.5	103.9	83.9	60.0	207.8
1984	188.8	179.3	161.1	130.8	185.3
1985	180.4	181.1	192.7	207.6	212.3
1986	180.0	171.9	154.7	112.9	221.2
1987	143.6	142.6	115.7	77.9	150.4
1988	107.8	108.0	80.2	33.6	146.7
1989	129.6	135.3	117.2	95.3	152.1

for a peacetime deficit ($74.1 billion) of unprecedented proportions. In the three fiscal years beginning with 1984 the deficit specified in the budget resolution averaged over $175 billion.

There are a couple of factors that have probably helped members feel politically less exposed in agreeing to large deficit numbers. First, in 1981 congressional budget resolutions began projecting "out-year" deficits. As table 4.2 shows, with the exception of the FY1985 resolution, these figures have projected future deficits to run at considerably lower levels than that for the current fiscal year. In 1980, for example, the FY1981 budget resolution projected a surplus of nearly $30 billion for FY1983 (the actual deficit was $208 billion). Large current deficits presumably appear less disturbing in the context of a brighter fiscal future. What really goes a long way toward preventing budgetary embarrassment for member of Congress, however, is a budget proposed by the president that also contains large deficit figures. This is especially the case for a Democratic Congress when the president is a Republican. In the same years the deficit in the budget resolution averaged $175 billion (FY1984–86), deficits called for by the Reagan administration averaged $183 billion.

As high as the deficit figures that the president and Congress have stipulated in their respective budget documents have been, they have rarely been high enough to accommodate the size of the deficits that actually accrued. As the figures in table 4.2 also show, from FY1976 through FY1989 the federal deficit averaged $30 billion more than the figures specified by ostensibly binding congressional budget resolutions. Congress, of course, need not explicitly vote to violate spending or deficit ceilings in order for this to occur. One recurrent source of downward bias in estimated deficits is the unrealistic economic assumptions upon which budget resolutions are often based (Calmes 1985). The FY1982 and FY1983 resolutions were extreme cases in this regard. Premised upon the Reagan administration's celebrated "rosy scenarios" of robust growth even as the economy was falling into a deep recession, their deficit forecasts were short by over $90 billion and $100 billion, respectively.[14] Congress has also resorted to one time savings, partial year funding for entitlement programs, payment deferrals, projected savings from "managerial reforms," and similar ploys to show lower spending and smaller deficits than the facts would justify. As with overly optimistic economic projections, this is not a specifically legislative foible. In many instances Congress has simply gone along with accounting fictions spun out by the Office of Management and Budget (Calmes 1990a).

Despite the ease with which a budget resolution's spending and deficit ceilings can be evaded, on many occasions Congress has explicitly voted to ignore the budget resolution, usually by voting to deactivate enforcement provisions in the Budget Act. In 1982, for example, the House voted to override the "deferred enrollment" provision that suspends further action on appropriations bills exceeding the first budget resolution's target figure. In 1984 it waived all enforcement provisions of the act for all appropriations bills. Budget resolutions are concurrent and not joint resolutions; they do not have the force of law. Thus another way to circumvent the "binding" spending ceilings is to not pass the requisite legislation. In 1983 Congress adjourned after failing to enact any of the many deficit reduction measures required by the reconciliation instructions included in the budget resolution it had adopted in June. Not surprisingly, those involved in the process have frequently concluded that it is an empty exercise. In the view of a minority staff member on the House Budget Committee, the budget process is "irrelevant" and "makes very little difference in what Congress would have done anyway" (quoted in Gregg 1981, p. 64). David Obey (D, Wisconsin) characterizes budget resolutions as "ethereal," with "no real connection to programmatic or tax reality" (Tate 1982, p. 1891).

It is something of a tribute to congressional faith in the procedural fix that by 1985 there was considerable sentiment for another try at designing a mechanism to restrain spending. Deficits in the previous

three years had run in the range of $200 billion and were projected
to remain at that level well into the future. After considering several
proposed reforms, in late 1985 Congress passed the Balanced Budget
and Emergency Deficit Control Act. Better known by the eponym of
Gramm-Rudman-Hollings, the measure called for steady reductions in
federal deficits, running at about 5 percent of GNP in FY1986, until
a balanced budget would be achieved in FY1993.[15] According to its
proponents, this law would eliminate the easy dodges of using overly
optimistic economic assumptions and bookkeeping gimmicks to arrive at
unrealistically small deficit forecasts. If the OMB determined that the
law's deficit targets were being breached during the course of the fiscal
year, automatic, "indiscriminate" cuts (distributed between domestic
and defense programs) would be triggered to bring spending back into
line.

For all the rhetoric about putting teeth in the budget process and
indiscriminate spending cuts, Gramm-Rudman-Hollings contained several very discriminate loopholes. As members were well aware of at the
time of its passage, much of the federal budget was immune from "sequestering," as the spending cut provision came to be called. Social
Security, federal pensions, food stamps, and interest payments on the
debt were exempted entirely, and any reductions in Medicare payments
were restricted to a maximum of 2 percent. Although Gramm-Rudman-
Hollings required the president's budget to meet its annual deficit target,
actual expenditures could exceed it by several billion dollars before cuts
were mandated. The effect of this was to give the president the job of
proposing cutbacks while allowing members of Congress to claim credit
for any benefits restored. Congress could also waive the deficit targets by
simply voting that the economy is in a recession. The ultimate defense
against the "automatic" cuts specified by Gramm-Rudman-Hollings, of
course, was to simply repeal the law itself. This is precisely what Congress did in late 1990. In legislation designed to lower the federal deficit
by $500 billion over the next five years, explicit deficit targets of the
previous law were scrapped in favor of multiyear ceilings on spending. Is
there any reason to believe that these caps will be any more successful in
binding Congress than the deficit targets of Gramm-Rudman-Hollings?
We do not think that there is.

In the years following enactment of the Gramm-Rudman-Hollings
Act deficits receded a bit, but starting in FY1990 the cost of funding the bailout of the Savings and Loan (S&L) industry pushed them
back to previously high levels. Any downturn in economic activity adds
further to deficit pressures. Although we are probably incurable opti-
mists, scenarios that we find vaguely plausible project deficits to begin
declining again over the next several years. Any downward trend in

deficits, though, is almost entirely a function of the growth in Social Security contributions resulting from the "Baby Boom" cohort moving into its peak earning years. Removing Social Security from the budgetary equation leads to forecasts of deficits persisting in the $200 billion range, as Senator Daniel Moynihan (D, New York) won some notoriety in pointing out.

It is nevertheless possible that Gramm-Rudman-Hollings exerted some drag on spending by keeping the size of the federal deficit a more salient consideration to members than would otherwise have been the case. Indeed, by our line of reasoning this is the most that such a law could ever accomplish. One thing that is certain, however, is that Gramm-Rudman-Hollings generated a veritable flowering of creative accountancy. To help Congress and the Bush administration meet the FY1990 deficit target, for example, the Department of Defense moved an October 1 payday to September 29 and the Department of Agriculture accelerated crop subsidy payments. This made the FY1989 deficit even higher, but that target had already been overshot and it was too late in the fiscal year for any funds to be sequestered. Proposals to move the cost of borrowing by the Resolution Trust Corporation "off-budget" also enjoy wide support (Redburn 1989).

Violating a previously agreed upon spending limit, in short, has proven not to be as embarrassing to members as proponents of the budget process might have presumed. On the surface, the reason for this would seem to be that funds appropriated in excess of previously adopted limits are usually for extremely popular programs—more money for the war against drugs, aid to victims of drought, hurricanes, and earthquakes, or support for the emerging democracies of Eastern Europe, to name a few. The fact that these expenditures are for such worthy causes, however, is only symptomatic of the fundamental reason why the congressional budget process, Gramm-Rudman-Hollings, and other expenditure limitation mechanisms have rarely succeeded as heristhetic devices for reducing spending and deficits: by and large, neither Democratic Congresses nor Republican presidents have wanted to use them in this way. For all but the four years of the Carter administration, the politics of budget resolutions in the House has taken the form of the Democratic majority against a Republican minority seeking to push the priorities of a Republican president (assisted from 1981 through 1986 by the GOP majority in the Senate). As such, their battles have generally not been over the size of the deficit per se. Rather, both parties have sought to blame federal deficits on each other's favorite policies. According to the Republicans, deficits result from excessive spending on the Democrats' domestic programs. The Democrats in turn blame budgetary shortfalls on the Republicans' penchant for too much defense spending and the

Reagan tax cuts. Introductory statements made by the two parties' contingents in the House Budget Committee (1983) Report on the FY1984 Resolution clearly reveal the battle lines the two sides have taken up year after year. The Democrats, on the one hand, begin with a blanket indictment of Reaganomics:

> The critical problems of unemployment, business failures and inequitable treatment of the majority of our citizens demand a bold and imaginative plan to promote economic growth and fairness and equity. The supply-side economic scenario promoted and implemented by this administration has failed. Pressing National needs in the areas of health, education, job creation and our physical capital structure have been sorely neglected. (p. 19)

The opening salvos of the Minority Report, on the other hand, attack the "liberal-Democratic Budget Resolution" as obviously inspired by a "longing to return to the days of the Great Society":

> In reporting a First Budget Resolution for Fiscal Year 1984 which calls for damaging tax increases, a crippled defense budget, and massive increases in domestic spending, the Majority on the House Budget Committee has failed the first important test of its ability to produce responsible budgetary recommendations despite its increased majority. Instead, the Majority seems to have devoted its attention to producing a first draft of the Democratic party's platform for the 1984 elections. If so, its obvious theme will be to return to the days of higher taxes, increased spending for whatever lobbying group can demonstrate its association with the mainstream of the Party's central headquarters, and depleted resources for this nation's defense programs. (p. 278)

The highly partisan nature of this language is to be expected in light of the nature of the Budget Committee. House Democrats plainly see it as a "leadership committee," acting on behalf of the majority party. Its job is to write a Democratic budget, which, throughout most of its history, has meant reordering the priorities of a budget submitted by a Republican president. The preferences of Budget Committee Republicans are given short shrift. According to Schick (1980), "From the start of markup in HBC through the completion of floor action, House Republicans have been outsiders, rarely courted or consulted by the Democratic majority" (p. 242). In order to insure that the preferences of committee members closely track those of the caucus as a whole, it and its counterpart in the Senate were designed to be more malleable than other committees. The chairman and all other members are reappointed by their party caucus at the beginning of every Congress. Members may serve only six years out of every ten, and members do not accrue seniority with continued service.

The best evidence as to the nature of budget resolutions is in the numbers themselves, reported in table 4.3. If anything, these figures understate the extent of the policy divisions between the parties. To some extent the president's budget incorporates expectations about

Table 4.3   Comparison of President's Budget and Congressional Budget Resolutions,[a] FY1976–88

| Fiscal Year | National Defense[b] | | | Domestic Programs[c] | | |
	President's Budget	CBR	Change	President's Budget	CBR	Change
1976	120.3	107.0	−11.1%	37.7	68.5	81.7%
1977	124.6	121.0	−2.9%	49.3	69.0	40.0%
1978	130.4	124.4	−4.6%	76.0	79.5	4.6%
1979	142.2	139.6	−1.8%	88.7	88.8	0.1%
1980	151.9	154.3	1.6%	101.9	118.2	16.0%
1981	178.7	206.6	15.6%	94.8	85.1	−10.2%
1982[d]	244.2	243.7	−0.2%	68.2	74.9	9.8%
1983	281.1	269.5	−4.1%	60.7	76.6	26.2%
1984	297.3	287.3	−3.4%	78.9	91.1	15.5%
1985	335.7	309.4	−7.8%	82.4	90.3	9.6%
1986	342.8	323.8	−5.6%	81.3	91.9	13.0%
1987	342.9	309.7	−9.7%	78.9	92.7	17.5%
1988	331.3	312.2	−5.8%	88.0	106.1	20.6%

[a]For fiscal years 1976-82, the congressional budget resolution figures are based on the second binding resolution. From FY1983 on, only one resolution was passed each year.

[b]New budget authority included under National Defense and International Affairs.

[c]New budget authority included under Energy, Natural Reserves and Environment, Commerce and Housing Credit, Transportation, Community and Regional Development, Education, Training, Employment, and Social Services.

[d]President's Budget figures for FY1982 incorporate the revisions submitted to Congress on 24 September 1981.

congressional action, and Congress adopts budget resolutions in the
knowledge that the president can veto appropriations bills flowing from
the various functional categories. Congressional budget resolutions from
FY1982 through FY1987, moreover, required the House Democrats to
reach compromises with the Republican Senate. Nevertheless, table 4.3
reveals that year in and year out, Democratic Congresses have used the
budget resolution to highlight their desire for relatively more domestic spending and relatively less spending on defense. In contrast, the
changes that congressional Democrats made to the Carter administration's budgets (FY1978–82) were generally quite modest and as likely to
be conservative in direction as liberal. The only substantial departures
from the Carter administration's proposals were additions to domestic
programs made in FY1980 and to national defense in FY1981. The first
is due in part to the successful efforts of liberal Democrats to boost
spending in this area, but much of it reflects an accommodation to the
rising tide of inflation that had inspired an "austere" Carter budget. The
FY1981 increases in defense—something of a "foreshock" to the rapid
rise in defense spending over the next several years—were prompted by
the fall of the Shah in Iran and the Soviet invasion of Afghanistan.

   Table 4.4 shows what many congressional scholars have noted previously: House Republicans have almost always been virtually unanimous
in their opposition to congressional budget resolutions. Their higher
rates of defection from the party's position leads Schick (1980) to stress
the extent of Democratic factionalism and disarray on budget votes.
A more telling interpretation of these figures, however, is that every
resolution House Democratic leaders have brought to the floor has been
brought with the knowledge that the majority they required had to be
constructed from the votes of Democrats alone.[16]

   Not surprisingly, the majority party leadership in the House has used
the Rules Committee to provide budget resolutions with an array of
parliamentary advantages. In many years the rule under which the resolution is considered permits the Republicans to offer only one or more
amendments in the nature of a substitute to the (Democratic) committee
bill. This induces something of a positive feedback loop, as the protective
rules make it even less likely that any Republican support is forthcoming.

   Required to review all budget-relevant legislation to insure its conformity with the budget process, the Rules Committee also plays the
role of enforcer. Most important legislation is budget-related, of course,
and most of it is in at least technical violation of the terms of the
1974 act. If they do not obtain the necessary waivers from the Rules
Committee, bills are likely to be decimated by points of order. At first
glance, the Rules Committee seems to be arbitrary and capricious in
its decisions. Sometimes waivers of a particular provision are granted to

Table 4.4   House Votes on Budget Resolutions by Party, FY1976–89 [a]

	Democrats		Republicans		Total	
Resolution	Yes	No	Yes	No	Yes	No
1976:1	197	68	3	128	200	196
1976:2	214	67	11	124	225	191
1977:1	208	44	13	111	221	155
1977:2	215	38	12	113	227	151
1977:3	225	50	14	119	239	169
1978:1	206	58	7	121	213	179
1978:2	195	59	4	129	199	188
1979:1	198	61	3	136	201	197
1979:2	215	42	2	136	217	178
1980:1	211	50	9	134	220	184
1980:2	212	52	0	154	212	206
1981:1	203	62	22	131	225	193
1981:2	201	45	2	146	203	191
1982:1	84	153	186	1	270	154
1982:2	70	150	136	50	206	200
1983:1	63	174	156	32	219	206
1984:1	225	36	4	160	229	196
1985:1	229	29	21	139	250	168
1986:1	234	15	24	155	258	170
1987:1	228	19	17	160	245	179
1988:1	230	19	0	173	230	192
1989:1	227	24	92	78	319	102

[a] Votes are on passage of the initial House version of the budget resolution, not on adoption of the conference report. Beginning with FY1983, Congress has adopted only one budget resolution each year, rather than the two originally prescribed by the Budget Act.

one bill but denied to the next. In May 1981, for instance, Rules blocked consideration of a supplemental appropriations bill until Appropriations removed $500 million for Department of Defense inflation adjustments and directed the Nuclear Regulatory Commission to speed up licensing procedures for nuclear power plants (Donnelly 1981a). Rules refused to allow the FY1987 omnibus continuing resolution to come to the floor and threatened to send its own version instead until Appropriations agreed to scrap the \$3.4 billion revenue sharing title (Wehr 1986a). Rules can invoke the Budget Act to stymie other committees as well. In 1985, for example, Rules denied Ways and Means "fast-track" consideration of their reconciliation bill because its counting revenues accruing to Superfund was explicitly forbidden by the budget resolution (Wehr 1985).

In contrast, a \$4.8 billion supplemental appropriations bill received Budget Act waivers even though it exceeded the FY1983 budget resolution, contained authorizing language, and funded unauthorized water projects (Sarasohn 1983). Throughout the years of the Reagan administration the Appropriations Committee routinely skirted budget resolution spending ceilings by funding commodity subsidy programs, food stamps, and other entitlements for less than the entire fiscal year. Such accounting gimmickry obviously violates the budget process, but the Rules Committee repeatedly failed to object.

If the Rules Committee is less than consistent in its enforcement of the congressional budget process, it is a mistake to think that its decisions are random. As one would expect from a committee that serves as an arm of the majority party leadership, its actions are heavily biased in favor of Democratic interests. What the Rules Committee assesses is not actually a bill's conformity with the Budget Act, but rather its conformity with the Democratic policy agenda. When Rules deems that the Appropriations Committee or other committees have acted in good faith vis-à-vis the Democratic caucus, they grant their bills waivers of spending ceilings, bans on authorization language, and any other requirements that they may fail to satisfy. If in their judgment this is not the case, the waivers are refused.

Summary

In his remarks to the House during the debate over the 1885 divestiture of the House Appropriations Committee, John Reagan (D, Texas) dismissed arguments that divestiture would lead to a surge in spending. He observed, "If it is the purpose of the House to be extravagant, that cannot be controlled by the committee from which the bills may come. If it is the purpose of the House to be economical in its appropriations, it will be so, whatever committee the bills may come from" (*Congressional Record*, 15 December 1885, p. 203). Although Reagan is more famous for the role he played in the creation of the Interstate Commerce Commission a few years later, the point he made on that day is an important one. Members of Congress cannot commit either themselves or future Congresses to binding levels of revenues, spending, or deficits. They cannot do so through structure, as the Guardian of the Treasury model of the House Appropriations Committee implies, nor through any formal procedure, such as the congressional budget process. Although Congress has made spending decisions under the auspices of many different procedures and organizational arrangements, none have served to prevent congressional parties from pressing on with their policy priorities.

CHAPTER FIVE

Congressional Parties and Committee Assignments

Many of the problems that are inherent in delegation can be avoided if principals are able to select as their agents individuals whose skills, attitudes, and other characteristics are appropriate for the tasks and responsibilities assigned to them. A good match between the person and the position reduces the need for costly monitoring, sanctions, and institutional checks. At the beginning of each Congress, the party caucuses decide on the size of the standing committees, on the ratio of majority to minority party members, and on which members should be assigned to fill which vacancies. Picking the right people for the right slots would thus seem to convey to congressional parties a superb opportunity for shaping committee decisions.

What does it mean, in the case of the House Appropriations Committee, for the party caucuses to assign the "right" people? The budgetary priorities established in the appropriations process are a major expression of party policy. Appropriations bills are "must pass" pieces of legislation; often considered under the pressure of impending deadlines, they are susceptible to a variety of agenda moves. The party caucus should be reluctant to entrust such important duties to members whose preferences over spending levels are unrepresentative of the caucus as a whole. Assuming that a reliable indicator of members' preferences across a wide range of policies is their position along a general, liberal-conservative continuum, we hypothesize that the congressional party, in order to achieve its desired policy goals, strives to make the median voter in its contingent on a committee coincide with the median voter of the caucus as a whole. In the context of appropriations, liberalism translates into a preference for more spending on domestic programs and less spending on the military. Going a step further, we posit that in the case of major committees such as Appropriations, the congressional parties seeks to replicate the entire distribution of policy preferences in the caucus. Doing so helps keep "peace in the family," as it allows caucus members across the entire ideological spectrum to infer that their views are fairly represented in committee (Masters 1961; Plott 1982). Our second hypothesis, then, is that in filling vacancies, the parties seek to align the distribution of preferences on the committee with the distribution of preferences in the caucus as a whole.

A key element of the abdication hypothesis is that instead of using assignments to shape committee decisions, the congressional parties accommodate as much as possible the desire of members to be assigned to committees with jurisdiction over programs of vital concern to their constituents. Once assigned to a committee, members are seen to have a "property right" that guarantees them their committee posts for as long as they want them. Although ostensibly made by the party caucuses, committee assignments are not used to further legislative objectives of the parties qua parties, and the composition of standing committees is largely the product of self-selection. In the case of most committees, this implies that their rosters are dominated by "high-demand" program advocates. In the case of House Appropriations, however, the prevailing Guardian of the Treasury model predicts self-selection by "low-demand" members, who presumably find cutting budget requests a congenial task (Stewart 1988). If so, conservatives would flock to Appropriations subcommittees with jurisdiction over domestic programs, and liberals would dominate those that oversee military spending. Because eleven of the thirteen Appropriations subcommittees in existence since the end of World War II focus predominately upon domestic spending programs, the Guardian of the Treasury model implies a conservative bias in the membership of the committee as a whole.

In this chapter we compare the merits of our hypotheses against those derived from the Guardian of the Treasury model by examining assignments to the House Appropriations Committee and to its various subcommittees made by the Democratic and Republican caucuses between the 80th (1947–48) and the 98th (1983–84) Congresses. We also examine assignments to the House Budget Committee since its inception in 1975. Before doing so, there are a few preliminary issues that need to be addressed. First, given the importance of assignments to Appropriations and other "power" committees to the parties' pursuit of their policy objectives, we would not expect them to assign to such committees members whose ideological predilections were not well known. The need for information of this nature prior to making assignments manifests itself in two important ways. First, the parties rarely assign members to Appropriations until they have observed them in action for a couple of terms. Fenno (1966) notes that only 15 percent of new members between 1947 and 1963 were named in their first year in Congress. In the 1965–83 period, 21 percent of the fifty-seven new Democrats were named in their first year, but only one of the thirty-eight Republicans was a freshman. As figure 5.1 illustrates, the reluctance to assign members until their policy preferences and other important characteristics have been ascertained results in a committee whose members have been in Congress longer than the average member. During the 1947–83 period, Appropriations Democrats had served in Congress an average of 11.9 years, compared with an average of 8.5 years for all House Democrats. Figures for the Republicans were 9.7 and 6.9, respectively.

Second, because a reliable indicator about what a congressman believes is where he comes from, party selection committees will often replace an outgoing member with someone from the same state. The Democrats were especially likely to follow this rule of thumb—49.5 percent of the 105 members they assigned to Appropriations were from the same state as their predecessor, compared to 29.1 percent for the GOP.[1]

In his analysis of the Ways and Means Committee, Shepsle (1978) points out that too great a reliance upon a "same-state" replacement

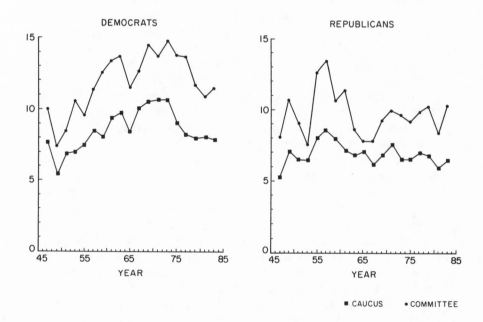

Figure 5.1 Average Years in Office, Party Caucuses vs. Their Contingents on the House Appropriations Committee

strategy would prevent committees from tracking changes in the geographic composition of the party caucus. If so, it could lead to a lack
of ideological representation as well. This has proven not to be a problem for the Democrats. As the data plotted in figure 5.2 indicate, their
contingent on Appropriations has closely mirrored the geographical composition of the caucus. Incremental growth in the number of positions
on Appropriations has helped in this regard, but Fenno reports that
the Democratic Committee on Committees did override the same-state
norm in order to make their contingent on Appropriations reflect the
declining share of southern members in the caucus (1966, p. 62). The Republicans, in contrast, allowed a large geographic imbalance to develop
on their contingent. Figure 5.3 shows that during the 1960s and 1970s
their contingent overrepresented the Midwest and underrepresented the
growing number of southern and border-state Republicans. By the 1980s
this imbalance had been redressed.

The issue of geographical balance confronts our analysis with a potentially damaging problem. Shepsle (1978) reported that the parties'
Committees on Committees have long been organized along geographical

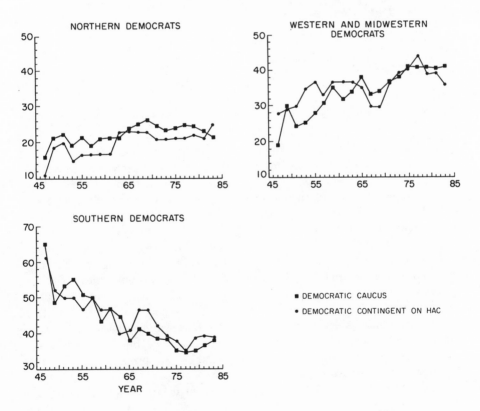

Figure 5.2 Geographical Balance of House Appropriations Committee Democrats

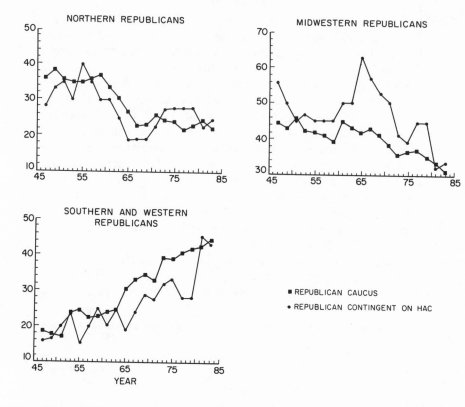

Figure 5.3 Geographical Balance of House Appropriations Committee Republicans

lines; zone representatives compete vigorously to get their regions' representatives their most preferred assignments.[2] Assume for the present that we find the two contingents on Appropriations to be ideologically very representative of their respective caucuses. It is entirely possible that those in charge of assignments care far more about geographical representation than about ideological representation, but because of the correlation between the two achieve ideological balance as a happy though unsought consequence of geographical balance. If so, the phenomenon upon which our analysis is focused—the ideological representativeness of party contingents on Appropriations—would be, well, epiphenomenal.

We concur that in the case of Appropriations geographical balance is an important desideratum in and of itself. Its recommendations concern not only *how much* is to be spent on various programs, but also *where* it is to be spent; members of Congress presumably want proper weight given to their preferences regarding both aspects of spending decisions. Several pieces of evidence, however, indicate that it is the signal it conveys about ideology that makes geography such an important consideration in assignments to Appropriations. First, we have already noted that the Democrats have made a much higher percentage of same-state replacements than have the Republicans. The most obvious explanation for this difference is the fact that the correlation between geography and ideology is much higher among congressional Democrats than among Republicans (Shaffer 1980). This also accounts for why it was the Republicans and not the Democrats who allowed a serious geographical imbalance to develop and to persist in their contingent.

The issue of geography raises another important problem for our explicitly partisan, ideological interpretation of assignments to the Appropriations Committee. Members of the committee, at least in their interviews with Fenno, cited several reasons as to why they had been chosen. Many reported that their party's Committee on Committees had picked them for geographical reasons—especially when the vacancy they were filling had been created by the retirement of a member from their own state. Others indicated they were chosen because they had the right personal style, most notably a willingness to work hard and an acceptance of the need for compromise (Fenno 1966, p. 26). Ideological considerations, however, were not perceived to have much at all to do with why they were named to the committee. How can we maintain our hypotheses about the parties seeking ideological balance on the committee when committee members themselves reject this as the reason for their selection?

We concede that committee members' perceptions are worth paying attention to, but consider the following scenario. Assume that a party, say the Democrats, currently has a contingent on the committee that is reasonably well balanced, but must fill the vacancies left by four departing members. Two of these members had been moderates, one an extreme liberal, and the remaining one moderately conservative. If they were replaced by a conservative, a moderate, and two moderate liberals, ideological considerations would appear to have played little or no role in their selection. After all, members with widely disparate policy views had been named to the committee simultaneously. Nevertheless, the Democratic contingent on the committee would remain nicely balanced.

Up to this point we have implicitly assumed that the congressional parties pursue identical assignment strategies, but otherwise act independently of each other. A prior decision must be made, however, as to the ratio of majority to minority members on each committee. During the time period covered by our analysis, the majority party has settled for a 3-2 ratio on Appropriations unless their margin in the chamber was even larger than 3-2. When this has occurred, their ratio has been adjusted upwards to approximate their seat advantage in the chamber.

Party ratios on Appropriations have therefore closely tracked party ratios in the House as a whole. As the figures plotted in figure 5.4 indicate,
the only sizable deviations occurred in the early 1950s, when the majority party's lower bound of 60 percent on the committee exceeded
narrower floor margins.

Most congressional observers have characterized House Appropriations as a holding company for distinct, highly autonomous subcommittees. Because of this we suspected that even though party ratios on
the full committee closely matched the floor ratios, the majority party
might have frequently occupied a disproportionate number of subcommittee slots. Indeed, in the 96th and 97th Congresses (1975–79) the
Democrats held 73 percent of all subcommittee slots, compared with
67 percent of the positions on the full committee. In a couple of other
Congresses, though, Democrats held two or three subcommittee slots
fewer than their margin in the chamber or on the committee would have
allowed. The discrepancies thus run in both directions, and in all other
years deviations between the percentage of subcommittee slots and the
percentage of slots on the full committee were virtually nonexistent.

But why wouldn't the majority party "stack" Appropriations, or other
standing committees for that matter? Of all the features of Congress that
exasperated Wilson, perhaps what annoyed him most was proportional
representation of the minority party on committees (1956, p. 87). This
arrangement, it turns out, is hardly atypical. A majority of parliaments
in the world afford proportional representation on committees to opposition parties (Inter-Parliamentary Union 1986). In many national legislatures the chairmanships of committees are distributed on a proportional
basis (Strom 1984). Why is this the case?

It is possible that majority parties accept proportional representation
of the minority on equity grounds; explaining why the Democrats in 1985
had agreed to reduce the size of their margins on many committees,
one staffer reported, "It may sound corny, but we were trying to be
fair" (Granat 1985, p. 141). He's right. It does sound corny. Another
reason for not doing so is that in all probability the votes aren't there
to do it. Assuming the Democrats are the majority party, reducing the
number of Republican slots would deprive conservative Democrats on
committees of the option (and threat) of forming a coalition with them.
Consequently, conservative Democrats might join the Republicans to
prevent majority party stacking of committees. More important, however, we believe that it would not be in the interest of any segment
of the majority party—liberals, moderates, or conservatives—to insist
on disproportionately large majority to minority ratios. Bills ultimately
come to the floor, where they are open to challenge from the Conservative Coalition or other interparty coalitions. It thus makes sense for the

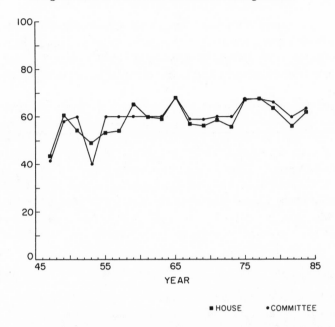

Figure 5.4 Percentage of Democrats in the House of Representatives
and on the House Appropriations Committee

majority party to make sure that these bills have already weathered such
challenges in committee. If the committee is an ideological microcosm of
the floor, members on both sides of the aisle will be satisfied that their
views were fairly represented in committee and that they are not likely
to achieve outcomes on the floor that they were unable to achieve in
committee. The value that both congressional parties derive from delegating legislative workload to their contingents on standing committees
is undercut if bills fashioned in committee can't survive on the floor.

This line of reasoning does not account for why the majority party
in Congress permits the minority party the right to make their own
assignments. What if the minority assigned doctrinaire extremists to
a committee in an attempt to extract more policy concessions from
the majority or to otherwise interfere with the normal workings of the
committee? The majority party's insistence upon a working majority
of at least 60 percent on Appropriations is no doubt motivated by a
desire to protect itself from this sort of mischief. It is also not obvious
that it is in the minority's interest to be represented by a badly skewed
committee contingent. At times the House Republicans have been able
to put their stamp on legislation—particularly when a Republican in the
White House stood ready to thwart Democratic policy initiatives. The

1981 and 1982 Reagan-backed budget resolutions remind us of this fact. For the Republicans, however, legislative victories rest upon their ability to provoke large numbers of Democrats to defect. A band of doctrinaire extremists is not likely to fashion proposals attractive to majority party waverers.

For this reason it would behoove the Republicans not to treat assignments in a totally cavalier fashion. Still, during the period covered by this study, the Republicans have almost always been the minority in the House. Even though they would seem to have nothing to gain from having ideologically skewed committee contingents, they probably also have less to lose. This consideration leads us to our third hypothesis: because of their inferior status, the Republicans tolerate greater ideological discrepancy (to the left or to the right) between their contingent on Appropriations and the caucus as a whole.

Ideological Composition of the Appropriations Committee

Have the congressional parties achieved a close fit between the distribution of preferences in their contingents on the House Appropriations Committee and the distribution of preferences in the caucus as a whole? Or has the committee displayed a consistently conservative bias, as the Guardian of the Treasury model would contend? The measures of general liberalism-conservatism that we use to test these rival hypotheses are the members' NOMINATE scores. As indicated in chapter 3, these scores are derived from scaling roll call votes with Poole and Rosenthal's (1985) Nominal Three-step Estimation procedure. Like all other such measures, the NOMINATE rankings are based solely upon what can be observed on the floor and do not reflect the behavior of members in committee. Variance between actions taken in these two different legislative arenas will compromise the value of these ratings as measures of ideological attributes. We must therefore assume that there is a very high correlation between members' public and private behavior.

Converting the raw NOMINATE scores into percentile rankings provides us with a good measure of the ideological representativeness of the two party contingents on Appropriations.[3] In order to determine whether parties align the median of their committee contingent with the caucus median we need only to determine the percentile ranking within their respective caucuses of the median committee Democrat and median committee Republican. The caucus percentile rankings of the median committee Democrat and median committee Republican from 1947 to 1984 are plotted in figure 5.5.

The median committee Democrat tracked the caucus median pretty closely prior to 1959 and again in the last few Congresses of the series,

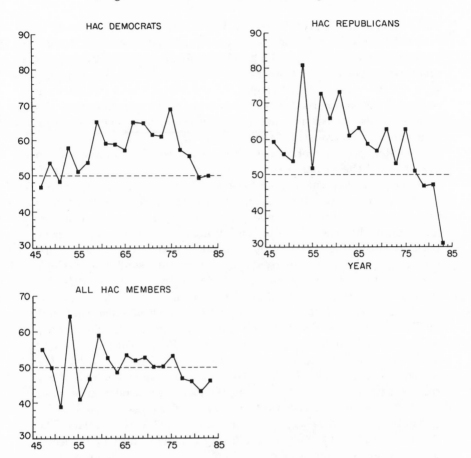

Figure 5.5 Percentile Rank of Committee Medians

but from the late 1950s until the late 1970s stood at or above the 60th percentile in the caucus. A Wilcoxon difference of medians test (Hogg and Craig 1978, p. 315) indicates that a deviation of this size, given the typical size of committee contingents, is usually significant at the $p < .05$ level. Through 1975, the median committee Republican was also significantly more conservative than the median caucus Republican, but moved sharply leftward after that. By 1983 the median Republican on the committee had dipped well into the liberal wing of the party.

Neither the Guardian of the Treasury model nor our median selection hypothesis imply that either party (let alone the Republicans) would have a committee contingent whose median was considerably more liberal than the caucus as a whole. We were thus troubled by these findings and correspondingly greatly reassured by the results of White's (1989) study of the ideological character of the Appropriations Committee between the 87th (1961–62) and 99th (1985–86) Congresses. Although his analyses are based upon Conservative Coalition support scores, he detects the movement of the Republican contingent to the liberal wing of the caucus as occurring at the same time as our analyses show. His figures similarly reflect the movement of the Democratic contingent away from the conservative side of their caucus.

Consistent with our other hypothesis, the Republicans do appear to have allowed their committee contingents to be ideologically less representative of their caucus than have the Democrats. Over this period, the median committee Republican deviated 11.2 percentiles on average from the caucus median, compared with only 7.8 for the Democrats. To be sure, the smaller size of the Republican contingent might have been a contributing factor. It also appears that the Republican caucus, especially in the middle years of this period, was less diverse ideologically than the Democratic caucus; going back to the raw NOMINATE scores, we see that the standard deviation of Republican scores was usually smaller than that of Democratic scores. On the one hand, this implies that a given change in roll call voting behavior would produce a bigger change in percentile rankings among Republicans than among Democrats, thereby making it harder to match the caucus median. On the other hand, the NOMINATE scores are based upon hundreds of roll call votes per Congress. Furthermore, the Pearson r correlation between percentile rankings across sessions of the same Congress averaged .94 for the Republicans—only slightly lower than the .97 for Democrats. The Republicans should have had no difficulty reliably identifying moderate members of their caucus. We therefore doubt that the larger average deviation in the percentile rank of their median committee member from the caucus median is artifactual.

These data thus support our hypothesis of larger deviations between the committee and caucus medians among the Republicans than among the Democrats. They tend not, however, to support the premise upon which the hypothesis was based. Contrary to our supposition that such slippage would result from their perennial minority party status, the most severe conservative bias in the Republican contingent occurred when they took control of the House in 1953!

Interestingly, the third series plotted in figure 5.5 reveals that the fit between the committee and the floor is much closer when we combine party contingents. The overall committee median differed from the overall chamber median by an average of only 4.4 percentiles. Earlier in this chapter we argued that it would be in the majority party's interest to make standing committees ideological microcosms of the parent chamber. It is tempting to speculate that the Democrats have sought to align the overall committee median with the overall chamber median and, in fact, have done a much better job of it than of aligning the median of their contingent with the caucus median. In this case, we think there is less to this finding than meets the eye. As long as the Republicans are given proportional representation on the committee (which they are) and as long as they are concentrated to the right of the Democrats (which is also the case during this period), the distribution of Democrats on the committee would have to be extremely nonuniform for them *not* to do a better job of matching the entire chamber median than of matching their own caucus median.

When we examine the overall distribution of each party contingent's percentile rankings, the patterns that emerge are very similar to those obtained from looking only at medians. Table 5.1 reports the percentages of committee Democrats in each Congress falling into each ideological quintile of the caucus. Table 5.2 reports the same data for Republicans.

Table 5.1   Ideological Distribution of Democrats on the House Appropriations Committee, 1947–84

Years	Liberal (0–20th)	Moderately Liberal (20–40th)	Moderate (40–60th)	Moderately Conservative (60–80th)	Conservative (80–100th)	n
1947–48	11.1	33.3	22.2	22.2	11.1	18
1949–50	11.1	22.2	22.2	25.9	18.5	27
1951–52	16.7	23.3	26.7	20.0	13.3	30
1953–54	10.0	30.0	15.0	20.0	25.0	20
1955–56	10.0	23.3	23.3	33.3	10.0	30
1957–58	16.7	23.3	13.3	23.3	23.3	30
1959–60	6.7	23.3	13.3	26.7	30.0	30
1961–62	13.3	20.0	20.0	23.3	23.3	30
1963–64	0.0	20.0	33.3	30.0	16.7	30
1965–66	2.9	23.5	26.5	23.5	23.5	34
1967–68	6.7	23.3	16.7	36.7	16.7	30
1969–70	6.7	16.7	20.0	33.3	23.3	30
1971–72	12.1	12.1	24.2	27.3	24.2	33
1973–74	6.1	12.1	27.3	30.3	24.2	33
1975–76	13.5	10.8	21.6	29.7	24.3	37
1977–78	16.2	13.5	27.0	27.0	16.2	37
1979–80	16.7	16.7	25.0	27.8	13.9	36
1981–82	15.2	24.2	21.2	24.2	15.2	33
1983–84	25.0	16.7	22.2	22.2	13.9	36

Table 5.2   Ideological Distribution of Republicans on the House
            Appropriations Committee, 1947–84

Years	Liberal (0–20th)	Moderately Liberal (20–40th)	Moderate (40–60th)	Moderately Conservative (60–80th)	Conservative (80–100th)	n
1947–48	12.0	16.0	24.0	20.0	28.0	25
1949–50	11.1	22.2	16.7	11.1	38.9	18
1951–52	20.0	25.0	10.0	10.0	35.0	20
1953–54	6.7	16.7	10.0	16.7	50.0	30
1955–56	10.0	15.0	35.0	5.0	35.0	20
1957–58	15.0	5.0	20.0	20.0	40.0	20
1959–60	15.0	10.0	20.0	25.0	30.0	20
1961–62	5.0	25.0	10.0	30.0	30.0	20
1963–64	10.0	5.0	30.0	35.0	20.0	20
1965–66	12.5	25.0	6.3	37.5	18.8	16
1967–68	19.0	14.3	19.0	19.0	28.6	21
1969–70	19.0	19.0	14.3	28.6	19.0	21
1971–72	18.2	13.6	13.6	27.3	27.3	22
1973–74	22.7	9.1	27.3	18.2	22.7	22
1975–76	22.2	11.1	11.1	38.9	16.7	18
1977–78	16.7	22.2	16.7	33.3	11.1	18
1979–80	22.2	16.7	27.8	16.7	16.7	18
1981–82	27.3	18.2	18.2	22.7	13.6	22
1983–84	38.1	23.8	23.8	4.8	9.5	21

As in the previous analysis of medians, these data reveal a conservative
bias among both committee Democrats and Republicans for most of
the period. An important difference is that the Democratic contingent
has tended to be overstocked with moderate conservatives, while the
largest category in the Republican contingent has tended to be extreme
conservatives. Also as before, these data indicate that by the 1980s the
Democratic contingent had become quite representative of their caucus
and that committee Republicans had become markedly more liberal than
theirs.

Our findings concerning the ideological representation of the House
Appropriations Committee are so far not very definitive. True enough,
the conservative bias in both the Democratic and Republican contingents on Appropriations during much of this period is exactly what the
Guardian of the Treasury model would lead us to expect. Nevertheless,
the bias among the majority party Democrats was usually not very large
and in many years was not present at all. In the last few Congresses in

our series, moreover, the Republicans were served by a contingent that was surprisingly liberal.

Part of the problem in evaluating this evidence is that we cannot tell whether the amount of ideological bias we observe is a little or a lot. For this reason it is useful to compare the Democratic and Republican contingents on Appropriations with those on the House Budget Committee. As indicated in the previous chapter, congressional parties strive to infuse their policy priorities into budget resolutions, and their efforts to do so have a major impact upon the informational content of the party label. This should give party leaders strong motivation to keep their contingents on the Budget Committee ideologically balanced. As also noted in chapter 4, positions on the Budget Committee are reassigned at the beginning of every Congress, and members must rotate off after a maximum stay of six years. These provisions have made for much higher turnover rates on the Budget Committee than on Appropriations. Between 1977 and 1983 the percentage of newly assigned members averaged 43 percent on the Democratic contingent and 56 percent on the Republican side. Party leaders are thus in a much better position to "fine-tune" the composition of the Budget Committee than they are in the case of other committees. Barring other considerations, we would therefore expect the ideological bias present on the House Budget Committee to be at the minimum attainable level.

Table 5.3 reports the distribution of percentile rankings by quintiles for both the Democratic and Republican contingents on the House Budget Committee, as well as the rankings of the median committee Democrat and Republican. The data reported here indicate that the Democratic contingent originally named to the committee in 1975 was very representative of the caucus. In the next two Congresses, however, Budget Committee Democrats were much more liberal than congressional Democrats in general. In the following years, the Democrats managed to bring the percentile ranking of the median committee Democrat back into the moderate 40–60 range. These findings replicate those of previous studies. Schick's (1980) analysis of the first six years of the committee, based upon a composite of ADA and ACA scores, also shows an initially balanced Democratic contingent that developed a pronounced liberal bias in the next two Congresses. Palazzolo (1988), in turn, reports that after the 1980 election, majority House Democrats assigned members to the Budget Committee with the expressed purpose of keeping it representative of the caucus as a whole. Across the entire 1975–84 period the median Democrat on Budget deviated an average of 9.7 percentiles from the caucus median, compared with 7.8 percentiles on Appropriations. In general, then, House Democrats have maintained a more representative contingent on Appropriations than on the Budget Committee.

Table 5.3   Ideological Distribution of Democrats and Republicans
             on the House Budget Committee, 1975–84

Years	Liberal	Moderately Liberal	Moderate	Moderately Conservative	Conservative	$\tilde{x}$
Democrats						
1975–76	4	2	4	4	3	52.9
1977–78	6	6	1	3	1	32.5
1979–80	7	3	3	2	2	31.4
1981–82	0	8	3	5	2	46.7
1983–84	2	7	5	4	2	43.7
Republicans						
1975–76	0	2	0	4	2	65.8
1977–78	0	2	1	2	3	64.7
1979–80	0	3	1	0	4	52.8
1981–82	0	4	3	1	4	52.8
1983–84	0	3	2	1	5	61.8

Republicans assigned in 1975 were considerably more conservative than the caucus and, with the exception of the 97th Congress (1981–82), stayed that way. Across the ten years of our series the median Budget Committee Republican deviated an average of 11.8 percentiles from the caucus median, a figure which is virtually identical to the 11.2 average percentile deviation between the caucus median and the median Republican on the Appropriations Committee.

How is it that the congressional parties have not done a better job of maintaining ideological balance on the ostensibly more malleable House Budget Committee? It could well be that the restriction on service that increases the supply of available positions on the Budget Committee each Congress simultaneously diminishes their attractiveness to members. The ability to fill a large number of openings every two years is not worth much if there is little demand for them or if demand comes disproportionately from an unrepresentative segment of the caucus. To be sure, Schick (1980) reports that in 1977 the House Democrats purposefully loaded their contingent on the Budget Committee with liberals in order to counterbalance the conservative bias on the Republican contingent. It is hard to see how they could have done so, however, if at that time conservative Democrats had been as adamant about adequate representation on the Budget Committee as they were in 1981.[4]

In evaluating our hypotheses about committee assignments it is thus critical to also consider the supply of and the demand for positions on House Appropriations. Previous research shows that Appropriations has long been one of the most sought after assignments in the House. Once on, members almost never request a transfer to another committee (Fenno 1966; Bullock and Sprague 1969). Despite claims that the committee is not as prestigious as it once was, recent data indicate that there is as much demand for assignments to Appropriations as ever. Over the past decade vacancies have continued to provoke many requests, and the "implicit queue" (members who desire a position but choose not to request one because they perceive the probability of the request being granted as too low) is quite long (Munger 1988). This excess demand creates a large pool of candidates from which party leaders may choose, increasing the likelihood that they will be able to assign members who match their ideological specifications.

Certainly, members requesting positions on Appropriations may be very atypical; perhaps it is only the more conservative members of each caucus who queue up for a slot. Overcoming selection bias of this nature may require "drafting" members. Indeed, nineteen of fifty-one Democrats assigned to Appropriations told Fenno they had not actively sought the position (1966, p. 67). These reports are suggestive, but we would caution against taking them at face value; in the heyday of Clarence Cannon, members may have believed that it was bad form to openly campaign for Appropriations and that playing hard-to-get would actually improve their odds of being chosen. All things considered, we doubt that the party caucuses have any real problems finding suitable candidates to serve on Appropriations.

But what about the supply side? Barring an all-out assault on current members' rights to continued service, the ability of parties to alter committee composition is determined by the number of vacancies.[5] Table 5.4 reports the total number of Democratic and Republican positions on the committee for each Congress during the period of our study and the number of vacancies that each party had to fill. As these data indicate, sometimes there are many vacancies and sometimes there are very few. In particular, years in which a party regained majority status (1949 and 1955 for the Democrats, 1947 and 1953 for the Republicans) meant a large expansion in the size of their contingent and thus large numbers of vacancies. Conversely, large reductions in the number of committee positions following the loss of chamber control left the parties with either few vacancies or none at all.

A better sense of what the parties have been able to accomplish with

Table 5.4   Vacancies on the House Appropriations Committee,
             1947–84

Years	Democrats		Republicans	
	Size of Contingent	Number of Vacancies	Size of Contingent	Number of Vacancies
1947–48	18	4	25	9
1949–50	27	12	18	0
1951–52	30	4	20	8
1953–54	20	0	30	13
1955–56	30	10	20	0
1957–58	30	5	20	3
1959–60	30	2	20	9
1961–62	30	4	20	2
1963–64	30	7	20	4
1965–66	34	11	16	5
1967–68	30	1	21	5
1969–70	30	2	21	3
1971–72	33	7	22	4
1973–74	33	4	22	5
1975–76	37	9	18	4
1977–78	37	4	18	2
1979–80	36	8	18	2
1981–82	33	6	22	7
1983–84	36	5	21	1

their contingents on Appropriations can thus be obtained by determining what transpired when they had a reasonable number of vacancies to work with. To do this we narrow our attention to those cases in which, given the ideological distribution of veterans returning from the previous session, there were sufficient vacancies to permit the party selection committees to position the committee median within 10 percentiles of the caucus median. Five times in our series (three for the Democrats, two for the Republicans), there were not enough vacancies for this to be accomplished. If we are right, then—when they are able to do so—the selection committees bring the median of their party's contingent into the moderate 40–60 percentile range. Conversely, the Guardian of the Treasury model implies that the selection committees instead allow any conservative bias on the committee to persist—or suffer one to be created, if it isn't there already.

As shown in table 5.5, the Democrats managed to move their median from outside of the middle quintile to inside of it in three of the six Congresses they could have done so. They also left well enough alone, in that their replacements never pushed their committee median from inside of the middle quintile to outside of it. The bottom line for the Democrats, then, is that they pegged the median of their contingent on Appropriations within 10 percentiles of the caucus median thirteen of the sixteen times they had sufficient vacancies to do so. As before, the Republicans were more likely to violate our expectations. They moved their committee median from outside of the middle quintile to the inside of it only one time out of five and moved it from inside of the moderate range to outside of it three out of twelve times.

A similar pattern emerges when we isolate the Congresses in our series in which the parties possessed a sufficient number of vacant seats to allow them to achieve an unskewed distribution of ideological rankings on the committee, that is, 20 percent from the extreme liberal quintile of the caucus, 20 percent from the moderately liberal quintile, and so forth. In identifying such cases we assumed that selection committees could place new members on the committee so as to achieve the most uniform distribution possible. A rank sums test (Hogg and Craig 1978) indicates that

Table 5.5   Location of Democratic and Republican Medians on Appropriations, before and after Filling Vacancies

| | Democrats | | Republicans | |
| | After: | | After: | |
	Within Middle Quintile	Outside Middle Quintile	Within Middle Quintile	Outside Middle Quintile
Before:				
Within Middle Quintile	10	0	9	3
Outside Middle Quintile	3	3	1	4

the Democrats managed to turn a significantly skewed distribution (i.e., we reject the hypothesis at $p < .05$ that the distribution of members on the committee was a random draw from the party) into one that was not significantly skewed five out of the eight times they could have done so. The Republicans managed this in only one of five Congresses. Another way of looking at these data is to determine whether or not the parties permitted the distribution of ideological rankings on their contingent to go from unskewed to skewed when there were enough vacancies to permit it. This is admittedly a demanding test of the conservative bias hypothesis, as the relatively small number of members in each party contingent makes it difficult to reject the null hypothesis that they are a random draw from the caucus as a whole. We could therefore identify only three Congresses in which the Democrats had sufficient vacancies to skew a previously unskewed distribution and eight such Congresses for the Republicans. In none of these cases did the parties do so.

Democratic Assignments

The findings so far suggest that the Democrats have generally succeeded in limiting the conservative bias in their contingent on Appropriations. The Republicans, on the other hand, have not been as successful in achieving an ideologically balanced contingent. Party intentions are probably revealed most clearly, however, by the characteristics of the individual members assigned to the committee. The data on Democratic assignments reported in table 5.6 reveal a moderate to slightly liberal cast in the distribution of new members at the time they were named. The Democrats assigned only half as many conservatives as they would have had they been choosing randomly from the caucus, but a significantly greater number of moderate liberals. Given the conservative bias which was usually present in their contingent, this mix of assignments strongly supports our hypothesis that the congressional party has sought to make the Democratic membership of the committee a more representative sample of the caucus.

But these data also present us with a puzzle. The 104 Democrats assigned to the committee from 1947 through 1984 are equivalent to three complete turnovers in the membership of their contingent. How could the conservative bias in their contingent persist for so long when most new members were moderate or liberal? Fenno's (1966) account suggests two possible answers to this riddle. The first is that the large number of Democratic moderates and liberals assigned to the committee served only to counterbalance a disproportionately large number of moderates and liberals who were leaving. This pattern would arise if during this period moderates and liberals from competitive districts—primarily

Table 5.6   Democratic Assignments to the House Appropriations
Committee, 1947–84

Years	Liberal	Moderately Liberal	Moderate	Moderately Conservative	Conservative
1947–48	1	3	0	0	0
1949–50	1	4	2	4	1
1951–52	1	1	1	1	0
1953–54	0	0	0	0	0
1955–56	2	4	3	0	1
1957–58	1	1	2	0	1
1959–60	0	2	0	0	0
1961–62	0	0	2	0	2
1963–64	1	3	3	0	0
1965–66	1	3	2	2	3
1967–68	0	0	0	1	0
1969–70	0	0	1	0	0
1971–72	2	2	1	2	0
1973–74	0	1	0	2	1
1975–76	2	2	1	4	0
1977–78	0	1	2	1	0
1979–80	2	3	0	2	1
1981–82	1	2	1	1	1
1983–84	1	1	2	1	0
Totals	16	33	23	21	11

located outside the South—were defeated more often than conservatives
from safe, one-party districts in the South. Indeed, Fenno's data indicate
that there was more turnover among committee liberals than among
conservatives. He reports that southern Democrats averaged 10.5 years
of service on the committee, compared with only 6.8 years for Democrats
from all other regions of the country (p. 60).

Our own analysis of committee turnover confirms the association between committee longevity and ideology in the 1947–64 period. Regressing the number of years of committee service upon members' ideological
rankings, we estimate that a committee Democrat at the 75th percentile
of his party could be expected to have spent 3.2 more years on the committee than a more liberal member at the 25th percentile. This implies
a higher turnover rate among liberal Democrats than among conservative Democrats and would seem to account for at least part of the
puzzle of the persistent conservative bias. In the years following Fenno's

study, however, southern Democrats did not exhibit greater longevity than non-southerners; between 1965 and 1984 the two groups averaged 12.3 and 12.4 years of committee service, respectively. More important, a closer look at the data in the earlier period reveals that the association between conservatism and longevity was largely a function of an event that took place before the beginning of the time series! This was the election of 1946, in which the Republicans regained control of the House for the first time since the New Deal. So many northern Democrats were defeated that nearly two-thirds of the surviving Democrats (on the committee and in the House as a whole) hailed from southern or border states. The election of 1946 is also why southern Democrats held a disproportionately large number of committee chairmanships from the 1950s through the 1970s. Regressing the number of years of committee service upon members' ideological rankings after excluding the survivors of 1946, we find that the the size of the estimated coefficient of the latter variable drops dramatically and is no longer statistically significant. Notwithstanding the longevity of Chairman Jamie Whitten, who has been on the committee since before the average American of today was born, this implies that conservative Democrats elected since 1948 have not served longer than moderates or liberals. In short, the greater longevity of conservative Democrats on Appropriations was confined to the early part of the series when the conservative bias was relatively small. Differential turnover rates thus account for little of the persistent conservative bias in the Democratic contingent on Appropriations.

Another possible reason as to why the Democratic contingent remained too conservative despite the addition of so many moderates and liberals is that members became more conservative after their assignment to Appropriations. If so, this would be an important exception to a large body of evidence which indicates that most members exhibit little change in their policy preferences over the course of their careers (Fiorina 1977; Poole and Rosenthal 1985). Whatever the case, socialization of liberal members into the norms of the committee is a major component of the Guardian of the Treasury view we are seeking to supplant. Fenno (1966) quotes many members who claim to have given up their free-spending ways after joining Appropriations. The following remarks are typical: "Yes, it's true. I can see it myself. I suppose I came in here a flaming liberal; but as the years go by I get more conservative. You just hate like hell to spend all this money. It's an awful lot of money. I used to look more at the program, but now I look at it in terms of money" (pp. 213–14).

If socialization by their elders into the "perceptual and logical underpinnings of budget cutting" (Fenno 1973, p. 97) does make Appropriations Democrats more conservative, we would expect to observe their position in the Democratic caucus moving rightward over time. But this is not the only reason why a member's percentile ranking might change. As we pointed out earlier, over the past thirty years the Democratic membership has become less southern, less rural, and presumably less conservative. As old members left and new members arrived after each election, the *relative* position of a member in the ideological spectrum of the Democratic caucus may have moved rightward even if his own preferences remained stable. To understand what has been happening to the Democratic contingent on Appropriations, it is necessary to distinguish between any socialization effects and a conservative shift produced by ongoing generational replacement.[6]

Evidence that Democrats entering Congress have been more liberal than those returning from previous sessions is presented in table 5.7, which lists the caucus percentile of the median member of each Democratic freshmen class from 1947 through 1984. As these figures indicate, thirteen of the nineteen classes of Democratic freshmen were more liberal (according to their voting records during their first term in office) than the Democratic caucus as a whole. The two most conservative classes, 1951 and 1967, were also the two smallest Democratic classes elected during this period.

The impact of each new vintage of Democrats upon the relative ideological position of their senior colleagues can be seen in figure 5.6, which plots the percentile rank of the median member of several electoral cohorts. All congressional Democrats who served between 1947 and 1984 are grouped into cohorts of similar size. The very large number of Democrats elected in 1948 and 1974 allows us to assign these classes to their own cohorts, but successive elections which yielded relatively few Democratic freshmen require us to combine as many as four classes

Table 5.7   Percentile Rank of Median Democratic Freshman, 1947–83

Class	Percentile	n	Class	Percentile	n
1947	50.1	38	1967	74.5	17
1949	38.7	109	1969	44.5	27
1951	62.0	25	1971	30.2	32
1953	50.0	41	1973	50.6	31
1955	45.3	38	1975	37.5	75
1957	33.3	29	1977	59.5	48
1959	40.2	64	1979	56.9	45
1961	47.0	28	1981	39.8	27
1963	31.5	39	1983	49.6	59
1965	43.1	73			

into a single cohort. The median for each cohort is plotted for each
session of Congress in which twelve or more individuals from a cohort
were present. As figure 5.6 illustrates, over the course of their careers
most cohorts of Democratic congressmen became more conservative relative to the caucus as a whole. This is not to say that their preferences
regarding federal spending or other issues became more conservative
in some absolute sense. Their policy preferences might actually have
become more liberal or, as most previous studies indicate, remained
stable. This evidence shows only that their position relative to all other
Democratic congressmen has tended to become more conservative. If
what we are concerned about is the ideological representativeness in the
committees' makeup, however, a member's relative position is the only
thing that matters.

In addition to the recurrent arrival of relatively liberal freshmen Democrats, the conservative drift of Democratic cohorts displayed in figure
5.6 could also be reflecting a lower rate of electoral attrition among
conservatives. A good way to check out this possibility is to assign each

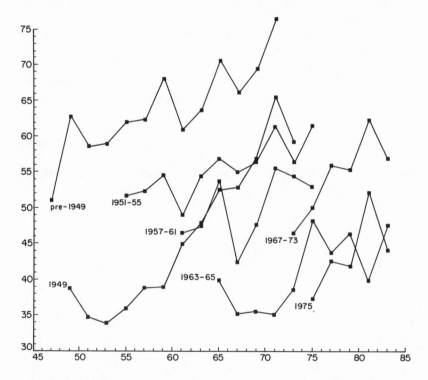

Figure 5.6 Liberal–Conservative Percentile Rank of
Median Cohort Member, House Democrats, 1947–84

Table 5.8   Electoral Survival Rates, House Democrats, 1947–84 (in percentages)

Term	Liberal	Moderately Liberal	Moderate	Moderately Conservative	Conservative
2d	82.2	84.0	77.1	80.6	85.2
3d	69.5	69.8	64.0	66.2	71.5
4th	61.0	62.6	52.7	55.7	64.4
5th	45.6	59.8	45.5	47.5	52.0
6th	46.0	52.8	42.4	42.6	39.1
7th	38.9	43.7	35.6	38.8	35.6
8th	33.7	34.0	30.5	34.0	34.7

member to an ideological quintile *within* the class of members initially elected the same year they were and then calculate the rate at which members of each quintile left Congress. As the data reported in table 5.8 indicate, during the period of our study attrition rates varied little across the ideological distribution of Democrats. Findings for the caucus as a whole thus parallel our findings for the Democratic contingent on the Appropriations Committee.

We are now ready to compare the relative merits of the generational replacement hypothesis with the socialization hypothesis. In order to do so we estimate a pair of equations. The first is for pooled cross-sections of Democrats serving on Appropriations in each Congress between 1947 and 1984:

$$Y_{it} = \alpha_j + \beta_j R_j + \beta_k C_k + \lambda z_{it} + \epsilon_{it} \tag{1}$$

where

$Y_{it} =$ member i's percentile rank in the Democratic caucus at time t;

$\alpha =$ a constant term;

$R_j =$ a battery of dummy variables registering the region of the country member i comes from (dummies are specified for the North, the Midwest, the South, and for border states, with Western members serving as the reference group);

$C_k =$ a battery of dummy variables registering member i's cohort, that is, the year in which member i was first elected to Congress;

z_{it} = the number of years member i had served on Appropriations by time t; and

ϵ_{it} = an error term.

As reported earlier in this chapter, the apparent tendency for conservative Democrats on Appropriations to serve longer than liberal members resulted primarily from the fact that the survivors of the 1946 election (an event which occurred prior to the beginning of our time series) were predominately southerners. This same phenomenon could also compromise our estimates of socialization effects, so we did not include in this sample members who had been on the committee prior to 1948.

The second equation is estimated with pooled cross-sections of all Democrats serving in Congress between 1947 and 1984:

$$Y_{it} = \alpha + \beta_j R_j + \delta_k C_k + \gamma_k C_k x_{it} + \lambda HAC_{it} + \zeta HAC z_{it} + \mu_{it} \qquad (2)$$

where, in addition to the terms defined previously,

$C_k x_{it}$ = for each cohort C_k, the number of years member i had served in Congress by time t;

HAC_{it} = a dummy variable indicating that member i was on the Appropriations Committee at time t; and

$HAC z_{it}$ = the number of years member i had served on Appropriations as of time t.

The logic of this analysis is as follows. The first equation is designed to show whether or not Appropriations Democrats, after accounting for differences in their percentile ranks due to regional factors and their electoral cohort, have tended to become more conservative over time. If so, the coefficient of z_{it}, which registers the number of years they have served on the committee, will be positive. If it is positive, the second equation should tell us whether it is due to committee-specific socialization effects, in which case the coefficient of $HAC z_{it}$ will be identical to the coefficient of z_{it} from the first equation. If it is instead registering a conservative shift in members' rankings due to generational replacement, the coefficient of $HAC z_{it}$ will drop to zero and the coefficients of the $C_k x_{it}$ terms will be positive. These latter measures register how long Democrats in each electoral cohort have been in Congress. The second pattern of results would thus indicate that Democrats on Appropriations have tended to become relatively more conservative over time, but at a rate no faster than all other members of their cohort.

Equations 1 and 2 can be estimated using ordinary least squares regression. Results are reported in table 5.9. The top number in each entry is the coefficient; the bottom number the standard error. Standard errors are estimated so as to be robust to heteroskedasticity (White 1980).

Turning to equation 1, the .29 coefficient of $HACz_{it}$, significant at the $p < .01$ level, indicates that after accounting for substantial differences associated with region and with electoral cohort, the caucus percentile

Table 5.9   Ideological Rankings of House Democrats, 1947–84

Variable	Committee		Caucus	
	Coefficient	Error	Coefficient	Error
c	29.05*	3.52	32.05*	1.61
North	−4.94	3.23	−4.45*	1.05
Midwest	−2.64	3.53	0.40	1.10
South	35.67*	3.50	43.71*	0.99
Border	21.91*	3.16	22.47*	1.27
C_k (Year elected):				
pre–1949	9.42*	3.61	−5.41*	1.81
1949	5.79	3.85	−2.94	1.88
1951–55	16.57*	3.28	−0.34	1.86
1957–61	16.64*	3.15	1.48	1.92
1967–73	8.37*	4.14	−2.44	2.22
1975	15.17*	4.13	2.47	2.71
1977–83	8.18*	4.67	4.67*	2.36
$C_k x_{it}$:				
pre–1949	—	—	0.29*	0.06
1949	—	—	0.45*	0.09
1951–55	—	—	0.24*	0.10
1957–61	—	—	0.51*	0.13
1963–65	—	—	−0.13	0.16
1967–73	—	—	0.42*	0.24
1975–83	—	—	0.70	0.45
1977–83	—	—	1.07*	0.55
HAC	—	—	3.26*	1.52
$HACz_{it}$	0.29*	0.13	0.17	0.13
n	458	—	4842	—
R^2	.47	—	.52	—

$* = p < .05$

rankings of committee Democrats did shift in a conservative direction over the course of their careers. In equation 2 the coefficient drops to .17 and is no longer close to conventional significance levels. It appears that the conservative shift exhibited by Appropriations Democrats is not the result of their being socialized into guardianship norms. Consistent with the generational replacement hypothesis, however, seven of the eight cohorts of Democrats register gains in relative conservatism over time. The average of these coefficients for Democrats serving on Appropriations during this period is .37. Multiplied by the average number of years members had been on the committee, an effect of this size implies that in any given Congress the relative positions of committee Democrats were about four percentiles higher, that is, more conservative, than at the time they were assigned to the committee. So too, however, were the relative positions of other Democrats serving on other committees who had entered Congress at the same time.

In light of these findings, the persistence of the conservative bias in the Democratic membership on Appropriations is no longer puzzling. After a decade in which the contingent had been quite representative of the caucus, the 1958 election sent a large and relatively liberal group of freshmen Democrats to Congress. With twenty-nine of the thirty available positions already filled by returning members, the committee became distinctly more conservative than the caucus. Although the party selection committees subsequently favored moderates and moderate liberals as positions opened up, each successive election usually signaled the arrival of more liberal freshmen into the caucus and the departure of veteran conservatives. For the next twenty years, new members added to Appropriations served to limit the conservative bias, but they did not completely eliminate it until the last few Congresses in our series.

This account leaves an important question unanswered. Why were the Democrats apparently satisfied with this strategy of only partial adjustment? If they really were intent on achieving an ideologically representative contingent on Appropriations, why did they not move more decisively against the conservative bias? A couple of Congresses in which they assigned liberals and only liberals would have made short work of it. This question is best answered, we think, after examining Republican assignments to the committee.

Republican Assignments

During the first half of the period covered by our study, the data on Republican assignments, reported in table 5.10, are what we would expect given the ideological balance of their contingent on Appropriations. A persistent conservative bias was created and sustained by continually

Table 5.10   Republican Assignments to the House Appropriations
Committee, 1947–84

Years	Liberal	Moderately Liberal	Moderate	Moderately Conservative	Conservative
1947–48	1	0	3	1	4
1949–50	0	0	0	0	0
1951–52	0	3	2	1	2
1953–54	0	1	1	3	8
1955–56	0	0	0	0	0
1957–58	0	0	0	0	3
1959–60	1	0	3	2	3
1961–62	0	1	0	1	0
1963–64	0	0	1	3	0
1965–66	1	3	0	0	1
1967–68	1	0	2	1	1
1969–70	0	1	0	1	1
1971–72	0	0	0	2	2
1973–74	1	0	2	1	1
1975–76	0	1	0	2	1
1977–78	0	1	1	0	0
1979–80	1	0	0	0	1
1981–82	2	1	1	2	1
1983–84	0	1	0	0	0
Totals	8	13	16	20	29

replenishing the Republican ranks with new conservative members. This
was probably accomplished simply by allowing John Taber to clear new
assignments (Fenno 1966, p. 70). The Republican assignment strategy
thus conformed closely to the dictates of the Guardian of the Treasury
model. Assignments in the second half of the series, in contrast, were
supportive of our hypotheses. After Taber's departure, a more balanced
mix of assignments made Appropriations Republicans a more representative sample of the caucus.

What the assignment data do not account for, however, is the post-
1975 metamorphosis of the Republican contingent. As shown earlier
(figure 5.5), between 1975 and 1983 the median committee Republican
moved from the 63d percentile rank in the caucus to the 31st! In 1983
nearly 40 percent of the committee Republicans fell into the extreme
liberal quintile of their caucus (table 5.2). It is not surprising that in
recent years junior Republicans have been sharply critical of their more
senior colleagues on Appropriations. Instead of supporting amendments

which would cut spending, the Republicans on Appropriations have often joined with their Democratic colleagues to defend the committee's
spending proposals (Wehr 1987, p. 1720).

There is nothing in Fenno's account or anywhere else in the congressional literature to suggest that committee Republicans are socialized
into a norm of fiscal extravagance. Even if they were, socialization effects
could hardly account for the magnitude of the change. If this shift toward
liberalism were caused by a collective change of heart, it would suggest
that committee Republicans had experienced something on par with a
visit from the Ghost of Christmas Past. We think that it is far more
likely that what occurred since 1975 in the Republican ranks is what
had been occurring for a longer period of time among Democrats—
change in the *relative* position in the caucus of committee members
after being assigned to Appropriations. Just as successive waves of relatively liberal freshmen Democrats produced a conservative shift among
committee Democrats, so would the arrival of relatively conservative
freshmen into the Republican caucus push committee Republicans in a
liberal direction. Data on the percentile rank of the median member of
each Republican class elected between 1947 and 1983, reported in table
5.11, exhibit exactly this pattern. Six of the classes of incoming freshmen
elected between 1947 and 1971 were more conservative than returning
Republican members, while seven were more liberal. The median member of every Republican freshmen class after that, however, was located
in the conservative wing of the party caucus.

The effects of generational replacement in the Republican caucus upon
the ideological representativeness of the party's contingent on Appropriations can be estimated by rerunning equations 1 and 2 on pooled

Table 5.11   Percentile Rank of Median Republican Freshman, 1947–83

Class	Percentile	n	Class	Percentile	n
1947	41.1	83	1967	47.3	59
1949	30.6	19	1969	76.8	21
1951	47.6	58	1971	48.6	22
1953	53.6	53	1973	65.1	45
1955	53.2	18	1975	56.5	18
1957	34.3	26	1977	60.2	23
1959	47.8	24	1979	63.8	38
1961	62.1	45	1981	54.9	54
1963	62.4	36	1983	67.2	24
1965	70.7	20			

cross-sections of committee and caucus Republicans. Because figure 5.5 indicates that generational effects were confined to the post-1975 period, we specify separate $HACz_{it}$ terms for the 1947–73 and 1975–83 periods respectively. Results are reported in table 5.12. One difference between the results here and those derived from the Democratic data are the much lower R^2 statistics. This is due to the fact that regional differences explain much less ideological variation among Republicans than among

Table 5.12 Ideological Rankings of House Republicans, 1947–84

Variable	Committee		Caucus	
	Coefficient	Error	Coefficient	Error
c	54.51*	4.47	54.46*	2.01
North	−21.99*	4.33	−17.73*	1.44
Midwest	1.16	3.89	3.23*	1.39
South	9.44*	5.02	16.95*	1.73
Border	9.00	8.15	0.94	2.30
C_k (Year elected):				
pre–1947	6.10	4.80	−6.12*	3.07
1947	8.18	6.63	−2.70	3.24
1949–55	14.43*	4.00	−0.49	2.32
1957–61	−2.85	4.45	−2.24	2.62
1969–73	5.19	4.95	3.35	2.80
1975–83	−8.11	6.24	3.17	2.86
$C_k x_{it}$:				
pre–1947	—	—	0.49*	0.16
1947	—	—	−0.08	0.34
1949–55	—	—	−0.04	0.14
1957–61	—	—	−0.20	0.21
1963–67	—	—	−1.06*	0.19
1969–73	—	—	−0.89*	0.33
1975–83	—	—	−1.55*	0.68
HAC	—	—	6.09*	2.27
$HACz_{it}$ (47–73)	0.27	0.31	−0.13†	0.26
$HACz_{it}$ (75–84)	−0.93*	0.27	—	—
n	392	—	3470	—
R^2	.24	—	.15	—

* $= p < .05$

†This estimate is for the entire 1947-84 period.

Democrats. The .27 coefficient of $HACz_{it}$ for 1947–73 suggests that during this period the rankings of Appropriations Republicans actually tended to drift in a conservative direction after their assignment to the committee. Given the standard error of .31, however, the more cautious inference is that the relative position of committee Republicans in the caucus did not move significantly in either direction. In contrast, the coefficient of $HACz_{it}$ during the latter period was −.93, which is significant at the $p < .01$ level. An effect of this magnitude implies that from 1975 on the typical Republican on Appropriations was dropping nearly two percentiles in the caucus every session.

The results we obtain from estimating the second equation confirm that the liberal shift of post-1973 committee Republicans is due to generational replacement. While the coefficient of $HACz_{it}$ in this equation is small and insignificant, coefficients of the $C_k x_{it}$ terms clearly register the effects of the successive waves of conservative freshmen entering the Republican caucus after 1973. The only one of the first four coefficients that clearly differs from zero is the .49 estimate for the cohort elected prior to the 1946 election. Almost all members of this cohort had left Congress by the early 1960s. Republicans elected since 1963, however, have seen their relative positions in the caucus shift to the left over time. When these coefficients are weighted according to the proportion of committee members in each cohort serving from 1975 on, they average −1.02—virtually identical to the −.93 coefficient for the analogous term in the first equation. In the latter year of our series then, Republicans on Appropriations have shifted leftward over time, but at about the same rate as all other Republicans in their electoral cohort.

Poole and Rosenthal's (1987) analysis of NOMINATE scores indicates that over the past several years the congressional parties have become increasingly polarized. The average Democrat has moved farther to the left, while the average Republican has moved farther to the right. Our findings thus corroborate theirs and indicate that the polarization is primarily due to ongoing generational replacement in the Democratic and Republican caucuses.

In the previous section of this chapter we questioned why the Democrats had not responded more aggressively to the persistent conservative bias in their contingent on the committee. Although the slightly liberal cast of their new assignments limited the bias, this partial adjustment strategy did not eliminate it until after the long streak of liberal freshmen classes ended in the late 1970s. One reason for their cautious approach, suggested more strongly by the Republican data than by the Democratic, is that an assignment strategy more aggressive than partial adjustment would also be riskier. Remember that during the 1975–83 period, the Republicans filled their vacancies on Appropriations with a very balanced group of members. When combined with the effects of generational replacement, these assignments actually made the Republican contingent on the committee *less* representative of the caucus! Imagine if in the late 1960s and early 1970s the Republicans had attempted to fully compensate for the conservative bias on their contingent with a disproportionately large number of liberal assignments. Given the long tenure of most committee members, it is likely that by the 1980s their contingent would have been even more out of line with the caucus. Responding in the meantime with a large number of conservative assignments might have balanced things out, but if the incoming freshmen classes had been relatively liberal, this would have sent the Republican contingent careening back into the conservative wing of the caucus. Unless those making committee assignments can accurately forecast changes in the ideological makeup of their party's caucus over the next several Congresses, strategies more aggressive than partial adjustment run the risk of overcompensating, first in one direction and then in the other.

Subcommittee Assignments

Long before the Subcommittee Bill of Rights was anything more than a gleam in the eye of the subservient junior committee member, the House Appropriations committee had delegated responsibility for each appropriations bill to a separate subcommittee. There is no reason to assume that our findings concerning the committee as a whole would be recapitulated at the subcommittee level. The manner in which House Appropriations operates also suggests that what we find out about subcommittee assignments is more important than anything concerning the membership of the full committee. It is the subcommittees that hold the hearings, formulate the bills, write the reports, and go to conference. In examining the assignment of members to Appropriations subcommittees we posit, as before, that the parties seek to align the median voter in their contingent on each subcommittee with the caucus median. As at the level of the full committee, the Guardian of the Treasury model holds that subcommittees include disproportionately large numbers of "low-demand" members. This implies a conservative bias on subcommittees that oversee funding for domestic programs, but it also implies that there should be a liberal bias on the subcommittees overseeing military spending.

Establishing and maintaining ideological balance on their Appropriations subcommittee contingents presents the party caucuses with a couple of difficulties that they do not face at the full committee level. First, individual subcommittees are only a fraction the size of the full committee. For that reason alone we should expect more variance between the caucus and subcommittee medians. (The relatively small size of subcommittees also precludes us from determining how well the entire distribution of preferences on a subcommittee approximates that of the party caucus. Second and more important, the party Committees on Committees do not directly make subcommittee assignments. Committee chairmen used to make them, but since the reforms of 1974 committee members choose assignments in order of seniority and are vested into whatever subcommittee positions they currently hold. In the case of Appropriations, these reforms basically ratified assignment procedures that had been followed informally on Appropriations since the ascension of George Mahon to the chairmanship in 1965.[7] Whatever the case, efforts by the parties to create ideologically representative contingents on Appropriations could be completely thwarted by the way in which committee members are assigned to subcommittees.

The fact that subcommittee assignments are now made in this manner raises the possibility that there may be a liberal bias on subcommittees with jurisdiction over domestic programs and a conservative bias on those which direct military spending. This is exactly the reverse of the pattern implied by the Guardian of the Treasury model and would presumably arise if interested members were allowed to self-select onto the subcommittee of their choice. The congressional literature, of course, has long seen the composition of most committees as primarily the product of self-selection, with Appropriations being something of an exception. It may be that after the departure of Cannon and Taber, the Appropriations Committee, at least at the subcommittee level, is not all that exceptional. Indeed, some observers believe that because of the change in assignment procedures Appropriations subcommittees no longer perform a guardianship role and have instead, through self-selection, become bastions of spending advocates (Smith and Deering 1984, p. 93). In the analyses that follow we therefore divide the data series into "Cannon" (1947–64) and "post-Cannon" (1965–84) segments in order to see if a tendency for assignments to facilitate guardianship has been driven out by a pattern of self-selection.

As at the full committee level, we proceed by first determining the caucus percentile rankings of the median members of each party contingent on each subcommittee. These data, reported in table 5.13, exhibit the same overall conservative bias present at the full committee level. Two-thirds of the entries in table 5.13 are over 50, indicating that the median member of the subcommittee party contingent was from the conservative wing of the caucus. Pooling both parties' contingents on all subcommittees for the whole period, we find that 44 percent of the medians are higher than the 60th percentile in their caucus, 24 percent are below the 40th percentile, and 32 percent are in the moderate 40–60 range.

Table 5.13   Average Floor Percentile of Subcommittee Medians,
              1947–84

Subcommittee	Democrats		Republicans	
	1947–64	1966–84	1947–64	1966–84
Whole Committee	55.2	59.1	64.1	53.7
Agriculture	56.2	69.8	50.6	70.0
Public Works	50.5	69.5	64.2	59.2
HUD-IO	60.9	53.2	62.9	44.6
Interior	36.9	56.2	64.4	29.0
Labor–HHS	42.3	51.3	78.3	43.6
Defense	75.5	69.8	64.2	58.8
Treasury	75.2	45.8	35.5	45.0
CSJJ	43.8	61.3	76.6	48.9
Foreign Operations	55.2	40.0	50.9	38.1
Military Construction	67.3	60.1	66.9	57.6
Transportation	—	39.1	—	35.4

Some of the data are also consistent with the hypothesis of a pattern of ideological self-selection. Defense subcommittee members, especially the Democrats, have been relatively conservative, while both Democrats and Republicans on Transportation have been relatively liberal. However, we see no evidence indicating that guardianship in the first half of the series had been replaced by the clustering of spending advocates in the second. Contingents on the Defense and Military Construction subcommittees were actually somewhat more liberal in the post-Cannon years than in the first half of the series. In other cases, subcommittees that were relatively liberal in the first half of the series were relatively conservative in the second half, or vice versa. Our findings concerning the Appropriations Committee as a whole indicate that throughout most of our series new members assigned by the Democrats tended to make their contingent more representative of the caucus, while those assigned by the Republicans generally did not. We can determine whether or not these patterns obtained at the subcommittee level by comparing the percentile rank of the median of the holdovers on each subcommittee with the percentile rank of the median after any vacancies had been filled. The results of this comparison, reported in table 5.14, reveal no systematic differences between the parties. Assignments made by both the Democrats and the Republicans narrowed differences between the

Table 5.14   The Effect of Filling Vacancies Upon the Position of the
Subcommittee Median vis-à-vis the Caucus Median

Party	Closer	No Change	Farther Away	n
Democrats	53.9	14.6	31.5	130
Republicans	60.3	8.3	31.4	121
Total	57.0	11.6	31.4	251

narrowed differences between the party caucuses and their contingents
in over half the cases. About 12 percent resulted in no change, as one
or more assignments to the left of the existing median counterbalanced
an equal number of assignments made to the right. In over 30 percent of
the cases the new members assigned to the subcommittee actually made
it less ideologically representative of the caucus. This is a big enough
fraction of the total to suggest that the parties are often unable to do
much about the composition of Appropriations subcommittees. A closer
look at the data, however, reveals that assignments that moved the subcommittee median farther away from the caucus median tended to occur
when the subcommittee median was very close to that of the caucus prior
to the filling of vacancies. In such cases it is obviously difficult to fill a
subcommittee vacancy without unfavorably perturbing the location of
the subcommittee median. This point can be made more precisely by
making before-and-after comparisons of the average percentile deviation
of the subcommittee median from the party caucus median in all three
circumstances, that is, when new assignments narrowed the difference,
left it the same, or increased it. In the case of the Democrats, when new
assignments narrowed the difference, the average percentile deviation of
the subcommittee median shrunk from 21.6 to 13.2. In the second case,
the average deviation remained at 18.4. And when the addition of new
members increased this deviation it expanded on average from 9.2 to
16.7 percentiles.

We cannot infer from this, however, that committee chairmen or party
contingents have purposefully sought to use subcommittee appointments
to create more ideologically balanced subcommittees. Selecting members
from the caucus at random (or, more plausibly, on the basis of other,
uncorrelated criteria) would produce a pattern of assignments similar to
that observed in table 5.14. In order to distinguish between purposeful
and random selection we estimate the following equation:

$$Y_i = \beta_j S_j + \delta M^{-i} + \epsilon_i \qquad (3)$$

where

Y_i = the percentile rank in the party caucus of each new member assigned to an Appropriations subcommittee;

S_j = a battery of dummy variables indicating the subcommittee to which the new member was assigned;

M^{-i} = the percentile rank of the median voter of the subcommittee party contingent excluding the new member; and

ϵ_i = an error term.

If new subcommittee members are pulled randomly from the caucus, their percentile scores should not be a function of the rankings of the other members already on the subcommittee. In this case δ, coefficient of the M^{-i} term, would be zero. A purposeful balancing of subcommittee membership, on the other hand, implies that relatively liberal members are assigned to subcommittees that are otherwise relatively conservative, and vice versa. If so, the coefficient of M^{-i} would be negative. In running equation 3, we separate the Democrats and the Republicans and also partition the data series into the "Cannon" (1947–64) and "post-Cannon" years (1965–84). Table 5.15 reports the estimated coefficients and (White robust) standard errors for these four equations. The percentile score variables Y_i and M^{-i} are entered as deviations from 50, so coefficients of the subcommittee dummies can be interpreted as deviations from the caucus median.

Looking first at the 1947–64 equations, we see that for both the Democrats and Republicans the coefficient of the M^{-i} term is negative, large, and significant. The tendency for new assignments to foster ideological balance on Appropriations subcommittees was thus greater than what would have been accomplished by drawing randomly from the party caucuses. An effect of the magnitude registered by these coefficients (both about −0.4) implies that a new member assigned to a subcommittee party contingent with a median in the 70th percentile of the caucus would have a rank about 12 percentiles lower than a member joining a group whose median was at the 40th percentile. To properly interpret these results, however, it is necessary to consider the different pattern of coefficients associated with the subcommittee dummies in the two equations. In the Democratic equation they were small and and tended to be negative, indicating that most new subcommittee members were moderate to slightly liberal. This is exactly what we should expect, given the moderate to liberal cast of new Democratic assignments to the full committee (table 5.6). A notable exception is the large positive coefficient of the Defense subcommittee, which reflects its attraction to

Table 5.15   Appropriations Subcommittee Appointments, 1947–84

Subcommittee	Democrats		Republicans	
	1947–64	1965–84	1947–64	1965–84
Agriculture	−1.60	17.83*	31.80*	14.10*
	(5.87)	(4.65)	(5.42)	(6.47)
Public Works	−11.71	15.81*	16.75*	7.81
	(7.13)	(6.22)	(6.92)	(10.76)
HUD-IO	11.75	−1.22	5.82	2.51
	(11.05)	(6.63)	(7.62)	(9.35)
Interior	−18.39*	8.28	15.91*	9.86
	(3.33)	(6.28)	(6.62)	(11.97)
Labor-HHS	−10.77	−2.30	39.58*	−15.33*
	(7.13)	(6.20)	(5.98)	(8.53)
Defense	22.83*	4.24	29.10*	6.59
	(3.63)	(4.73)	(4.40)	(7.33)
Treasury	6.41	−2.81	−13.12*	8.47
	(10.61)	(6.00)	(7.25)	(8.13)
CSJJ	−1.53	−1.71	28.22*	−7.96
	(6.03)	(9.54)	(11.83)	(8.79)
Foreign	1.58	−17.54*	5.91	−3.74
Operations	(7.47)	(5.48)	(7.60)	(6.24)
Military	—	10.16*	—	11.48*
Construction		(4.87)		(5.99)
Transportation	—	−13.37*	—	−6.83
		(4.71)		(11.90)
M^{-i}	−.42*	.09	−.37*	.14
	(.14)	(.10)	(.11)	(.13)
R^2	.18	.24	.27	.14
n	81	181	104	99

$* = p < .05$

conservatives. This indicates that in the 1947–64 period the moderating effects of new Democratic assignments to the full committee filtered down to most of the subcommittees.

In contrast, coefficients of most dummies in the first Republican equation are large and positive, indicating a strong conservative bias in their subcommittee assignments during this period. This too is almost a necessity given the bias in their assignments to the full committee. To state that Taber sought ideological balance on Republican subcommittee contingents, however, is a bit of a misnomer. It is more accurate to describe Republican assignments during this period as efforts to insure that each subcommittee contingent remained sufficiently conservative. Conversely, coefficients of the subcommittee dummies in the second equation are much smaller and frequently negative, reflecting the ideologically balanced assignments of the post-Taber years.

Turning attention back to the coefficients of the M^{-i} terms, we see that in both equations for the 1965–84 period they are indistinguishable from zero and thus consistent with the random selection model. One possible reason why ideological considerations appear to have disappeared as a criterion for subcommittee assignments is the change in subcommittee assignment procedures discussed earlier; even though no rampant self-selection appears to have occurred, the randomness of the second half of the series does represent a change from the first half. Another possibility is that these results primarily reflect the large increase in the average size of Appropriations subcommittees. From rosters of three Democrats and two Republicans in 1949, many subcommittees in 1984 had eight Democrats and five Republicans. Because of the larger rosters, the percentile rankings of subcommittee medians are necessarily perturbed less by the addition of new members. In the context of our regression analysis, this implies that the coefficient of M^{-i} should decrease as subcommittee size increases. Whatever the case, it should be kept in mind that even random selection of new members from the caucus serves to prevent highly unrepresentative committees and subcommittees.

In general, then, our findings concerning assignments to the Appropriations Committee carry through to the subcommittee level. During the entire 1947–84 period the liberals and moderates that the Democrats tended to assign to Appropriations limited the extent of the conservative bias present on the committee as a whole and on most subcommittees. The Republicans, in contrast, maintained a strong conservative bias in their contingent on virtually every subcommittee in the 1947–64 period by making predominately conservative assignments. The balanced nature of their assignments in the 1965–84 period, in turn, translated into more balanced subcommittee contingents.

In addition to the Subcommittee Bill of Rights, another potentially consequential reform, enacted in 1974, was the requirement that chairmen of Appropriations subcommittees be approved by the Democratic caucus at the beginning of each Congress. This has not been a mere pro forma exercise. Jamie Whitten faced serious opposition from the caucus in 1975, a year in which three committee chairmen did lose their positions. He managed to retain the chairmanship of the Agriculture subcommittee by agreeing to transfer jurisdiction over the Environmental Protection Agency to another subcommittee. Robert Sikes, chairman of the Military Construction subcommittee and a strong advocate of defense spending, lost his post in 1977 following a censure by the full House. Although there is no reason to believe that he would have been ousted had it not been for his ethics violations, it is also the case that many Democrats opposed Sikes on policy grounds. The misconduct charges thus provided a convenient way of getting rid of him.

Given that the threat of removal is not an empty one, we hypothesize that this reform has discouraged Appropriations subcommittee chairmen from occupying too extreme a position in the caucus and that their NOMINATE scores would therefore move closer to the median of the party caucus. Table 5.16 reports the average pre-1975 and post-1975 percentile rankings of subcommittee chairmen whose tenure overlapped the institution of this reform, or who became chairmen after 1975. According to these data, the 1975 reform has had little effect on the relative position of subcommittee chairmen in the party caucus. What movement there is actually runs counter to our expectations, in that eight of the nine who were to the right of the median prior to 1975 moved even farther away after 1975. We interpret this not as evidence that these individuals' own policy preferences were changing, but rather that their positions were shifting relative to an increasingly liberal Democratic caucus.

Our analyses have not uncovered a tendency for domestic subcommittees to be stacked with conservatives or for military subcommittees to be stacked with liberals. The rationale for such a strategy (implied by the Guardian of the Treasury model) is to create subcommittees whose members' ideological predilections run against program and spending advocacy. Another way of placing "low-demand" members on subcommittees is to assign members whose constituencies have little stake in the programs over which the subcommittee has jurisdiction. This is the eponymous Cannon-Taber norm, inspired by the two committee patriarchs who reportedly lived in fear and loathing of the "interest-sympathy-leniency" syndrome alluded to previously. Assignments based on the Cannon-Taber norm would minimize the the extent to which committee members encountered "moral hazard" in making spending decisions.

Fenno's account provides little indication as to what share of subcommittee assignments adhered to the Cannon-Taber norm; Schick (1980) asserts that "even in the heyday of fiscal control" such assignments were exceptions rather than the rule (p. 432). By our cursory examination of the economic and demographic characteristics of their districts, many members of Appropriations subcommittees appeared to have had no obvious constituency-oriented interest in the subcommittee to which

Table 5.16 Average Party Percentile Ranking of Subcommittee Chairmen before and after 1975 Reforms

	Before 1975	After 1975
Whitten, Agriculture	87.9	82.6
Bevill, Public Works	81.1	83.1
Boland, HUD-IO	45.3	43.7
Yates, Interior	22.1	10.4
Flood, Labor HHS	42.0	48.0
Natcher, Labor HHS	64.9	70.3
Mahon, Defense	75.0	87.7
Addabo, Defense	33.5	22.7
Steed, Treasury	69.9	73.9
Roybal, Treasury	9.6	11.0
Slack, SCJJ	65.8	73.5
Smith, SCJJ	53.8	57.2
Long, Foreign Operations	52.7	58.2
McKay, Military Construction	66.3	77.8
McFall, Transportation	41.0	41.4

they were assigned. This was true in the Cannon-Taber era as well as in subsequent years. Other subcommittees appeared to have large numbers of "interested" members. Judging whether or not a particular subcommittee assignment followed the Cannon-Taber norm, however, is extremely problematic. As Shepsle (1978) notes, committee jurisdictions are "diverse, heterogeneous, and, consequently, very imperfectly correlated with particular social interest" (p. 77). We find it implausible that a member could find nothing of interest to his constituents in the jurisdiction of any subcommittee. Fred Santangelo (D, New York) of East Harlem, for example, developed a much more positive attitude about being on the Agriculture subcommittee when he discovered that it oversaw funding for school lunch programs as well as for soil conservation (Fenno 1966, pp. 215–19). Something else to consider is the possibility that members with no obvious constituency-interest reason for being on a sucommittee are there because there were no vacancies on the "right" subcommittees. To examine this and several other related questions, we need information on initial requests for subcommittee assignments and on requests for transfers. Until then, a thorough study of the Cannon-Taber norm is best left as a topic for subsequent research.

Summary

In line with the House Appropriations Committee's reputation for being
the Guardian of the Treasury, over much of the 1947–84 period both
parties' contingents on the committee exhibited a conservative bias. The
bias on the Democratic contingent was usually small, however, and in
both the early years and later years of the period was not present at all.
Data on assignments, moreover, indicate that the Democrats made a sustained effort to make their contingent on the committee representative
of the caucus. The modest conservative bias that was often present persisted in spite of the moderate to liberal cast of newly assigned members.
Because of the steady infusion of relatively liberal newcomers into the
Democratic caucus, the relative position of committee Democrats, like
that of other Democrats of their vintage, tended to move rightward from
one Congress to the next. An assignment strategy of partial adjustment
to these trends limited the extent of the resultant bias, but did not
eliminate it until the 1980s.

The Republicans usually exhibited a much larger rightward bias than
did the Democrats, although by the 1980s the GOP contingent was considerably more liberal than the caucus as a whole. Prior to 1965 or so,
this substantial conservative bias was maintained by continually filling
vacancies with members drawn disproportionately from the conservative
wing of the caucus. In contrast, Republican assignments in the second
half of our series were very representative of the caucus at the time they
were made. The dynamics of generational replacement were at work here
as well, but they were moving in the opposite direction; the arrival of
several successive classes of conservative Republicans into the caucus
pushed the relative position of veteran committee Republicans far to
the left of the caucus median.

Although these findings could have been undermined by various patterns of self-selection of committee members to Appropriations subcommittees, our findings at the subcommittee level generally recapitulate
results for the full committee. The liberals and moderates that the
Democrats tended to assign to the committee limited the extent of
the conservative bias present at the subcommittee level as well. The
Republicans' predominately conservative assignments in the first half of
the series maintained a strong conservative bias in their contingent on
virtually every subcommittee. The balanced nature of their committee
assignments in the second half of the series translated into more balanced
subcommittee contingents.

In the case of the majority party Democrats, the weight of the evidence is thus supportive of our hypothesis that congressional parties
seek to make their contingents on the House Appropriations Committee

ideologically representative of the caucuses as a whole. In the case of
the Republicans, our expectations are borne out only in the second half
of the period of our study. In the first half, the data on the Republican
contingent is much kinder to the Guardian of the Treasury model of
the committee than it is to ours. In the case of both parties, however,
differential rates of replacement in the caucus versus the committee contingent worked to create discrepancies between the ideological composition of one group relative to the other. The congressional parties could
have dealt more decisively with ideological biases that developed and
persisted on Appropriations, but more aggressive assignment strategies
also run the risk of repeatedly overadjusting, first in one direction, then
in the other. The result would be a very polarized committee that might
not perform nearly as well as a committee biased slightly in one direction
or the other.

The final matter we need to consider is the generalizability of our findings concerning House Appropriations. By our argument, assignments
to this and other major committees are the subject of party scrutiny
because their jurisdictions subsume the major issues that divide the
parties—taxes, the budget, and the tradeoff between domestic and military expenditures. But what about committees whose jurisdictions are
dominated by issues that do not divide Democrats from Republicans? In
the case of these committees it would seem to make little sense for parties
to worry much about ideological considerations in making assignments.
A quick look at the standing committees in the contemporary House,
however, indicates that there are few committees of the latter type. One
committee traditionally identified as largely "constituency-oriented" is
House Interior and Insular Affairs. According to McCurdy (1989), prior
to 1970 this assessment was correct; the Democratic and Republican
contingents were both dominated by members who were interested primarily in multiple-use water projects. As the two parties came to adopt
starkly different policy positions regarding the environment, however,
their committee contingents quickly came to reflect these differences.
The difference between the League of Conservation Voters' ratings for
the average committee Democrat and average committee Republican
grew from a mere 5 points in 1972 to more than 60 points by the mid-
1980s. At the same time LCV scores became highly correlated with
more general ideological measures such as ADA scores and thus with
major party policy differences. With Interior and Insular Affairs off the
list, the only committee left which would not seem to traffic much in
partisan controversy is Merchant Marines and Fisheries. We therefore
think our findings concerning Appropriations are far more the rule than
the exception.

CHAPTER SIX

Looking Backward:
Conference Committees and Amendments
to Appropriations Bills

"The Institutional Foundations of Committee Power"

The data analyzed in the previous chapter indicate that congressional parties can use selection procedures to keep their contingents on the House Appropriations Committee reasonably representative of the caucus as a whole. But they clearly cannot "fine-tune" the ideological composition of the committee, and committee members are in a position to behave opportunistically no matter how representative party contingents are of their respective caucuses. It would thus be unwise for parties to rely solely upon assignments to manage the delegation of legislative authority to committees, and of course they do not. The three other basic mechanisms for limiting agency losses—monitoring and reporting requirements, institutional checks, and contract design—are also employed.

Like most other committees, Appropriations and its subcommittees are required to publish the transcripts of their hearings. This amounts to hundreds of thousands of pages annually—about 30 percent of the total output of all House committees. Unfortunately, the value of this information is often compromised by long publication lead times; subcommittee hearings on appropriations bills and even the texts of the bills themselves may not be printed until well after the measures have been passed and the money committed.[1] It is thus a crucial feature of congressional organization that non-committee members can avail themselves of multiple sources of information in considering legislation. For each appropriations subcommittee, one or more authorizing committees reviews the same agencies, hears from the same witnesses, and makes recommendations in the same areas of policy.

In addition to reporting requirements, the House Appropriations Committee confronts some important institutional checks. Even though appropriations bills are privileged, they usually need waivers of one or more points of order and thus the blessing of the Rules Committee. This has been especially true in recent years when so many bills have gone to the floor in violation of the Budget Act or without the necessary authorizing legislation. The Speaker can also hold up appropriations legislation by referring it to another committee.[2] Like any other piece of legislation, an appropriations bill is in for rough sledding if not backed by the majority party leadership.

In principle, though, the fact that committees have been delegated only the authority to make recommendations and not final decisions would seem to foreclose the possibility of the congressional parties absorbing significant agency losses. Some contracts call upon agents to take actions that are irrevocable or that can be modified only at great cost. In other cases agents do things that principals cannot possibly do for themselves, for example, surgery. But that would not seem to be the case here. The task delegated to the Appropriations Committee, and indeed to all other standing committees, is to recommend legislation, which chamber majorities can either accept or alter as they see fit. How could legislation that is objectionable to a majority on the floor ever pass? Or, as argued in the previous chapter, how could the Appropriations Committee act as a Guardian of the Treasury to achieve lower appropriations figures than would otherwise be preferred? If a majority of members on the floor want to appropriate more to an agency than the House Appropriations Committee recommends, presumably they can simply vote to do so.

According to Shepsle (1988), a defining feature of the "Textbook Congress" is that they just don't. Goodwin (1970) and many others observe instead that members routinely "defer" to committees on matters within their jurisdiction and refrain from offering amendments. By most reports norms of deference also inform the internal workings of the Appropriations Committee. Most bills move from subcommittee to the floor after a markup in full committee so brief and perfunctory that most observers see it as little more than a ritualistic formality. If so, the congressional parties, in delegating the management of legislation to their members serving on committees, have apparently abdicated their perogative to influence or to amend committee proposals. In a regime of reciprocal deference, committees need not worry about challenges to their bills on the floor. This might be tolerable in the case of some committees in some policy areas, where the collective interests of the majority party are undefined or nonexistent. It would hardly seem tolerable in the case of the House Appropriations Committee.

Shepsle and Weingast (1987a) accept "deference" as an accurate description of standard congressional operating procedure, but point out that its existence is hard to explain from a social choice point of view. Specifically, several basic theorems imply that for any proposal, there almost always exists an alternative proposal that a majority of voters prefer. It could be that committee proposals avoid picking up amendments because they are confined to policy jurisdictions that non-committee members don't care about, but the myriad interdependencies among policy areas makes this highly improbable. A more likely possibility, consistent with much of the literature on committees, is that deference is a self-enforcing norm, a pattern of cooperation that emerges naturally in "repeat-play" conditions. Congressional members, in other words, refrain from offering and supporting amendments to other committees' proposals in the expectation that proposals brought to the floor by their own committee will be similarly deferred to. A highly influential statement of this thesis is the case Axelrod (1984) makes for the conditionally cooperative "tit for tat," a strategy that dictates behaving cooperatively on the first round of an encounter and subsequently responding in kind to the other player. Cooperation is reciprocated with cooperation, defection with defection.

Shepsle and Weingast reject this explanation on theoretical grounds, as do we. Consider what happens when someone playing tit for tat, after exchanging a series of reciprocally cooperative moves with another person, encounters a noncooperative move. Tit for tat dictates that he or she respond in kind and that reciprocal defection continue until the end of the game. The problem is that at the time players face the choice of either defecting in response to defection or returning to cooperation, it is in their best interest *not* to play tit for tat but rather to seek a return to cooperation. The threat of defection in response to defection is not credible and thus cannot in and of itself induce cooperation. In technical terms, this problem is one of subgame perfection (Selten 1975). So-called "grim" strategies can ensure cooperation by somehow locking in defection, that is, a defection by either player leads both players to defect until the end of the game. This makes defection so costly that it is effectively deterred (Friedman 1986). Grim strategies are themselves problematic, in that rational people are understandably reluctant to enter into arrangements in which their welfare is determined, to such a great extent, by the actions of others with whom they may have little in common.

In the spatial model of committee-floor interaction that Shepsle and Weingast develop, "deference," that is, the acceptance of committee proposals without amendment, is instead the equilibrium of an institutional arrangement that puts committees in a strategically favorable position vis-à-vis the rest of the chamber. Like all such models, theirs has elements that are stylized and abstract, and lacks much of the complexity and detail of real-world settings.[3] The purpose of such models, however, is not to reproduce actual institutions and practice as faithfully as possible, but to expose the basic elements of the decision-making process as clearly as possible. The assumptions upon which their model is premised are as follows (technical aspects of these assumptions are discussed in the appendix to this chapter):

1. Members have well-behaved, "Euclidean" preferences, favoring points closer to their ideal points over those farther away.

2. Members have common knowledge about each others' preferences, about the rules and sequence of the legislative process, and thus know with certainty which outcome will occur for any action they choose.

3. A committee has sole authority to make proposals in its jurisdiction. This assumption, often referred to as "exclusivity," necessarily requires that committee jurisdictions are nonoverlapping.

4. A bill can be passed by the legislature if and only if it is first recommended by the committee with jurisdiction. This is usually referred to as the "gatekeeping" assumption.

5. In seeking enactment of their legislation, there are no constraints on the nature and membership of the chamber majority that the committee may choose to assemble.

Figure 6.1, which depicts a unicameral, three-person legislature in which member 2 is the committee, reveals the consequences of these assumptions. The points labeled z_1, z_c, and z_3 represent the most preferred policies (ideal points) of the three legislators. We assume that the loss of utility to each member as the policy moves away from that person's ideal point is proportional to the distance from that ideal point (this allows indifference contours $P_i(x)$ to be represented as circles). The point x^o represents the status quo, which remains the policy in place if the legislature takes no action. It is located on the contract curve between the ideal points of the committee (member 2) and member 1.

The set of all points in X that command a majority when paired against x is defined as $W(x)$, that is, the "win set" of x. Thus the win set of some point $x \in X$, given that two votes make a majority in a three-person legislature, is composed of all points in the intersection of any two of the preference sets $P_1(x)$, $P_c(x)$, and $P_3(x)$. The win set of the status quo, $W(x^o)$, consists of the two "petals" that are composed

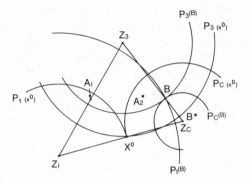

Figure 6.1 Shepsle and Weingast's "Foundations of Committee Power"

of the points preferred to x^0 by members 1 and 2 and by members 2 and 3, respectively.

In figure 6.1, the committee, if it were able to offer "take it or leave it" proposals to the legislature, would offer B^*, which is the closest the committee (member 2) could get to its ideal point and still win a majority (member 3 prefers the proposal B^* to x^0 and would side with member 2). It is easy to see that this "closed rule" situation maximizes the strategic advantage of the proposer. However, if an "open rule" prevails and amendments are permitted, the committee's possession of exclusivity and gatekeeping authority do not provide the same strategic advantages. The committee is only able to guarantee that points such that $x \in P_c(x^0)$ are proposed and that proposals such that $x \notin P_c(x^0)$ never go the floor. Thus it can keep a motion like $A_1 \in W(x^0)$ off the floor, thereby frustrating the preferences of a majority in the chamber (members 1 and 3, represented by their preference set around z_1 and z_3).

If the committee "opens the gate" by proposing some $B \in P_c(x^0)$, amendments made to the proposal may yield an outcome, $A_1 \in W(x^0)$, where $A_1 \notin P_c(x^0)$. If the committee were to propose B, for example, it could be amended to some point in the left petal, such as A_1, that would defeat both B and x^0 in majority votes. Such amendments make the committee worse off than they are under the status quo. In a multidimensional setting such as that portrayed in figure 6.1, there is generally no voting equilibrium—hence the expectation generated by social choice theory that voting in a majority rule institution like Congress should be marked by a chaotic cycle of amendments and counteramendments. If the policy space is unidimensional, any proposal brought to the floor loses out to the median voter's ideal point. In neither situation, under an open rule, does the committee enjoy any advantage vis-à-vis the rest of the chamber once legislation has gone to the floor.

According to Shepsle and Weingast, though, committees derive a strategic advantage from the requirement that in a bicameral legislature both chambers must agree to an identical piece of legislation in order for it to be enacted. Their model thus incorporates the possibility of a conference committee, namely, a committee of members drawn from both chambers that is authorized to reconcile differences between different versions of a bill. Abstracting from actual congressional practice, they assume that conference committees are composed of the members of the committees that originally proposed the legislation. If amendments picked up on the floor leave the legislation they originated no longer to their liking, committee members, in their role as conferees, can, they hope, persuade the other chamber's conferees (presumably like-minded members drawn from the corresponding committee) to repair the damage. Although they assume that initial floor consideration of a bill takes place under an open rule, Shepsle and Weingast nevertheless posit that conference agreements are considered under a closed rule. At a minimum, the committee can cast an ex post veto by simply refusing to reach an agreement in conference. The committee is thus insured an outcome that is an element of $P_c(x^0)$ or x^0.

Shepsle and Weingast's model thus formalizes the vision of the "runaway" conference that has long been the subject of legislative horror stories. Echoing sentiments shared by members of the House and the Senate since the first conference committee huddled in private, William Fulbright's (D, Alaska) observations suggest that the Shepsle-Weingast model accurately captures some congressional *Realpolitik*:

> It is clearly evident, Mr. President, that to save the world and the people of this country from disaster, all that is needed is to reconvene, preferably in secret, only those incomparable sages, the conferees of the Appropriations Committee. From their deliberations the same results would be achieved and without the expense and trouble to everyone that is involved in going through the archaic ritual of pretended legislation. It is quite clear that regardless of what the common members of this body may wish, the conferees make the decision. (quoted in Longley and Oleszek 1989, p. 6)

Longley and Oleszek recount several other examples of conferees working to undermine legislation that had been approved by the chamber they were ostensibly representing. It was his deep distrust of this peculiar institution that reportedly inspired George Norris (R, Nebraska) to wage a successful campaign back in his home state for the ultimate defense against legislation by conference committee—a unicameral legislature (Norris 1945, p. 35).

Although the conference occurs at the end of the sequence, expectations about what will occur there inform the prior beliefs and behavior of both committee and non-committee members. Suppose, for instance, that in figure 6.1 committee bill B provokes the floor amendment A_1. As noted earlier, $A_1 \in W(B) \cap W(x^0)$ with member 1 and member 3 preferring A_1 to both B and x^0. However, $A_1 \notin P_c(x^0)$, and if A_1 passes, the committee will invoke its ex post veto and reinstate x^0. A vote for A_1, then, is tantamount to a vote for the status quo. But both the committee (member 2) and member 3 prefer B to x^0. Despite preferring A_1 over B, member 3 therefore joins with member 2 to defeat amendments like A_1. What we have here, then, is the classic expression of deference—even amendments with majority support on the floor do not pass if they are opposed by the committee.

The key implication of the Shepsle-Weingast model is that the committee never actually needs to bring the brute force of an ex post veto to bear. Anticipating the response of the committee acting as conferees, non-committee members refrain from offering amendments that the committee would reject in conference or that would provoke the committee to collapse the conference entirely. After all, why bother to offer amendments to a bill if the result is to either revert to the status quo or to get a similar bill back later under a closed rule? What appears to be deference to the committee is actually an equilibrium response (or, more accurately, non-response) to an unfavorable strategic situation. Shepsle and Weingast describe their model as revealing the "institutional foundations of committee power." If in fact congressional parties have conceded this much of the agenda to their contingents on the standing committees, what we really have here are the institutional foundations of abdication.

An Alternative Model of Deference

According to Krehbiel (1987), the Shepsle-Weingast model does not accurately reflect actual congressional practice, especially as it pertains to the resolution of interchamber differences. He points out that nine out of ten bills passed by Congress do not even go to conference. Indeed, there is no need for a conference if both chambers pass identical versions of a bill. This simple fact is of considerable strategic importance. Referring back to figure 6.1, the two chambers could each adopt a point in A (the shaded area) and there would be no opportunity for the committees to "fix" the bill in conference. Krehbiel identifies several other features of actual conference procedures that are not incorporated into the Shepsle-

Weingast model: (1) House rules require the Speaker to appoint conferees who are generally supportive of the legislation involved; (2) like all other committees, conference committees can be discharged, that is, forced to report a bill because a majority of members have petitioned that they do so; (3) a majority of members can vote to recommit a conference report, with or without instructions to the conferees. As vividly illustrated in the saga of H.R. 3128, the actual procedures for resolving interchamber differences, which may involve amendments between the chambers either before or after a conference, can be byzantine beyond belief (Bach 1986a).

In response to Krehbiel's critique, Shepsle and Weingast (1987b) point out that major pieces of legislation, namely, what *Congressional Quarterly Weekly Report* refers to as "key votes," are much more likely than less important bills to go to conference. Virtually all appropriations legislation is acted upon by a conference committee. Our purpose here, however, is not to arbitrate the controversy over the extent to which the Shepsle-Weingast model mimics actual congressional practice. Rather, we intend to show that an observationally equivalent pattern of deference is the equilibrium of a very different strategic environment than the one described by Shepsle and Weingast. Our model adds a prior stage and a posterior stage to their model. In the prior stage, the majority party in each chamber establishes the chamber's rules and organization. Through screening and selection procedures, monitoring and reporting requirements, institutional checks, and contract design, the party seeks to secure a satisfactory agency relationship with its contingents serving on standing committees. In the posterior stage, that is, after the legislative process has concluded, the majority party reviews the policy choices that have been made and determines whether any changes need to be made in its relationship with any or all committees.

Returning to the three-member unicameral legislature displayed in figure 6.1, we assume that members 1 and 2 constitute the majority party. They must decide which one of them is to be assigned to the committee, and because we have no criteria for this choice we assume they choose member 2. In agreeing to delegate authority to make proposals in X to member 2, the members of the majority party (i.e., members 1 and 2) agree to a compensation schedule for member 2. Member 2 is to be given, in utility terms, $R > 0$ if the outcome of the legislative process x^e, satisfies the following:

$$x^e \in \Theta = p_1(x^0) \cap p_2(x^0)$$

If x^e does not satisfy this condition, then member 2 receives a sanction, S. The payoffs to members 1 and 3 are simply their utility for the choice

$u_1(x^e)$ and $u_3(x^e)$, respectively. For member 2, the payoffs are $u_2(x^e)+R$ if $x^e \in \Theta$ and $u_2(x^e) - S$, if $x^e \notin \Theta$.

In figure 6.1, the Shepsle-Weingast model predicts an outcome such as A_2. Notice that the committee and member 3 form the winning coalition to pass A_2. The other member of the majority party, member 1, is made worse off relative to the status quo by the choice of A_2. For making this choice, the committee receives a sanction or some other undesired change in the nature of its relationship with the majority party, such as the assignment of new members, additional reporting requirements, new procedural checks, etc. For that reason the committee (member 2) may prefer the reversion point of the status quo to A_2. Because the preferred-to sets of the members of the majority party intersect at only one point in this example, that is, $P_i(x^0) \cap P_2(x^0) = x^0$, the only outcome in which the committee avoids negative consequences is the status quo, that is, $x_e = x^o$. In this case, majority party members on the committee, by anticipating the reaction of the rest of the caucus, make a choice that is inferior, at least from their point of view, to what could be achieved in the situation modeled by Shepsle and Weingast.

We present another example in figure 6.2. The Shepsle-Weingast model predicts that the committee could enforce the choice of something like A_1. But an outcome outside of the shaded area would again result in negative consequences for the committee. The committee thus proposes a bill like B. Member 3 might offer an amendment to change the bill to something like A_1, thereby making both members 2 and 3 better off. But the committee would actually vote against such an amendment, for it knows that the ultimate consequence of its vote would be adverse changes in its relationship with the party. The sophisticated strategy for

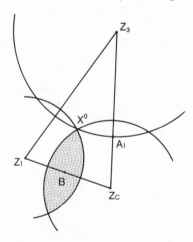

Figure 6.2 An Alternative Model of Deference

the committee is to propose B and defend it against amendments, but we would not expect either member 1 or 3 to offer amendments to the committee's bill in the first place.

In equilibrium, then, the committee proposes B and it is accepted without an amendment being offered—a pattern of "deference" that is observationally equivalent to that implied by the Shepsle-Weingast model. But in this case the nonappearance of amendments arises not from an agenda game that confers strategic advantage upon the committee, but rather from a well-managed delegation of authority from party to committee. Indeed, delegating to committees only to redo their work on the floor undercuts the rationale for delegating in the first place. Offering and passing amendments requires non-committee members to expend time and effort in monitoring committee activity, in obtaining new information, and in striking new bargains. These were precisely the costs that delegation was intended to minimize.

Floor Amendments to Appropriations Bills, FY1948–85

So far we have seen that observationally equivalent patterns of deference can emerge from very different strategic environments—one that favors committees vis-à-vis the chamber and one that does not. Before considering further the theoretical basis of deference, it is a good idea to determine just how stylized the "stylized fact" of deference is. How accurate is it to describe the treatment appropriations bills receive on the House and Senate floors as one of deference to the committees that report them? If such bills are substantially altered by floor amendments, our concern over this particular manifestation of the abdication hypothesis may be misplaced.

Data collected by Bach (1986b) and reproduced in table 6.1 suggest that, in the realm of appropriations at least, deference is a much less accurate description than it used to be. From a low of fourteen in 1965, the number of amendments offered on the House floor reached one hundred forty in 1980. The House also became increasingly likely to adopt amendments to appropriations bills. Over ninety amendments were adopted in 1980, compared with only four in 1966. Trends in amendments to appropriations bills appear to parallel those of amendment activity in general. Smith (1989) reports that in the 93d Congress (1973–74) the proportion of House bills subject to an amendment attempt peaked at nearly 30 percent. Although the rate has fallen off some since then, it remains much higher than in the 1950s, when only about one bill in twenty was subject to amendment attempts on the House floor. Smith's data also reveal a corresponding increase in the success rate of floor amendments.

Bach's data also show that the number of floor amendments offered

Table 6.1   House Amendments to Appropriations Bills, 1963–82

Year	Total Number of Amendments	Amendments per Bill	Winning Percentage of Amendments
1963	39	3.2	30.8
1964	24	2.0	25.0
1965	14	1.2	35.7
1966	43	3.6	9.3
1967	63	4.5	22.2
1968	55	4.2	29.1
1969	70	5.4	30.0
1970	45	2.8	17.8
1971	66	4.7	36.4
1972	83	5.9	16.9
1973	58	4.5	17.2
1974	70	5.0	35.7
1975	57	4.4	33.3
1976	93	6.2	48.4
1977	74	5.7	37.8
1978	113	8.7	47.8
1979	130	10.0	50.0
1980	140	11.7	65.0
1981	116	9.7	65.5
1982	47	4.7	61.7
Total	1400	5.4	40.4

Source: Bach 1986b.

to appropriations bills decreased sharply in 1982, and amendment frequency remained at the low level of approximately five per bill through the rest of the 1980s. This decline might seem to mark a return to the more deferential atmosphere of the 1950s, but most of it is attributable to a major change in House rules, adopted by a strict party-line vote, in early 1983 (Bach and Sachs 1989). By the late 1970s, appropriations bills, which had traditionally moved to the floor under an open rule, had become the frequent target of "limitations amendments." These riders, which forbade funds to be used for particular activities, were especially popular among Republican members as a ploy for forcing

House Democrats to vote on controversial issues. Federally funded abortions were frequently the target, but these amendments also concerned busing, affirmative action, and the ban on saccharin. The rules change now allows limitation amendments to be offered only after all other amendments have been disposed of and a nondebatable motion for the Committee of the Whole to rise and report the bill has failed. Most of the decline in amendment activity in appropriations legislation is thus a response to the parliamentary barriers that the majority party in the House has erected against this type of amendment.

A shortcoming of the Bach time series is that it stretches back only to 1963. Also, there are no comparable figures for the Senate. Another, more important limitation is that all amendments are afforded the same importance. But all amendments are not created equal; an amendment to add a $5,000 preliminary study to the Corps of Engineers budget is given the same weight as a 5-percent across-the-board reduction in the Labor, Health, and Human Services bill. To gain a better sense of the actual impact of amendment activity on committee proposals, we compare the appropriations amounts recommended in House and Senate Appropriations Committee reports between FY1948 and FY1985 for seventy agencies and programs with the amounts that were subsequently adopted by the House and Senate. As shown in table 6.2, this sample contains 33 of the 36 analyzed by Fenno (1966).[4] The thirty-seven additional entities, which include regulatory agencies, housing programs, and divisions of the State and Defense Departments, add substantially to both the size and scope of the original sample. Many agencies in Fenno's sample were subsequently merged into or subsumed by larger entities, and most of the additional agencies did not exist until well into the time period. We also omit the data from certain agencies for certain years because of major discontinuities in their appropriations due to reorganization, for example, the Bureau of Mines, Fish and Wildlife, or, in the case of the Census Bureau, the distortive effects of the decennial census.

The percentages of agencies and programs in our sample whose budgets were altered each year by House and Senate amendments are plotted in figures 6.3 and 6.4, respectively.[5] For the whole period, the percentage receiving amendments in the House is virtually identical (14 percent) to the percentage of agencies and programs amended in the Senate. The most striking feature of the House data is the U-shaped curve in activity, with a trough in the 1960s and peaks in the early 1950s and 1980s. From 1963 on, our data coincide with Bach's, but his series obviously did not register the earlier peak. Amendment activity in the Senate oscillates over most of the period within a range of about 5 percent to 20 percent, but then it, too, increased significantly in the late 1970s.

Table 6.2 Sample of Federal Programs and Agencies, FY1948–85

Fenno's Agencies	Years of Existence
Food and Drug Administration	1948–85
Geological Survey	1948–85
Census Bureau[a]	1948–85
Federal Bureau of Investigation	1948–85
Immigration and Naturalization Service	1948–85
Federal Prison System	1948–85
Bureau of Customs	1948–85
Bureau of the Public Debt[b]	1948–85
Secret Service	1948–85
Internal Revenue Service	1948–85
Patent Office	1948–85
Coast and Geodetic Survey	1948–66
National Bureau of Standards	1948–73
Bureau of Narcotics	1948–69
Bureau of the Mint	1948–85
Bureau of Labor Statistics	1948–85
Bureau of Employment Standards	1948–68
Extension Service	1948–85
Farmers Home Administration	1949–67
Soil Conservation Service	1948–85
Forest Service	1948–85
Bureau of Reclamation	1948–85
Bureau of Land Management	1948–85
National Park Service	1948–85
Bureau of Indian Affairs	1948–85
Fish and Wildlife Service[c]	1948–85
Bureau of Mines[d]	1948–85
Bonneville Power Administration	1948–75
Office of Education	1948–85
Office of Vocational Rehabilitation	1948–68
Rural Electrification Administration[b]	1948–85
Public Health Service	1948–69
Weather Bureau	1948–66

[a]Except decennial years.
[b]Salaries and expenses only.
[c]Except 1972–74.
[d]Except 1975–76.

Additional Programs and Agencies	Years of Existence
Occupational Safety and Health Administration	1974–83
Commodity Futures Trading Administration	1977–83
Environmental Protection Agency	1975–83
Drug Enforcement Administration	1975–83
National Highway Traffic Safety Administration	1972–83
National Science Administration	1954–83
Justice Dept. Legal Activities and Gen. Admin.	1948–85
General Services Administration	1948–85
Civil Aeronautics Board	1948–85
Federal (Power) Energy Regulatory Commission	1948–85
Interstate Commerce Commission	1948–85
Nuclear Regulatory Commission	1977–83
Federal Communications Commission	1948–85
Federal Trade Commission	1948–85
Securities and Exchange Commission	1948–85
Coast Guard	1948–85
Federal Maritime Commission	1964–83
Maritime Administration	1952–83
Foreign Miliary Assistance	1955–83
National Oceanographic and Atmospheric Admin.	1972–83
National Aeronautics and Space Administration	1961–83
Corps of Engineers	1948–85
Military Construction	1960–83
Atomic Energy Commission	1948–75
Economic Development Administration	1967–83
HUD Commission Planning and Development	1973–83
HUD Housing Programs	1977–83
Rural Waste Water and Disposal Grants	1968–83
Small Business Admin. Bus. Loan & Inv. Fund	1971–83
Consumer Product Safety Commission	1975-83
State Dept. Administration of Foreign Affairs	1958–83
State Dept. International Orgs. & Conferences	1958–83
State Dept. International Commissions	1958–83
Defense Procurement	1961–83
Defense Personnel	1961–83
Defense Operations and Maintenance	1961–83
Defense Research and Development	1961–83

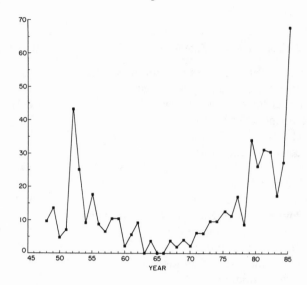

Figure 6.3 Percentage of Agency Budgets Altered by House Amendments

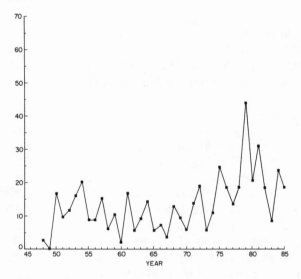

Figure 6.4 Percentage of Agency Budgets Altered by Senate Amendments

In the last years of our series, then, both chambers became increasingly
likely to alter the budget figures recommended by their Appropriations
Committees. This upward trend is associated with three important developments. The first is the appearance of amendments calling for across-
the-board (ATB) percentage reductions in entire appropriations bills or,

on some occasions, for "targeted" cuts confined to specific subsets of agencies within a bill. Although House Republicans routinely sponsored amendments of this type as early as 1966, few ever passed until the last half of the 1970s. Many amendments that purported to make ATB cuts actually did no such thing. House amendments to the Transportation and State, Commerce, Justice, and Judiciary bills for FY1968, for example, called for cuts of 5 percent from amounts requested by the president. The bills reported by the House Appropriations Committee, however, had already reduced the bills' spending totals by more than the requisite amount. There were also ATB amendments that were riddled with loopholes. Some called for cuts, but exempted all expenditures "required by law" (FY1978 Foreign Aid, House). Another exempted all contract authority and left details to the conferees (FY1975 Transportation, Senate). Other ATB reductions were mooted when large amounts of a bill's funding had previously been eliminated due to lack of authorizing legislation (FY1979 State, Commerce, Justice, and Judiciary, House). Our amendment data do not reflect these measures, which we view to be primarily blue smoke and mirrors. Had we included them, the observed increase in floor activity would have been greater.

Second, in the latter years of our series the House and Senate often had two chances to modify appropriations figures recommended by the Appropriations Committees. The first came when the original bill was reported to the floor. The second came at the end of the session when the bill, having failed to achieve final passage, returned along with all other stalled appropriations legislation in the form of an omnibus continuing resolution. Unlike ordinary appropriations bills, omnibus continuing resolutions frequently move to the House floor under the cover of restrictive rules. Because of such rules and the time pressures that attend consideration of these last-minute bundles of "must-pass" legislation, committee recommendations usually pick up fewer amendments the second time around. Still, of the 117 changes to agency budgets made on the House floor between FY1979 and FY1985, twenty of them (17 percent) affected continuing resolutions.[6] In addition to budgetary changes wrought by amendments per se, our data also reflect the effects of points of order that were successfully lodged against some appropriations bills. Usually raised in objection to the absence of prior authorizing legislation, points of order effectively set the budgets for affected programs to zero. Of the 117 changes to agency budgets made on the House floor from FY1979 to FY1985, twenty-one of them (18 percent) were produced by points of order.

How dramatically have these amendments affected spending totals? Table 6.3, which aggregates the data by presidential administration, indicates that except for the first few years and last few years in our

Table 6.3   Floor Changes in HAC Recommendations, FY1948–85

			Administration			
	Truman	Ike	JFK LBJ	Nixon Ford	Carter	Reagan
> 2% Cut	6.9	1.0	0.5	0.7	4.3	13.7
0–2% Cut	6.2	1.3	0.9	2.3	2.1	2.6
No Change	82.7	91.1	97.3	90.7	82.8	76.8
0–2% Increase	2.7	2.9	0.9	3.9	8.6	5.2
> 2% Increase	1.5	3.7	0.5	2.3	2.1	1.7
n	260	382	440	432	233	233

series, most measures adopted by the House altered agency budget totals by less than 2 percent. These data also present some new problems
for the the Guardian of the Treasury model of the House Appropriations Committee. If that depiction were correct, then the House, in its
amendments, should rarely decrease the committee's recommendations.
The committee, after all, supposedly leans against the prevailing pressures for more and more spending. What table 6.3 shows, however, is
that in the instances in which the House altered the committee's recommendation for an agency or program, 58 percent were cuts and 42
percent were additions. Even during the Fenno years (FY1948–62) the
House decreased funding levels recommended by the committee more
often than it raised them.

    The figures reported in table 6.4 show that the Senate has been even
less likely to adopt changes larger than 2 percent to the agency and program budgets proposed by its committee. When we compare amendment
activity across different types of agencies, we find that in both the House
and Senate, public works agencies and Department of Defense programs
were somewhat more likely to be amended. There are a couple of good
reasons for this. Until the latter part of our time period, committee
reports concerning public works agencies—most notably the Corps of
Engineers and the Bureau of Reclamation—recommended appropriations at the level of individual projects. This required the specification
of several hundred individual line items, making it highly likely that at
least a few of the lines "at risk" would pick up an amendment. Similarly,
the higher probability of amendments to Defense programs primarily
reflects the vast size of the Pentagon budget (usually broken down into
a few dozen large titles) relative to most other agencies in our sample.

    Looking across both tables, we see that the highest frequency of large

Table 6.4   Floor Changes in SAC Recommendations, FY1948–85

| | Administration | | | | | |
	Truman	Ike	JFK LBJ	Nixon Ford	Carter	Reagan
> 2% Cut	1.2	1.0	0.5	1.2	3.4	3.9
0–2% Cut	0.8	0.3	1.8	1.9	5.2	4.3
No Change	90.8	89.0	91.8	88.0	75.5	80.2
0–2% Increase	5.4	6.8	4.5	7.2	15.0	9.2
> 2% Increase	1.9	2.9	1.4	1.9	0.9	2.4
n	260	381	440	432	233	207

changes were made during the first Reagan administration, when the House made cuts of 2 percent or more in nearly one-seventh of the agency budgets proposed by the committee. As pointed out above, most of these cuts reflect instances in which the House upheld a point of order that completely eliminated agency funding from a bill. It is a serious mistake to take the effect of such actions at face value. Those who filed points of order against appropriations lacking prior authorization did so quite literally to protest the lack of prior authorization, which they saw as a serious breakdown in sound legislative practice (i.e., an intrusion upon their committee's jurisdiction). Few if any of the individual members who voted to uphold these points of order actually desired to eliminate the budgets of the agencies involved (e.g., the entire State and Justice Departments). Everyone was surely aware that the deleted appropriations would be restored when the legislation came around again, either in the form of a continuing resolution or in the conference report.[7] In short, what appear to be the most drastic changes to committee budget recommendations were made with full confidence that such actions were of little or no consequence as far as agency budgets were concerned.

Data on amendments to appropriations bills hardly suggest a consistent pattern of "deference." On the contrary, amendment activity has varied considerably across time, across chambers, and across agencies. But the evidence does not indicate that bills are routinely rewritten on the floor, either. Amendments tend to be small in percentage terms or, in the case of across-the-board cuts that have already been made or points of order that delete appropriations for a few days until the continuing resolution reinstates them, lacking in substance. That appropriations committees appear to get most of what they want approved on the floor means that Shepsle and Weingast can salvage something, but the same evidence can be interpreted as showing that majority party members of the Appropriations Committees are usually good at anticipating what the rest of their caucus will support. Just as two highly contradictory models generate the same prediction of no floor amendments to committee bills, the actual facts provide as much support to one as they do to the other.

The extent to which House Appropriations or any other committee can exploit strategic features of the legislative process to achieve more favorable outcomes thus remains an open question. We obviously need to do more than to count amendments and to note whether they are large or small. The surest route to making progress on this front is to build upon the key insight of the Shepsle-Weingast model: what happens to a bill on the floor depends upon what is expected to occur later in conference. This leads us, in the following analysis, to assess the consequences of floor amendments in a radically different way. Rather than calculate how amendments affect the bill they are directed against, we gauge the consequences they have for the conferees.

Back to the Future: Conference Committees and the Scope of Legislation Restriction

> When I go to the conference as a representative of the Senate, I represent the Senate viewpoint as vigorously as possible, even though it may not be in accord with the vote or votes I cast on the floor of the Senate. I conceive that to be the duty of the conferee. (Richard Russell, D, Georgia, quoted in Oleszek 1984, p. 208)

> I have been in this body long enough to beware of the chairman of a committee who says in an enticing voice, "Let me take the amendment to conference," because I think that is frequently the parliamentary equivalent of saying, "Let me take the child into a tower and I will strangle him to death." (Paul Douglas, D, Illinois, quoted in Fenno 1966, p. 610)

Whether or not members accept the claims of Russell or share the suspicions voiced by Douglas, they are keenly aware that the necessity of the House and Senate agreeing to identical legislation places the committees coming back from conference in a strategically strong position. Both chambers have adopted a host of rules and precedents to limit their exposure to conference committee opportunism. One of the most important of these is the "scope of legislation" restriction, which forbids conferees from reaching agreement on matters that lie outside the provisons of the original House or Senate bills. Similarly, conferees may not undo an agreement between the chambers by reconsidering a provision that both chambers passed in identical form (Oleszek 1984, p. 209).

Although the scope of legislation restriction is open to some interpretation when the language of companion bills is at issue, its application is straightforward in appropriations legislation.[8] If the House bill would appropriate $100 million to an agency and the Senate bill specifies $120 million, the conferees must reach an agreement inside the interval formed by the two numbers. Failure to do so requires them to report an "amendment in technical disagreement," to be voted on separately from the conference report. This restriction on the range of bargaining, which we henceforth refer to as the interval rule, applies to individual line items. Agreements concerning an agency's total budget can and often do stray outside of the range defined by House and Senate figures, even though agreements on all the individual line items that make up its budget are in compliance. Although we encountered seven cases in our appropriations data in which the conferees offered amendments in technical disagreement (all were routinely approved), the only open violation of the scope of legislation constraint occurred in the conference report on the Commerce, Justice, State, and Judiciary FY1984 appropriations bill.[9]

An important implication of the interval rule is that floor amendments to committee proposals can have very unequal force in constraining conferees. Consider a line item for which the House accepted the Appropriations Committee's recommendation of $10 million, but for which the Senate Appropriations Committee recommended $15 million. An amendment adopted by the Senate to cut the $15 million recommendation to $12 million would be binding on the conferees, for it shrinks the range over which they may bargain. An amendment to increase the line to $18 million, in contrast, is not binding, for it expands their bargaining range. There is no reason that the conferees need move off their contract curve into this new range ($15 million to $18 million) in order to reach an agreement.

If, as the Shepsle-Weingast model posits, floor amendments are conditioned upon expectations about what will occur in conference, we would expect to observe far more amendments of the first sort, that is, those that impose binding constraints on appropriations conferees by increasing the minimum number or decreasing the maximum number. Other than whatever symbolic or public relations value there might be in it, there is no legislative gain per se in offering amendments of the second type, that is, those that lower the minimum or raise the maximum and thus fail to reduce the conferees' bargaining range. Furthermore, when amendments of this type do occur, we would not expect the conferees to agree to a figure in the newly created bargaining area, for it presumably lies outside the contract curve of the two committees.

The data used to examine these hypotheses are line-item amendments made to committee recommendations for the domestic agencies in our sample between FY1948 and FY1979. For the House there are a total of 252 line-item amendments made to 125 agency budgets, for the Senate a total of 271 amendments made to 152 agency budgets. The number of line items per agency ranges from one to nearly eight hundred (the Army Corps of Engineers budget for FY1962). Contrary to expectations derived from the Shepsle-Weingast model, the figures reported in table 6.5 provide no evidence that knowledge of the interval rule informs the prior adoption of amendments to appropriations bills. On the positive side, nearly 80 percent of all line-item changes made on the House floor were to increase the minimum figure or to lower the maximum, and to thus shrink the range of bargaining. But over two-thirds of the Senate amendments expanded the range of bargaining by raising the maximum number, and an additional 10 percent lowered the minimum. The fact that these actions could be ignored by the conferees appears to have discouraged neither the appearance nor the adoption of such amendments.

The conferees do not behave as predicted, either. In nearly half the occasions that they were given the opportunity to do so, they reached agreement on a figure in the range created by a nonbinding amendment. Conferees, in the realm of appropriations at least, frequently appear to be successful advocates of their chamber's position—and not their own—even when the rules do not force them to do so. If so, the specter of "irresponsible" conferences subverting the preferences of congressional majorities should not be considered a chronic threat to the congressional parties' pursuit of their policy objectives.

The above analysis assumes that spending choices are unidimensional. If so, any proposal by the committee, other than the chamber median,

Table 6.5 House and Senate Amendments to Domestic Line Items and their Effect on Conference Agreements, FY1948–79

	House Amendment	Outside Committees' Interval	Senate Amendment	Outside Committees' Interval
Minimum Down	18%	31%	10%	67%
Minimum Up	65%	—	8%	—
Maximum Down	13%	—	13%	—
Maximum Up	4%	45%	69%	46%
n	271	—	215	—

is vulnerable under an open rule to floor amendments to change the committee's recommendation to the floor median. But this also means that there is no available strategy that makes the committee better off than that of reporting its sincere preferences, and we can therefore interpret the analysis in table 6.5 as a refutation of the Shepsle-Weingast model. This is something we cannot do, however, if we adopt the assumption that the choice space is multidimensional. In such settings, it is conceivable that the committee can gain some advantage by misrepresenting its preferences when reporting proposals to the floor.[10] The simple analysis in table 6.5, which assumes that the two committees' recommendations define the endpoints of their contract curve, cannot be applied straightforwardly to multidimensional settings where misrepresentation can be an important component of committee strategy.

The problem is illustrated in the following three figures. As in previous examples, figure 6.5 portrays a simple three-person legislature, where H_1, H_C, and H_3 represent the ideal points of the three members over the choice space $X = |R^2|$. Also as before, let member 2, represented by H_C, be the committee, and let x^0 be the status quo. The preference sets, $P_{H1}(x^0)$, $P_{HC}(x^0)$, and $P_{H3}(x_0)$ represent the preference sets of members 1, 2, and 3 with respect to x^0. The win set with respect to x^0, $W_H(x^0)$, consists of the two petals defined by the intersections of $P_{H3}(x^0)$ with $P_{Hc}(x^0)$ and $P_{H1}(x^0)$ with $P_{H3}(x^0)$. It is the shaded area in figure 6.5.

Two new important points are the committee's recommendation, R_H, and B_H, the final bill approved by the House. What is the optimal recommendation, R_H, for the committee to report? If the agenda sequence is unknown to the committee, or if the agenda sequence is established

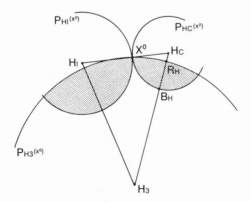

Figure 6.5 Decision Making in the House

after the committee reports its bill, R_H, no strategy exists that can make
the committee better off than sincerely reporting its ideal point. But if
the committee knows who is to offer what amendments and in what
order, it can choose its recommendation so as to have the final bill, B_H,
come as close to its ideal point, H_C, as possible. As a consequence, the
committee may strategically misrepresent its ideal point. This sort of
strategizing on the part of the committee, of course, requires the strong
assumptions that are needed to characterize a collectivity as a single
entity with stable preferences. In figure 6.5, R_H is drawn so that it is
the optimal feasible outcome from the committee's point of view (i.e.,
$R_H = H_C$); B_H has been drawn so that the committee is left indifferent
between this proposal and the status quo, x^0.

We next add to this an identical model for the Senate, portrayed in
figure 6.6, whose three members have ideal points represented by S_1,
S_C (member 2 is the committee), and S_3. The Senate chooses over the
same policy space $X = |R^2|$ as the House, and the status quo, x^0, is also
the same. Let $P_{S1}(x^0)$, $P_{SC}(x^0)$ and $P_{S3}(x^0)$ be the preferred-to sets
of senators 1, 2, and 3 with respect to x^0. The win set for the Senate
with respect to x^0, then, is the intersection of these sets: $W_S(x^0) =
P_{S1}(x^0) \cap P_{SC}(x^0)$ or $P_{S1}(x^0) \cap P_{S3}(x^0)$ or $P_{SC}(x^0) \cap P_{S3}(x^0)$. R_S is
the recommendation of the Senate committee, also selected to be its best
feasible alternative. Depending upon the agenda sequence, the Senate-
passed bill B_S will be on the contract locus between S_C and S_3, as
constrained by the preference sets of S_C and S_3, or between S_C and S_1.
For the purposes of this illustration, we put B_S on the contract locus

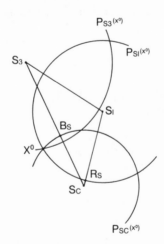

Figure 6.6 Decision Making in the Senate

between S_C and S_3 at the point at which S_C is indifferent between B_S and x_0.

Figure 6.7 combines elements of the separate House and Senate models to yield a schematic diagram of what happens in conference. The House bill, B_H, and the Senate bill, B_S, define the scope of legislation (the rectangle formed by the dotted lines) over which the conferees may bargain. Because the conferees are also constrained to choose a point that lies in the House and Senate win sets, the feasible set is reduced to the shaded area in the figure. The necessary condition for the conference committee to report a bill (rather than fall back to the status quo by failing to reach an agreement) is:

$$P_{HC}(x^0) \cap P_{SC}(x^0) \cap W_H(x^0) \cap W_S(x^0) \cap IR(B_H, B_S) \neq \emptyset,$$

where $IR(B_H, B_S)$ is the set of points allowable under the scope of legislation restriction. In this case, the contract locus between the two committees' ideal points, H_C and S_C, is actually outside the constraints imposed by the interval rule. This means that the best the committees can achieve for themselves is a point on the line segment $Z_1 Z_2$.

In this example, as in Shepsle and Weingast's, the House and Senate committees use the conference procedure to make themselves better off

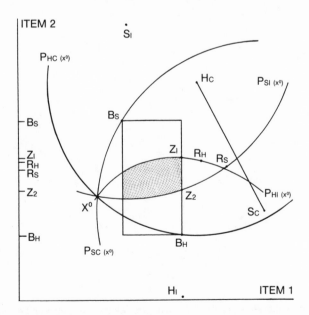

Figure 6.7 The Conference Committee and the Scope of Legislation

at the expense of floor majorities in both chambers who had supported
B_H and B_S. But more important, the liability in our previous one-
dimensional analysis of the scope of legislation restriction is now apparent. Because both committees had strategically misrepresented their
preferences in originally reporting their recomendations R_H and R_S to
the chamber floor, when we map the multidimensional choice environment portrayed in figure 6.7 onto a single dimension, for example, item
2, the conference choice may be greater than the recommendations made
by either the House or Senate committees, since $Z_1 > R_H > R_S$ on item
2. This makes it appear, in choosing a point such as Z_1, which for item
2 lies outside of R_S and R_H, that the conferees have chosen a point that
is inefficient for them but better for one of the chambers (the Senate, in
this example). We interpreted such evidence in table 6.5 as a refutation
of the Shepsle-Weingast model. As just shown, however, what we observe
may merely be an artifact of projecting a multidimensional choice space
onto a single dimension.

Fortunately, under certain circumstances outcomes in the multidimensional analysis can be mapped straightforwardly to the outcomes on the
individual line items. Consider the situation, illustrated in figure 6.8,
where both S_1 and S_3 are up and to the right of S_C. Under these
circumstances, the committee might choose to recommend something
on the contract locus between itself and senator 1, or the committee

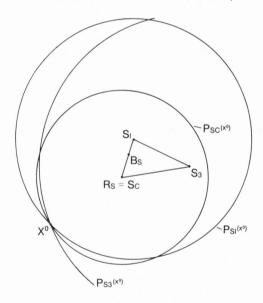

Figure 6.8 The Senate Appropriations Committee and the Senate

might recommend something between S_C and S_3. It would never be to the committee's advantage to recommend a point not on one of these two contract loci. Thus in figure 6.8 the Senate committee recommends something like R_S, and an amendment alters this proposal to the point B_S. The Senate bill thus sets funding on both items 1 and 2 at levels that are at least as high as the Senate committee had recommended. If we observe that the Senate acts to amend the committee's recommendation by increasing spending on one or more line items, while leaving spending on all other items at a level at least as high as that recommended by the committee, then it must be true that the committee's recommendation, R_S, proposed spending at or above the level the committee actually prefers, S_C, on every item in X.

We can thus avoid the artifact revealed in figure 6.7 by restricting our analysis to those cases where (1) the Senate committee's recommendations for all line items in an entire program or agency were less than or equal to the figures approved by the Senate as a whole, and (2) the recommendations for each line item made by the House committee, as well as the figures approved by the House as a whole, were less than or equal to the figures proposed by the Senate committee.[11] This situation is pictured in figure 6.9.

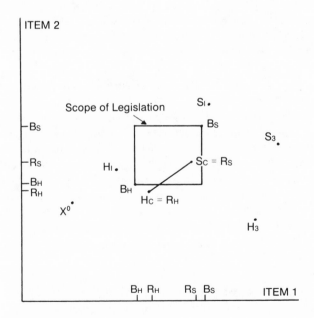

Figure 6.9 Application of the Interval Rule to Two Dimensions

According to the Shepsle-Weingast model, the committees in figure 6.9 would prefer to restrict their negotiations to the contract curve defined by the line segment drawn between H_C and S_C. In this case, almost the entire contract curve is within the constraints of the scope of legislation and the intersection of the House and Senate win sets (for the sake of clarity we did not draw them in). If, as the Shepsle-Weingast model presumes, the conferees choose only from the feasible part of the contract curve between H_C and S_C, it follows, under the general conditions illustrated in figure 6.9, that the conferees would never choose more than R_S, the Senate committee's recommendation, for any item in the bill.

As reported previously, there are 144 Senate amendments in our appropriations data that increased the maximum number for a line item. In other words, the Senate committee's proposal was as high or higher than the House figure, and the Senate amendment made the figure even higher. The circumstances required by our test—that this same ordering be observed for all line items in the agency—left us with 104 amendments. Restricting our attention only to these cases, we find that the conferees chose to spend more than the amount recommended by the Senate Appropriations Committee in 49 percent of the cases. This is actually a larger proportion than the previous result of 46 percent. In nearly half the test cases, then, the House and Senate conferees agreed to a figure that in terms of the Shepsle-Weingast model was too high. In such cases, members of both chambers' committees could have complied with the interval rule and still reached an agreement on a figure less than or equal to the Senate committee's recommendation, but chose not to do so.

Why would House and Senate Appropriations conferees behave in this manner? As we see it, the tip-off comes from considering the following two things. First, it is the Speaker of the House, the leader of the majority party, who appoints conferees. By simply following the time-honored convention of sending members of the relevant subcommittee, the Speaker is assured that his party's majority on the conference committee is at least as large as it is in the chamber as a whole. Second, a large majority of the seemingly anomalous appropriations conference agreements occur when the conferees agree to a spending figure that is higher than we would otherwise expect. If the conferees from House Appropriations truly were Guardians of the Treasury, these are obviously not the kind of outcomes that we should observe.

What is going on, then, is that the Democratic party leadership in the House exploits the closed rule consideration of conference agreements to obtain higher levels of spending on domestic programs and agencies than they can obtain in the original House bill, which is usually considered under an open rule. This also accounts for Fenno's finding that agreements reached in Appropriations conferences were considerably more likely to be closer to the higher figure going in (usually the Senate bill) than to the lower figure. Nagler (1989) comes to the same conclusion in his analysis of House-Senate conferences on minimum wage bills. In 1972, 1973, and 1977, the House adopted amendments sponsored by Richard Erlenborn (R, Missouri) that significantly weakened the legislation. The Speaker, however, sent the members of original subcommittee to conference, who, according to Nagler, "were able to produce a proposal closer to the original committee proposal than the House passed bill by accepting substantial proportions of the more liberal Senate bill" (p. 74). House Democrats, in short, were able to use the conference to obtain legislation that could not get through the House under an open rule.[12]

Shepsle and Weingast are absolutely correct in positing that the conference process provides a major source of leverage in congressional policy-making. It is not the originating committee, however, that obtains this advantage. It is the majority party. The answer to the question that has long vexed congressional scholars—Who wins in conference committees, the House or the Senate?—is thus neither. Given their hold on both chambers during most of the past sixty years, the real winners of conference committee proceedings have usually been the Democrats.

Summary

Floor amendments are presumably the ultimate safeguard against unacceptable committee recommendations, but one of the key stylized facts that constitute the Textbook Congress is that floor amendments are seldom offered and rarely adopted; noncommittee members instead typically ratify the recommendations of each others' committees in a pattern of reciprocal deference. According to Shepsle and Weingast, committees induce this nonresponse through the ex post veto and through the opportunity to return to their chamber with conference agreements that are considered under a closed rule. But the observation of little amendment activity is consistent with very different models of the legislative process. The actual data on House and Senate amendments to appropriations bills, furthermore, reveal that the number of amendments offered, the number of amendments adopted, and the number of agency budgets affected by floor amendments have varied considerably over time and across chambers—hardly a consistent pattern of deference. Our analysis of House-Senate conferences reveals that the conference process is, as Shepsle and Weingast posit, the source of strategic advantage in the legislative process. It is the majority party that exploits this advantage, however, and not the originating committees. A fundamental element of the abdication hypothesis can be summarily dismissed.

Appendix

Preferences

Prefence relations among alternatives in X are commonly defined as follows. R_i is a binary preference relation, where $x_1 \, R_i \, x_2 \, (x_1, x_2 \in X)$ is defined to mean that individual i prefers x_1 at least as much as x_2. R_i is a complete and transitive weak-order over X. Completeness means that for every pair of alternatives x_1 and x_2 in X, either $x_1 \, R_i \, x_2$ or $x_2 \, R_i \, x_1$. Transitivity means that for any three alternatives x_1, x_2, and x_3 in X, if $x_1 \, R_i \, x_2$ and $x_2 \, R_i \, x_3$, then $x_1 \, R_i \, x_3$.

Indifference can be defined by using the definition of R_i. Let I_i represent indifference, and $x_i \, I_i \, x_2$ if and only if $x_1 \, R_i \, x_2$ and $x_2 \, R_i \, x_1$. An individual may also strictly prefer (as opposed to weakly prefer) one outcome to another, that is, $x_1 \, P_i \, x_2$. Let $x_1 \, P_i \, x_2$ if and only if $x_1 \, R_i \, x_2$ but not $x_2 \, R_i \, x_1$.

These binary preference relations can be used to define preference and indifference sets for each individual over alternatives in X. Define $P_i(x) \subset X$ to be individual i's preference set with respect to $x \in X$, where individual i strictly prefers all outcomes in $P_i(x)$ to x, that is, $P_i(x) = \{y \in X | y P_i x\}$. We can define the weak-preference set, $R_i(x)$, and the indifference set, $I_i(x)$ similarly. Spatial models of legislative choice generally assume that $P_i(x)$ is convex and open and that $I_i(x)$ is closed. Thus, if $x_1 \, P_i \, x_2$, then there exists an arbitrarily small neighborhood around x_1 that is entirely in $P_i(x)$. Also, it follows that the union of $P_i(x)$ and $I_i(x)$, that is, $R_i(x)$, is closed and convex. We also assume that indifference sets are "thin" and that indifference contours are continuous. Under these conditions, the weak-order, R_i, the strict-order, P_i, and the indifference relation, I_i, adequately represent preferences between pairs of alternatives when these sets are finite.

It is often more convenient to represent preferences in a manner consistent with the definitions of R_i, I_i, and P_i by defining an ordinal utility function, $u_i(x)$, for individual i over the set of alternatives X. To each element of X, $u_i(x)$ assigns a real number such that for all x_1 and x_2 in X, $u_i(x_1) \geq u_i(x_2)$ if and only if $x_1 \, R_i \, x_2$. If $u_i(x)$ is concave, it has a unique maximum. This maximum, that is, the alternative that stands highest in the individual's preference order, is called an ideal point and is denoted as z_i. Thus $z_i \, R_i \, x_j$ for all x_j in X. Euclidean preferences are a particularly well-known functional form for $u_i(x)$. Specifically, in policy space $|R_n|$, $u_i(x_j) = [\Sigma_k = 1^n (z_{ik} - x_{jk})^2]^{1/2}$, where z_{ik} is the kth dimension of z_i and x_{jk} is the kth dimension of outcome x_j in X.

Sincere and Sophisticated Voting

An alternative x_1 in X is Pareto-optimal for the set of persons $N' \subseteq N$, if there does not exist another outcome x_2 in X such that everyone in N' prefers x_2 at least as much as x_1, and someone in N' strictly prefers x_1 to x_2. An outcome $x \in X$ is a Condorcet winner if, for some other $y \in X$, the number of people who strictly prefer x to y exceeds the number who strictly prefer y to x. In other words, no motion can defeat a Condorcet winner in a majority vote, and no amendment agenda can lead away from it.

A sequence of votes in an agenda tree can be represented by an agenda tree, which at each stage compares two alternatives. For example, with four alternatives, A, B, C, and D, we can have an agenda that first pits A against B. The winner is then pitted against C in the second stage. If A or B beats C in the second stage, voting ends. If C wins in the second stage, then the third and final vote is between C and D.

To see how agendas affect outcomes, consider a three-person legislature whose preferences over the alternatives, $X = \{A, B, C, D\}$, are ordered as follows: member 1 prefers D to B, B to C, and C to A; member 2 prefers B to C to A to D; and member 3 prefers C to B to D to A. The set of actions at each stage in the agenda comprises two alternatives (vote for the right-hand branch, vote for the left-hand branch). Thus the left-hand branch at the first node contains A, C, and D, and the right-hand branch contains B, C, and D. At the first stage, then, members are voting for $\{A, C, D\}$ against $\{B, C, D\}$. Suppose each member, at each agenda stage, votes sincerely, that is, for their most preferred alternative. Since these two sets differ only in that A is replaced by B in the second set, all three members vote for the right branch $\{B, C, D\}$. The comparison at the second stage is $\{B\}$ versus $\{C, D\}$. Since a majority prefer either C to B or D to B, the collective choice will be the right branch, $\{C, D\}$. The final choice favors C over D. But the Condorcet winner is B. This means that a majority prefer B to the outcome generated by sincere voting.

If members vote sophisticatedly, they anticipate how their choice at each stage affects the final outcome. Assuming that voting occurs simultaneously, so that no one can condition their vote on the decisions of others at that stage, we can start at the bottom of the agenda tree and work up to determine the "sophisticated voting equivalent outcome" of each alternative at each stage. In the last stage no one ever has an incentive to vote other than sincerely, but in this example member 1 will vote sophisticatedly in the first stage. Because C beats A at the second stage, a vote for A is, in the end, a vote for C, that is, the sophisticated equivalent of A at stage one is C. On the other hand, since B beats C

in the second stage, the sophisticated equivalent of B is B in the first stage. Thus a majority will vote for B at stage one and then for B again at stage two. Doing so, however, requires member 1 to vote for B at stage 2, even though he prefers D to B. Under sophisticated voting, the outcome is the Condorcet winner. See Enelow and Hinich (1984) for a more comprehensive discussion of these matters.

CHAPTER SEVEN

Congress and the Budget Bureau

Congressional Abdication to the Executive Branch

In "Congressional Responses to the Twentieth Century," Huntington (1965) observes that "the congressional role in legislation has largely been reduced to delay and amendment ... the initiative in formulating legislation, in assigning legislative priorities, in arousing support for legislation, and in determining the final content of the legislation has clearly shifted to the executive branch" (p. 23). Moe (1985) offers a similar assessment: "As government has taken a far more positive role over the years in addressing a wide range of social problems—and as Congress has shown itself quite incapable of institutional coherence and political leadership—the president has increasingly been held responsible for designing, proposing, legislating, administering, and modifying public policy, that is, for governing" (p. 239).[1] By this view, the nation has been fortunate that at critical junctures, members of Congress have been sensible enough to acknowledge their institution's inadequacies and, in a wide range of policy areas, have handed over to the president tasks and responsibilities that Congress itself could not effectively discharge. As a consequence, according to Sundquist (1981), Congress has lost many of its original policy-making functions simply by abdicating them to the president: "The powers of the modern presidency were not wrested by self-seeking chief executives from a struggling but ultimately yielding Congress ... on the contrary, every transaction embodying a shift of power and influence was one of mutual consent, for the shifts were made pursuant to law, and Congress wrote and passed the laws" (p. 155).

In the realm of appropriations, the key episode in the saga of congressional abdication is widely regarded to be the passage of the Budget and Accounting Act of 1921. This legislation assigned to the president the task of formulating a unified budget and created a new agency, the Bureau of the Budget, to assist him in carrying out this task. Henceforth, funding levels proposed in the president's budget would be the starting point in the annual appropriations process. Agency requests for appropriations would not come to Congress until they had been filtered through the Budget Bureau. In Pfiffner's (1979) words, the creation of the Budget Bureau marks the "beginning of the domination of the budgetary process by the institutionalized presidency" (p. 15).

As with the delegation of policy-making authority to the Appropriations Committee and to all other standing committees within Congress, the grant of authority made from Congress to the Budget Bureau was in principle limited to that of proposing legislation—in this case, the amount of appropriations each department and agency should receive. (Throughout this chapter we use the term "Budget Bureau" to refer either to the Bureau of the Budget or to its successor, the Office of Management and Budget, created in 1970.) Members of the House Select Committee that reported the Budget and Accounting Act stressed the limited nature of the delegation they were recommending:

> The proposed law does not change in the slightest degree the duty of Congress to make the minutest examination of the budget and to adopt the budget only to the extent that it is found to be economical. If the estimates contained in the President's budget are too large, it will be the duty of the Congress to reduce them. If in the opinion of Congress the estimates are not sufficient, it will be within the power of Congress to increase them ... [The bill] provides for no restrictions on the part of Congress to modify the proposals of the President but, on the other hand, seeks to have such proposals come before it in such a form, so itemized, classified, and supported by detailed data, as will enable it more effectively to perform this function. (House Select Committee on the Budget 1921a, pp. 6–7)

According to Sundquist (1981), though, such conveyances of authority are hardly innocuous:

> [A]ny delegation to the executive of authority to act on matters on which the Congress has customarily acted is a shift of power from the legislative to the executive branch. Even if Congress delegates to the president no more than the responsibility to recommend, to the extent that the recommendations are not seriously reviewed and therefore become controlling, the exercise of governmental power has moved between the branches. (p. 12)

In the case of legislative authority delegated to standing committees within Congress, the abdication hypothesis derives from the premise that a regime of reciprocal deference shields committee proposals from hostile takeovers on the floor. Here the abdication hypothesis posits a similar pattern of deference, as Sundquist's remarks point to, by Congress to the president in budgetary matters (Peterson 1985). The title given to the Brookings Institution's annual (1970–83) series of analyses of the president's budget—*Setting National Priorities*—is, as White (1990) observes, testimony to the extent to which his recommendations were seen to define the major features of fiscal policy. Or, as Kiewiet (1983) put it not too many years ago, "It is the president who is primarily responsible for the general thrust of economic policy, whether it be the 'guns and butter' policies of Lyndon Johnson or the 'Reaganomics' of the current administration" (p. 126).

The abdication hypothesis draws additional credence from the growth of the bureau's legislative role, beyond the explicit statutory charge of melding agency requests for appropriations into the president's annual budget, to that of reviewing proposals for substantive legislation. Under "central clearance," as Neustadt (1954) described this arrangement, the bureau's ruling that a proposal emanating from the executive branch was "not in accord with the program of the President" was meant to bar its submission to Congress. The ostensible rationale for this innovation was that the Budget Bureau's job is to make budgetary recommendations and that virtually all legislation eventually has at least some effect upon either revenues or expenditures. Especially pertinent here is the fact that the original proposal to extend central clearance by the bureau to substantive legislation came from the House Appropriations Committee only a few months after the bureau was established. As Neustadt explains in his classic treatment on the subject, the committee and the bureau "had a clear mutuality of interest in closing off, as nearly as might be, all avenues to action on appropriations save their own. Substantive congressional committees, no less than executive agencies, were potential conspirators against the exclusive jurisdictions conferred by the new budget system. Facing common dangers, the system's beneficiaries made common cause. Central legislative clearance was a principal result" (p. 643). By this line of reasoning, the abdication of policy-making authority within Congress to the House Appropriations Committee complemented and reinforced the abdication of policy-making authority from Congress to the executive branch. Although the bureau's role in clearing legislation was not fully consolidated until the Roosevelt administration, in subsequent years the scope of central clearance expanded to include all proposed executive orders and proclamations, oral testimony and written reports of executive officials who were to appear before congressional committees, and finally, during the Reagan administration, to proposed rules and regulations. It was through the growth of central clearance, according to Sundquist, that the president institutionalized his role as "Chief Legislator" (1981, p. 138).

Responsible for both the preparation of the president's budget and coordination of his legislative program, it is only natural that the Budget Bureau came to have what Heclo (1975) calls "special Presidential status" (p. 80). Its first director, Charles Dawes, certainly saw himself as an agent of the president and, moreover, as something of a first among equals in this regard: "The Director of the Budget, in gathering information for the use of the President, acts for the President, and his calls upon the chiefs of bureaus and other administrative officers for purposes of consultation or information take precedence over the Cabinet head of a department, or any head of an independent organization" (Dawes 1923, p. 8).[2]

Nothing in the public record suggests that any of Dawes's successors have envisoned the job in a substantially different way. Transfer of the bureau in 1939 from Treasury to the newly created Executive Office of the President thus constituted a formal recognition of its uniquely presidential orientation. When the Bureau of the Budget became the Office of Management and Budget in the early 1970s, its director, Roy Ash, informed the House Government Operations Committee that nothing had changed in this regard, stating, "The OMB director serves as the personal agent of the President in the performance of presidential duties" (*Congressional Quarterly Weekly Report*, 14 April 1973, p. 860). David Stockman (1986) reports passing up another cabinet post in hopes of the OMB directorship, believing that he could do more to further the "Reagan Revolution" in that capacity than in any other. One consequence of the bureau's close identification with the president is that the one's problems quickly become the other's. Berman (1979) reports that by the end of the Nixon administration, OMB was "cordially hated." Conversely, the Reagan administration suffered considerable embarrassment from publication of Stockman's confessions in *The Atlantic Monthly*, and of course the Bert Lance scandal seriously damaged the public standing of Jimmy Carter.

From the beginning, however, its proponents saw the bureau as something more than a mere advocate for the president's favorite policies, coming up with the numbers to rationalize whatever it was that he wanted to do. Its mission was instead to provide impartial policy analysis and independent judgment, to be "less concerned about the short-term political ramifications of who believes what how strongly, and more concerned with the substance of the policy issues themselves"(Heclo 1975, p. 82). In other words, the bureau should serve the presidency, not whoever happened to be president. Dawes laid the groundwork for the development of this ethos, asserting that "the Bureau of the Budget is impersonal, impartial and non-political, and thus it must always remain" (1923, p. xi). After serving several presidents of both parties, the bureau came to be perceived, at least by those who worked there, as a bastion of "neutral competence" (Heclo 1975, 1984). Neustadt (1954) relates the special care that Harry Truman took to insure that the bureau's legacy for dispassionate analysis remained after his own term in office had ended:

> In 1951, Truman appointed as Budget Director a top Bureau careerist, Frederick J. Lawton, charging him specifically, though not publicly, to batten down the institution, readying it for the transition ahead. There was to be no more expansion in politically charged directions. The Bureau's reputation for "nonpolitical" expertise, its institutional respectability, were to be guarded at all costs, thereby preserving its utility to the next president." (p. 664)

According to Neustadt, Truman's foresight paid off. After initial mistrust of the Budget Bureau ("holdovers schooled for twenty years in Democratic policies"), the Eisenhower administration was able to tap its valuable "resources of careerist expertise" (p. 666).

Neustadt, Heclo, Berman, and other scholars who have studied the Budget Bureau are perfectly aware that neutral competence is a fragile commodity. Pressure from the administration to be "politically responsive" can be overwhelming. During the Nixon administration, political appointees called program associate directors (the much maligned "PADs") were inserted into the chain of command, and another layer of appointees was interposed between the director and the careerists soon after Carter took office (Berman 1979, p. 118). In the view of these scholars, however, it is crucial for the bureau to guard the flame, because independent judgment and analysis are the most valuable products it can offer a president. As Heclo (1984) puts it, "The test of a staff serving the presidency as an ongoing institution is not its responsiveness to one set of demands, but its ability to respond to one set of demands without diminishing its capacity to respond to the next" (p. 286). If the president cannot get a straight answer from the Budget Bureau, according to this line of reasoning, he is not going to get a straight answer anywhere else.

One difference between the delegation made to the bureau and that made to the House Appropriations Committee is that the "special presidential status" of the bureau would seem to make the extent of the abdication that has occurred plainer to see. But the bureau's association with the ideal of neutral competence means that this new manifestation of the abdication hypothesis shares a common thread with the one considered previously: as in the case of the House Appropriations Committee (at least according to the Guardian of the Treasury model), a major policy-making role has been handed over to an entity whose mission is supposed to transcend the mere prosecution of partisan politics.

As before, we reject the abdication hypothesis in favor of an alternative interpretation: that members—in particular, those of the majority party—have delegated to the Budget Bureau the authority to prepare a budget and to oversee the president's legislative program in order to better achieve their own policy objectives. We proceed with our case against the abdication hypothesis by first reconsidering the political origins of the 1921 Budget and Accounting Act. It bears repeating that our intent in this endeavor is not to determine whether the president has become more powerful than Congress, or whether and when the balance of power between the two branches has shifted from one to the other. As we argue elsewhere, the success of delegation has nothing to do with the appearance of power. Principals can be highly successful in using delegation to pursue their interests, yet appear passive and ineffectual relative to their agents.

Political Origins of the Budget and Accounting Act

In order to properly appreciate the nature of the delegation made to the Budget Bureau by the Budget and Accounting Act, it is important to remember that Congress has always delegated the job of formulating budget requests to officials in the executive branch. In the first years of the Republic, estimates (that is, requests for appropriations) were compiled and transmitted to Congress by Secretary of the Treasury Alexander Hamilton. Following his departure, individual departments submitted their requests directly to the House Ways and Means Committee (or to the Appropriations Committee, after its creation in 1865). In 1879 Congress directed once again that departmental estimates be submitted through the Secretary of the Treasury, and in 1884 it consolidated this grant of authority to Treasury by stipulating that estimates of appropriations and deficiencies "shall be transmitted to the Congress through the Secretary of the Treasury and in no other manner."

According to most budgetary historians, nineteenth-century presidents generally chose not to review the spending estimates that federal agencies submitted to Congress; Treasury, in turn, merely went through the pro forma motion of collecting agency budget requests and forwarding the resultant agglomeration to Capitol Hill. There is, then, a flip side to the abdication hypothesis that posits a pre-1921 regime of presidential passivity. As Fisher (1975) characterizes this longstanding view of this literature, "Presidents and their Secretaries of the Treasury were passive bystanders during those years, mechanically forwarding budget estimates to Congress without revision or comment" (p. 9). Fisher categorically rejects this notion, noting that presidents, including John Quincy Adams, Van Buren, Tyler, Polk, Buchanan, Grant, and Cleveland, revised budget estimates before they were submitted to Congress. Others who did not formally revise estimates nonetheless related their views to Congress as to what should be done with them. And if presidents were not always intimately involved at the beginning of the annual appropriations process, they always have been at the end. Beginning with Andrew Jackson in 1830, several nineteenth-century presidents vetoed appropriations bills that contained provisions they found objectionable.

It is clear, then, that the Budget and Accounting Act did not initiate presidential involvement in the appropriations process. Nor was the act the first piece of legislation to delegate to the president the task of formulating a budget to be submitted to Congress. In 1909, the Republican 61st Congress approved the following provision in the FY1910 sundry civil appropriations bill:

> Immediately upon the receipt of the regular annual estimates of appropriations needed for the various branches of the Government it shall be the duty of the Secretary of the Treasury to estimate as nearly as may be the revenues of the Government for the ensuing fiscal year, and if the estimates for appropriations, including the estimated amount necessary to meet all continuing and permanent appropriations, shall exceed the estimated revenues the Secretary of the Treasury shall transmit the estimates to Congress as heretofore required by law and at once transmit a detailed statement of all of said estimates to the President, to the end that he [the president] may ... advise the Congress how in his judgment the estimated appropriations could with the least injury to the public service be reduced so as to bring the appropriations within the estimated revenues, or, if such reductions be not in his judgment practicable without undue injury to the public service, that he may recommend to Congress such loans or new taxes as may be necessary to cover the deficiency. (quoted in Stewart 1989, pp. 179–80)

If this was not an executive budget, it was certainly the moral equivalent of one. At President Taft's behest, the Secretary of the Treasury continued to submit budgets to Congress (after ordering agencies to make cuts) until a Democratic Congress specifically forbade him to do so in 1913 (Stewart 1989). Any further innovations in the manner in which agency estimates were submitted to Congress were put off by the intervention of World War I.

The Budget and Accounting Act thus built upon practices that had already been implemented in the previous decade and simply redelegated the authority to formulate appropriations requests and to compile other budgetary data to the newly created Bureau of the Budget. There were many reasons for this decision. Above all, however, it was a product of the Republican party's desire to demonstrate their commitment to the ideals of fiscal retrenchment and restraint. Passage of the Budget and Accounting Act occurred only a year after the House had voted to reverse the reforms of 1885 and to return jurisdiction over all annual spending bills to the House Appropriations Committee. Both innovations were inspired by the same tenets of reformist faith and were clearly envisioned by the measures' proponents as logical corollaries of each other.[3] The bureau, they claimed, would be an effective instrument of retrenchment. Costs would be cut dramatically as the bureau applied scientific principles of management to put government operations on a "business basis." Acting in conjunction with each other, the committee and bureau would ferret out waste and inefficiency by insuring that each item of expenditure was considered in relation to all other competing demands upon the Treasury. Under the previous regime, federal expenditures had emerged as the product of countless disjoint, independent decisions, with no single entity responsible for seeing how all the pieces fit together. To those familiar with the Guardian of the Treasury model of the Appropriations Committee, the arguments made for establishing the Bureau of the Budget have a familiar ring.[4]

As indicated earlier, the Republicans, most notably Taft, had been pressing for an executive budget for some time. Committed to high, protectionist tariffs, they had long been, at least relative to the Democrats, willing to countenance higher expenditures in order to prevent resulting federal surpluses from threatening tariff rates. This had been an electoral liability in an age in which "economy" was a motherhood issue, and they were determined to make a break with it. After winning the House and Senate in the election of 1918 and the White House in 1920, several other considerations bolstered their commitment to retrenchment. First, there was the unprecedented cost of the war. Federal spending had risen from $740 million in FY1916 to $18.9 billion in FY1919, and the federal debt from $971 million to over $24 billion. By May of 1918, monthly deficits incurred by the Treasury—approximately $1 billion—were significantly larger than the entire annual budget in the years prior to the war (Kennedy 1980). "The deficit budgets of 1917, 1918 and 1919," as Brady and Morgan (1987) put it, "created an untenable fiscal situation" that required swift, decisive action (p. 230).

A second factor was the shift that had occurred in both the level and the incidence of federal taxation. In 1913, the Democrats, holding the White House and both Houses of Congress for the first time in twenty years, enacted the Underwood Tariff, which lowered rates to levels that had not been seen since before the Civil War. To make up for lost revenue they simultaneously imposed taxes on individual and corporate net income, a move made possible by the ratification of the Sixteenth Amendment.[5] The rates were initially established at very low levels, but increased dramatically during World War I. Revenues collected from the taxes on corporate and personal income rose from $128 million in FY1916 to $3.95 billion in FY1920 and accounted for roughly two-thirds of federal receipts. The share of revenues raised from customs duties correspondingly dropped from about one-third to less than 6 percent. The progressive nature of the income tax meant, of course, that it fell disproportionately on Republican constituents. What the Democrats referred to as the "conscription of wealth," the Republicans denounced as a "monstrosity" promoted by "Bolsheviks intent upon wrecking the financial structure of the country" (Livermore 1966, p. 60).[6] Attitudes about spending, in short, are a function of where the money comes from.

Third, the Republicans confronted an executive branch bureaucracy that was composed primarily of Democratic appointees. Although Woodrow Wilson had long been a staunch advocate of civil service reform, as president he found patronage a valuable currency in mustering support for his legislative program. According to Skowronek (1982), Wilson halted Taft's attempt to "blanket in" 36,000 postal employees in the South and West. Albert Burleson, Wilson's Postmaster General, then cleared the subsequent merit appointments with congressional Democrats. The Civil Service Commission's extension of protections guaranteed under the 1912 Lloyd-LaFollette Act was thus implicated, as Skowronek puts it, in a "Democratic party spoils raid" (p. 195). As Skowronek goes on to note, all of the major bills Wilson favored "carried explicit provisos against the merit classification of administrative personnel. Internal revenue officers, the Federal Trade Commission, the Agricultural Credits Administration, the Tariff Commission—all the great institution-building accomplishments of Wilson's first term—bore the stamp of the spoilsmen" (pp. 195–96). Republican calls to increase government efficiency effectively meant reducing the number of Democratic holdovers in the executive branch and independent agencies.

Under the Republicans, federal spending declined steadily during the 1920s. With solid majorities in the House and Senate, they brought total spending down from $6.2 billion in FY1920 to $3.8 billion in FY1929, the final year of the Coolidge administration. During the same period they reduced the federal debt from $24 billion to under $18 billion. The total number of federal employees was cut quickly from 593,000 in FY1920 to 448,000 in FY1922 and remained at that level for the rest of the decade. The Bureau of the Budget stood as a tangible, institutional commitment to this program of retrenchment. In its first year of operation its director, Charles Dawes (1923) pointed to a number of cost-savings measures that the bureau had brought about: reducing civilian personnel at the War Department, for a savings of $23,069.20; getting the Interior Department to refrain from printing some maps that would have cost $679.00; disconnecting three telephones at the State Department, thereby saving $27.00. But Dawes, a former military man, believed that the best way to lead was by example and therefore directed more attention to cutting costs within the bureau than anywhere else. His martial background also manifested itself in his concern over the *espirit de corps*. To this end he established the Business Organization of the Government, a forum of cabinet officers and senior Budget Bureau officials, that held semi-annual pep rallies to bolster the fighting spirit in the war against waste and extravagance.

His successor, Herbert Lord, was, if anything, even more zealous than Dawes in the pursuit of cost-cutting. In his Annual Report for 1924, Lord pointed to the large savings the bureau had realized by using discarded furniture found in the basement of the Treasury Building, by using obsolete forms and envelopes for scratch paper, by taking special care in turning off the lights, and by issuing employees only one pencil at a time (they were required to surrender the stub of their old pencil before receiving a new one).[7] Lord allegedly remained after hours to patrol employee offices, confiscating superfluous paper clips and pads of paper. Starting with twenty-five employees, the bureau staff had grown to only forty by the beginning of Roosevelt's second term. The bureau's self-imposed austerity regimen, of course, meant that it could function as little more than a demonstration project. As Neustadt (1954) observes, during the Coolidge and Hoover administrations, the bureau's role in clearing legislation consisted of little more than the routine assertion that proposals implying new financial commitments were in conflict with the president's program. Not until the Roosevelt administration, when the president assigned the bureau sole responsibility for advising him to either sign or to veto enrolled bills, did the bureau's clearance role effectively extend to substantive policy.

Central Clearance and the Abdication Hypothesis

The creation of the Budget Bureau thus marks a milestone in the transformation of the Republican party into the party of fiscal conservatism. But even after one accepts that the origins of the bureau are to be found in the partisan politics of the first quarter of this century, its subsequent evolution would seem to provide plenty of justification for retaining the abdication hypothesis. Above all, as indicated earlier, there is the widespread view that Congress tends to defer to a substantial degree to the estimates contained in the president's budget (Kiewiet 1983; Peterson 1985). By most accounts, such deference is not deference per se, but rather a consequence of the informational advantages the Budget Bureau derives from its clearance of agency appropriations requests. Hubert Humphrey (D, Minnesota) was only one of many members since 1921 who have complained about this. "The president's budget," he asserted, "comes before us as a total package, conceived in secrecy and delivered in the middle of the night, in the cloak of darkness" (*Congressional Quarterly Weekly Report*, 10 February 1973, p. 314).

The bureau's clearance of executive branch testimony would seem to further bolster its strategic advantage. Agency officials appearing before appropriations subcommittees are there to defend the estimates the Budget Bureau has approved, not to make a case for what they actually consider to be necessary and appropriate for carrying out their agency's mission. Those who fail to be team players in this regard presumably face the threat of retribution from the bureau in the next year's budget review. Typical of the complaints members have expressed about this is that made by then member of the Government Operations Committee, Jack Brooks (D, Texas), during the Nixon adminstration: "The refusal of the executive branch to permit its witnesses to convey to congressional committees their forthright opinions on matters coming before us," he charged, "is detrimental to the entire government process" (quoted in Havemann 1973, p. 1589). This arrangement would seem to leave Congress dependent upon whatever information the Budget Bureau deems to be fit for their consumption. As in the case of Shepsle and Weingast's portrayal of committees, then, congressional "deference" to appropriations requests cleared by the Budget Bureau is a product of the bureau's strategically favorable position vis-à-vis Congress.

Another major source of support for the abdication hypothesis, as indicated earlier, is the extension of the bureau's clearance role from budgetary matters to the president's entire legislative program. In the views of Sundquist and other scholars, acquiescence to this innovation greatly augmented the extent to which Congress had abdicated policy-making capabilities to the executive branch. As members complained in the final days of Roosevelt's presidency, "bills originating in the departments have had the green light before the committees, and bills originating with the members have been an idle fantasy" (Lester 1969, p. 55). During the Kennedy administration, the tasks of defining the major features of the president's legislative program and of tracking its progress in Congress moved from the Budget Bureau to the White House staff (Gilmour 1971). In one form or another, that is where those responsibilities remain. The bureau retains substantial responsibilities for legislative clearance, however, and in the realm of appropriations its original responsibility for "correlating" agency budget estimates remains intact.

We have a number of objections to this line of thinking about the legislative role of the Budget Bureau. Above all, we have grave doubts about the bureau's ability to see to it that all the information Congress receives about appropriations requests is supportive of the figure put forth in the president's budget. Even if the bureau were somehow able to insure that Congress never heard a discouraging word, we submit that it is perfectly safe for members to assume that (1) what agency heads requested from the Budget Bureau was greater than the figure appearing in the president's budget; (2) agency heads would be happy to receive an increase in appropriations over the figure appearing in the president's budget; and (3) they have some very specific ideas about how they would spend the additional appropriations.

Congressional members do not need to rely upon deductive reasoning in these matters, however, because there is simply no way that the bureau or any other entity in the exective branch can choke off the flow of communication between Congress and executive agencies. First of all, threats to punish disloyalty are not entirely credible. Say, for example, that an agency official succeeds in obtaining a big increase in appropriations by persuading the members overseeing his budget that the bureau had made unconscionable, draconian cuts in his requests. If the bureau retaliates the next year by cutting his requests even more, he can make the same argument again and presumably win an even larger increase. Eventually, of course, the agency's appropriations can be held in check by the veto. But this is the president's constitutional prerogative, not an outgrowth of the Budget Bureau's clearance of appropriations requests.

Second, Congress can simply mandate that federal agencies or the Budget Bureau provide desired information. It has voted, for example, to require several agencies, including the International Trade Commission, the Federal Maritime Commission, and the Consumer Product Safety Commission, to submit budget proposals concurrently to the Budget Bureau and to Congress. Congress and its committees can also subpoena witnesses to obtain information that is otherwise not forthcoming, but executive branch personnel almost always appear voluntarily. Some oversight committees such as Government Operations swear in witnesses as standard procedure, but most forego such legal technicalities. Recognizing this, the Budget Bureau has generally limited its clearance of executive branch testimony to prepared remarks and written reports. Even here it is unwise to be too heavy-handed. As demonstrated in the recent case of the bureau ordering a NASA scientist to water down his report on the climatological consequences of continued emission of greenhouse gases, overzealousness by the bureau in this regard can embarrass the administration and provoke charges of censorship. On occasion it has provoked Congress to forbid the Budget Bureau from reviewing testimony of agency officials prior to their appearance before the committee. Besides, as OMB Director Richard Darman observed, the information is going to get out anyway (Hager 1989).

The answers witnesses give in response to direct questioning by committee members, in contrast, are not covered by central clearance and it is hard to see how they could be. Of course, executive branch officials who for one reason or another desire to adhere closely to the administration's line can do so under questioning just as readily as in their written reports and prepared testimony. But most executive branch officials find that they can convey the information they want to without engaging in open defiance of the bureau. Several different accounts of appropriations subcommittee hearings all report that after initial protestation, an appropriate display of discomfiture, and token effort at resistance, the agency head dutifully reports to the subcommittee precisely how much he requested from the bureau. What is a bit odd about all of this, which Fenno describes as a "ritual mating dance" (1966, p. 303), is that in all likelihood the members of the subcommittee already knew what the agency had requested of the Budget Bureau well before the hearings were underway. Prior to the hearings, agencies typically send the relevant subcommittee extensive budgetary data, "adding details to what appears in their formal budget requests submitted by the chief executive" (Rosen 1989, p. 52). White (1990), similarly, reports that agency and committee staff personnel rarely experience difficulty in communicating with each other; as a number of them assured him, the telephones work fully as well in Washington, D.C., as they do in the rest of the country.

But if information does flow so freely from the agencies to Capitol Hill, what accounts for members' protests about the Budget Bureau stifling information? In our view, these complaints are not about information. They are about making policy. Uncooperative witnesses make it difficult to establish the kind of "legislative history" committees need to direct agency activities through what Kirst (1969) characterizes as "nonstatutory techniques." These include such things as warnings, recommendations, expressions of concern or unhappiness, and prods for policy initiation. Such methods permit greater administrative flexibility, and, as Kirst notes, they are especially useful to the Appropriations Committee as a mechanism for including substantive legislation in an appropriations bill. What nonstatutory techniques essentially boil down

to, however, are informal agreements between the committee and agency
as to what the agency is to do in the upcoming year. An official's refusal
to acknowledge that his agency could do anything useful with additional
funding, or that there are some lower priority programs that could get
by with less funding, or that certain activities could probably best be
covered by contingency funds is tantamount to a refusal to bargain in
good faith. If policy-making were not the issue here, it would be hard
to account for why Congress has been so adamant about forbidding the
Budget Bureau from altering the transcripts of testimony *after* it has
been given to a committee. Such prohibitions appear in the FY1988 omnibus continuing resolution (P.L. 100–202) and in the FY1989 Treasury,
Postal Service, and General Government Appropriation Bill (P.L. 100–
440). Obviously, in such cases, the problem is not one of information. In
order to know that a transcript has been altered it is necessary to know
what the witness had said in the first place! The problem with altering
transcripts is that it compromises the ability of the committee to direct
agency activities through nonstatutory means.

   Whatever informational filter the bureau is able to interpose between
executive agencies and Congress through its clearance of budget requests
and supportive testimony is thus a highly permeable one. It is hardly
surprising, then, that the estimates (appropriations requests) presented
in the president's annual budget are not graven in stone. As revealed
by the data in table 7.1, Congress rarely appropriates the same amount
of money to an agency that the president requested. In the FY1948–85
period less than 10 percent of the estimates in our sample of agencies
(listed in table 6.2) made it through Congress without being changed.
The changes Congress makes, furthermore, can be substantial. In the
Kennedy, Johnson, Nixon, Ford, and Carter administrations, approximately 30 percent of the estimates in the president's budget were either
cut or increased by over 5 percent. In the Truman and Reagan administrations, the corresponding figure was over 50 percent. Indeed, when we
confine our attention to the extreme case of the budgets Truman submitted to the Republican 80th Congress, we find that nearly 90 percent
of his agency estimates were cut by more than 5 percent.

   This is in sharp contrast, of course, to the data on floor consideration of House and Senate Appropriations Committee recommendations.
Although we rejected characterizing them as indicative of a consistent
pattern of deference, the data in tables 6.3 and 6.4 did show that between
80 and 90 percent of the appropriations figures reported by the committees are adopted by their chamber without amendment. Floor changes
are often very small, furthermore, and many of the large ones (produced
by points of order objections) are illusory. The data in table 7.1 should
not be pushed too far. They do not reveal, for example, whether final

Table 7.1   Congressional Changes in Presidential Budget Estimates,
             FY1948–85

	Administration					
	Truman	Ike	JFK LBJ	Nixon Ford	Carter	Reagan
> 5% cut	52.7	25.3	27.0	17.1	15.0	15.3
2%–5% cut	21.5	13.5	20.9	14.8	12.8	11.5
0–2% cut	14.6	23.7	28.1	29.4	24.8	10.6
No change	5.0	16.4	8.2	8.8	7.7	6.0
0–2% increase	2.7	7.0	8.6	8.3	16.2	11.5
2–5% increase	1.5	4.2	3.4	8.3	9.0	10.6
> 5% increase	1.9	9.9	3.9	13.2	14.5	34.5
n	260	384	441	432	234	235

appropriations are closer to what the president wants or closer to what
Congress wants; the president's budget incorporates expectations about
congressional action, and Congress makes appropriations in the knowledge that the president can veto bills he finds unacceptable. A thorough
analysis of the various factors that affect final appropriations decisions is
taken up in the next chapter. Suffice it to say for now that the submission
of the president's budget is the first word in the annual congressional
appropriations process, not the last.

Just as the bureau cannot use central clearance to stifle information,
neither can it be used, by the bureau, the White House staff, or any other
entity in the executive branch, to block legislative initiatives. Neustadt
(1954) himself makes this observation, citing Taft-Hartley as a prominent example of legislation considered and enacted by Congress (over
a veto) that never received favorable clearance. Even during the high
point of the bureau's legislative clearance role, congressional committees
routinely called upon executive branch departments and agencies to provide "technical drafting services" which, as long as they did not carry
an explicit endorsement, were exempt from clearance (p. 644). It is a
mistake, then, to see central clearance of substantive legislative proposals
as something akin to the "gatekeeping" capabilities that congressional
committees are often assumed to have. Traditionally it has been nothing
more and nothing less than a requirement that the president stake out his
position in advance of congressional consideration. Given that he must
ultimately accept or reject any legislation that Congress passes, this is

valuable information indeed. As several political scientists have explicitly recognized, Congress accepts central clearance of executive policy
proposals because it serves the interests of its members. Heclo (1984)
makes this point as clearly as we could ever hope to: "It should never
be forgotten that Congress agreed to increase the president's budgetary
responsibilities as a means of helping the legislature do its work. Any
executive budget process that strikes members of Congress as more of a
hindrance than a help in their jobs is likely to be disregarded" (p. 256).
We would add only that Heclo's observation holds for the clearance of
substantive legislative proposals as well.

A good way to appreciate the extent to which the bureau's traditional clearance role serves congressional interests is to consider how
Congress has responded when the bureau has instead invoked central
clearance to stymie members' policy objectives—particularly those of
the majority party. Backed by a Republican Senate that was very much
in favor of "regulatory relief," in early 1981 Ronald Reagan issued Executive Order 12291, which directed executive branch agencies to conduct
a cost-benefit analysis of all major rules and regulations. The order
authorized the Office of Information and Regulatory Affairs (OIRA)
within OMB to monitor compliance. OIRA had been created by the
Paperwork Reduction Act of 1980 to oversee federal information policy,
records management, telecommunications and data processing, and to
review all agency proposals to collect information from the public. The
order necessarily exempted independent agencies, such as the Interstate
Commerce Commission, as well as any regulation issued in response to
a court order. Executive Order 12498, issued in January 1985, further
broadened the scope of OIRA's purview to include "pre-rulemaking activities" such as hearings, data gathering, statistical analyses, or other
undertakings that might eventually point to the desirability of new or
revised regulations.

Whatever might be implied by cost-benefit analysis in theory, OIRA
clearly took it as a mandate to block (or, more accurately, to delay
indefinitely) a wide variety of regulatory initiatives opposed by the administration but favored by congressional Democrats and most of the
party's major constituencies—labor unions, consumer advocates, envi-
ronmentalists, and minority groups. Its targets included Occupational
Safety and Health Administration (OSHA) standards for workplace exposure to toxic or carcinogenic substances and rules requiring worker notification of such exposure, Department of Energy regulations regarding
nuclear waste disposal, FDA standards governing the content of infant
formula, Department of Transportation requirements to place air bags in
automobile steering columns, EPA regulations concerning air and water
quality, and many others.

House Democrats reacted to this application of central clearance, which they saw as an assertion of an executive veto over proposed regulations, in a strong and predictably negative fashion. In principle they could write any agency rule or regulation into law, thereby providing a statutory basis for agency action and bypassing OIRA review. In reality this was not a strategy that was likely to pay off, given the presence of a Republican in the White House and, through 1986, a Republican majority in the Senate. Republican opposition also blunted the efforts of House Democrats to strike at OIRA directly. In 1986 the House Appropriations Committee, at the behest of Energy and Commerce Committee Chairman John Dingell (D, Michigan) and other leading House Democrats, dropped all funding for OIRA in FY1987 appropriations legislation. (OIRA had been operating for three years without reauthorization.) OIRA ultimately received new authorization and new funding in the FY1987 omnibus continuing resolution, but this legislation made future administrators of the office subject to Senate confirmation and stipulated that any funds OIRA received on the basis of authorization under the Paperwork Reduction Act could be used solely to review information collection requests (Hook 1986). The bill did not forbid OIRA from continuing to review proposed regulations, and President Bush has threatened to veto legislation that would (Morehouse 1989).

Another recourse was to go to court. In 1985 Dingell and the chairmen of four other House committees filed an *amicus curae* brief in *Public Citizen vs. Rowland*, a suit brought to the D.C. Circuit in 1985 to force OSHA to issue standards covering short-term exposure to ethylene oxide. In this document the chairmen charged that OSHA's decision to drop the standard had been "dictated by OMB" and was indicative of a "systematic usurpation of legislative power" (Davis 1985). The court eventually ruled in the plaintiffs' favor, and the standards were duly issued in April 1988.

Congressional Democrats also succeeded in placing limits on OIRA (or OMB) supervision of regulatory activity and information gathering in certain policy areas. The House Committee on Banking, Finance, and Urban Affairs' (1985) report accompanying the FY1986 reconciliation bill ordered OMB to stop interfering with regulations governing low-income housing programs administered by the Department of Housing and Urban Development and by the Farmers Home Administration, as well as with the collection of racial and ethnic data on the families being served by these programs. The committee noted that "this provision, like many of the amendments in the bill, is necessary because the Office of Management and Budget has been interfering in a very destructive way in the efforts of the Secretary of HUD and Agriculture to carry out their obligations under the laws governing discrimination" (p. 14). Legislation alluded to earlier—the 1988 omnibus continuing resolution and the FY1989 Treasury, Postal Service, and General Government Appropriations Act—directed OMB to refrain from challenging the Bureau of Alcohol, Tobacco, and Firearms' "administrative and/or regulatory methodology," its labeling rules (credited with keeping contaminated wine off the shelves), and its monthly collection of alcoholic beverage statistics. The same bill also instructed OMB not to interfere with the Department of Agriculture's issuance of marketing orders. Most recently, 1990 legislation reauthorizing vocational education programs stipulates that whenever OMB review significantly delays the release of reports and surveys mandated by the bill, the General Accounting Office is to determine whether or not there are legitimate grounds for the delay.

Perhaps more important than these statutory limitations, however, is that congressional Democrats appear to have achieved some sort of working relationship with OIRA and its regulatory review activities. First of all, many congressional Democrats appreciate that central clearance of regulatory initiatives can serve the interests of their consituents as much as those of the Republicans. The beleagured businessman is not the only one who confronts overlapping, contradictory regulations or the tedium of filling out forms to supply an agency with information that another agency has already coded into machine-readable form. For their part, OMB and OIRA administrators have adopted a far less confrontational approach to regulatory review than their predecessors took in the early 1980s. During her tenure as head of OIRA, Wendy Lee Gramm undertook a number of reforms to make information about OIRA and its activities more accessible to Congress and to the public (Rovner 1986). Current OMB Director Darman has also promised to not to use OIRA review as a cover for derailing regulations that the administration does not favor (Morehouse 1989). What these developments portend is a return to central clearance along the traditional lines described by Neustadt. Rather than a synonym for veto, regulatory review is to be used as a way for the president to make his policy priorities known, to signal what he will find acceptable or unacceptable, and perhaps even to create some order out of what both liberals and conservatives have described as the regulatory thicket through which American businesses and consumers seek to find their way.

Divided Government

It is tempting to view the recent conflict between Congress and OMB over regulatory review through the prism of the abdication hypothesis. Designed by Congress to be a small, elite agency that would provide badly needed assistance in making appropriations decisions, it eventually became a major roadblock to the implementation of regulations that Congress had authorized federal agencies to make. It would seem to be a classic case of Madison's dilemma, of an agent working against the principal rather than for him. As we hope to have shown, however, this conflict is not the product of an ill-considered decision to delegate that eventually went awry, but rather of divided government.

In this respect there is nothing new here. Other actions taken by the bureau have led to conflict whenever a president of one party was pushing in one direction and Congress (or at least one chamber) organized by the other party was pulling in another. In the 80th Congress, when the Republicans took control of both chambers, Harry Truman used the Budget Bureau to stall congressional directives to pare back the federal workforce. Much to the chagrin of the Republican majority on the Appropriations Committee, the Budget Bureau maintained that it would take until at least March 1949 to issue even a preliminary study on where personnel might be reduced (House Approprations Committee 1948). This rearguard action succeeded, of course, as the Democrats were swept back into office in the 1948 elections.

Under Eisenhower, the bureau sought to restrict spending on several programs favored by the Democratically controlled Congress. At his direction, the bureau "put into reserve" (impounded) funds Congress had voted for these purposes. Congressional Democrats added provisions to appropriations bills to force release of these funds, most notably those in the highway trust fund. In 1958 another controversy flared when the Budget Bureau instructed the General Services Administration to enter into lease-purchase contracts for federal office buildings. The House Appropriations Committee directed that the GSA instead finance the construction or purchase of office buildings through direct appropriations. The Budget Bureau continued to insist on lease-purchase, however, and its director, Maurice Stans, was subsequently reprimanded by Appropriations in its report on the FY1959 Independent Offices bill (House Appropriations Committee 1958). Congress approved the bill, halting lease-purchase contracts. Congressional Democrats sent a couple of other shots across the bureau's bow during the Eisenhower administration. In 1955, a House Government Operations subcommittee held hearings on measures proposed by Appropriations Chairman Clarence Cannon (D, Missouri) to abolish the Budget Bureau and to assign its functions to a new agency under congressional control (*Congressional Quarterly Weekly Report*, 1 July 1955, p. 781). In 1958, another Democrat on House Appropriations, Daniel Flood (D, Pennsylvania), introduced a bill to abolish the bureau. In 1959, the House Government Operations Committee asked the General Accounting Office to conduct a comprehensive audit of the Executive Office of the President (including, of course, the Budget Bureau). The investigation was dropped after John Kennedy became president.

The biggest conflict, of course, occurred during the Nixon adminstration, when OMB ran impoundments and was at the center of the responsiveness campaign. In 1974 Congress made the director (and deputy director) subject to Senate confirmation.[8] We discuss the subject of impoundments in much greater detail in chapter 9, so there is no need to say more about it here.

In light of the many policy disputes that have involved the Budget Bureau during periods of divided government, it should come as little suprise that it is predominately during these times that observers have lamented the erosion of the bureau's neutral competence. The symptoms most commonly associated with excessive demands from the administration for political responsiveness include the departure of long-time bureau staff people to other agencies and poor morale among those who remain. Due to his close association with the president who appointed him, it is more often than not the director who is singled out as a political animal insufficiently responsive to the bureau's need to preserve a reputation for objectivity: "Career staffers complain that Darman, who is widely known for his own intellectual talents, neither respects nor appreciates their work or views. Instead he acts alone or with a few political associates to plot strategy and work up the budget numbers that fit his strategic purpose" (Calmes 1990, p. 93). Although these complaints concern the current director, similar things have been said about many of his predecessors. Previous Republican administrations that confronted a Democratic Congress have all been charged, in one way or another, with placing too much value on political responsiveness and too little on preserving the bureau's capacity for solid, objective policy analysis (Berman 1979; Helco 1975, 1984).

Summary

What has appeared to many to be Congress's abdication of responsibility for policy-making to the president has in fact been delegation designed to aid congressional parties in pursuing their policy goals. The bureau continues in its role of clearing of budget requests, substantive legislative proposals emanating from executive departments, and even of proposals for new rules and regulations because it serves congressional interests for the bureau to do so. This is the case even during periods of divided government, when a president of one party confronts a Congress controlled by the other. When the Budget Bureau has been at the point of conflict between the two branches, the majority party in Congress has often sought to alter the nature of the delegation to the Budget Bureau. These changes have included making the director and other top officials subject to Senate confirmation and a number of restrictions on the way the bureau exercises its authority, as in the case of impoundments and regulatory review by OIRA.

CHAPTER EIGHT

Congressional Parties and Appropriations Decisions

In the previous several chapters we have presented our case against the abdication hypothesis. We have argued that it is beset by serious theoretical problems and that it does not provide an adequate explanation for major changes in the House Appropriations Committee and for other budgetary reforms (chapter 4). It also does poorly in accounting for the pattern of party assignments to the Appropriations Committee (chapter 5), for floor amendments to appropriations bills (chapter 6), and for the manner in which Congress has delegated budgetary and other legislative responsibilities to the Budget Bureau (chapter 7). We have presented our case for an alternative view of the appropriations process that sees congressional parties as having coherent, stable policy priorities and that recognizes the delegation of authority, both internally to standing committees and externally to the executive branch, as a means of achieving those policy objectives. In this chapter we turn our attention to the bottom line—the amount of appropriations awarded each year to the myriad programs and agencies of the federal government. Evidence that domestic spending increases more quickly when the Democrats control Congress, other things being equal, and that it contracts (or at least expands more slowly) when the Republicans have a majority would provide the capstone to the case that we are seeking to make.[1]

This is not the first study to examine the responsiveness of spending decisions to the partisan composition of Congress. Indeed, it is not even the first in this book. The analysis undertaken in chapter 4 led us to conclude that the post-1885 growth in federal expenditures was primarily the product of Republican-sponsored increases in veterans' pensions and not the consequence of the divestiture of the House Appropriations Committee. These data are confined to the late nineteenth century, however, so it would be unwise to infer from them much about the Congress of today. A more contemporary source of evidence is the time series of congressional budget resolutions examined in chapter 3. As reported there, congressional Democrats have adopted resolutions paring tens of billions of dollars from Republican presidents' requests for military spending while adding tens of billions to their requests for domestic programs. But these data also have their limitations. Subsequent appropriations legislation often violates the terms of the budget resolution, and in any case the congressional budget process only began in 1975.

There are also several previous studies, by ourselves and others, that directly examine the effect of congressional parties upon appropriations decisions and other budgetary outcomes (Davis, Dempster, and Wildavsky 1974; Auten, Bozeman, and Cline 1984; Kiewiet and McCubbins 1985a, 1985b, 1988; Kamlet and Mowery 1987; Lowery, Bookheimer, and Malachowski 1985). In most of these efforts the partisan balance in Congress is measured as the number or percentage of congressional seats held by one party or the other—usually just in the House, but sometimes the average of the House and Senate. None of these studies, either by ourselves or others, provide much of a rationale as to why they employ the percentage of seats type of measure. The problem with proceeding in this fashion is that a party's share of seats is, at best, only a rough guide as to spending preferences in the chamber.[2] Such measures certainly do not reveal anything about the effectiveness with which the majority party in the House or the Senate pursues its budgetary priorities. The specification of a percentage of seats measure in a linear regression of appropriations figures upon partisan composition and other variables is particularly problematic in this regard. In estimating such an equation, the effect of an increase in a party's percentage of seats from 55 percent to 59 percent is constrained to be the same as an increase from 48 percent to 52 percent. Alternatively, a case in which one party holds 53 percent of the seats in both chambers cannot be disinguished from one in which they hold 58 percent in the House but only 48 percent in the Senate.

If there is any validity to the claims we have made about the ability of the majority party to pursue its policy priorities, the possession of a majority is in and of itself of critical importance. In the House, majority status means the Speakership, the chairmanship of all committees and subcommittees, and all the strategic advantages that holding these posts implies. To be sure, the size of a party's majority may also have a significant effect upon appropriations; more Democrats may in fact lead to more spending on nondefense activities. It is essential, however, that we initially take into account which party has a majority in each chamber.

Even if congressional parties do overcome the many problems of delegation we have discussed, the consequences of one party holding a majority versus the other may be overshadowed by the many other factors that influence congressional spending decisions. Above all, final appropriations figures necessarily reflect the preferences of the president, who must ultimately approve or reject the spending decisions Congress has made. Previous research has identified several other variables that can be expected to affect the marginal value members attach to the dollars appropriated to various agencies.[3] Chief among these is the state of the economy. Although there is no real consensus in macroeconomic theory on fiscal policy, probably the most common view in the field is that governments should decrease spending to lessen upward pressure on prices but increase it if output and employment growth become too sluggish. To the extent members accept Keynesian prescriptions, higher rates of unemployment should thus lead Congress to award higher levels of appropriations to government programs and agencies. Conversely, higher rates of inflation should prompt members to choose lower levels of appropriations.

In responding to economic conditions in this manner, members may be motivated purely by the desire to do the right thing. We suspect, though, that they also want to be seen by voters as doing the right thing. Fluctuations in the nation's economy clearly affect the outcomes of both congressional elections (Kramer 1971) and presidential elections (Fair 1978). The campaign decisions of incumbents and potential challengers, as well as the behavior of contributors, also bear out this fact of political life (Jacobson and Kernell 1981). Most of the evidence concerning voters' reactions to economic conditions suggests that voters respond retrospectively to past conditions, but that they tend to have short memories (or, more precisely, that they discount the past fairly rapidly). If members have similarly high discount rates, we would expect unemployment and inflation rates from the recent past—say the previous six months—to be weighted heavily in the choices they make over appropriations.

Another factor that might affect members' calculations is the electoral calendar. As the salience of electoral imperatives (raising money and garnering votes) increases with the proximity of election day, we would expect members to become increasingly anxious to channel government benefits to their constituents, or at least less anxious to cut benefits. Specifically, then, we hypothesize Congress to be more generous in its treatment of agency budgets in election years than in nonelection years. There are a couple of other factors, conversely, that might induce Congress to be less generous in appropriating money to domestic programs. One is the jump in military spending that occurs when the country mobilizes for war. The other is a large federal deficit in the preceding year's budget. Though deficits do not impart much cost in the year of their occurrence, voters probably suspect that in the long run they may lead to higher taxes, higher inflation, or higher interest rates. If nothing else, there are the opportunity costs associated with paying interest on the debt; revenues devoted to debt service could presumably be spent in ways that are politically, if not economically, more efficient.

Data and Estimation

The data we use to test the hypotheses we have just sketched out are the president's requests and congressional appropriations figures from FY1948 through FY1985 for the sixty-three nondefense agencies listed previously in table 6.2. This sample includes agencies from most federal departments and functions, but accounts for, at most, one-fourth of total federal spending. Because of this, and also because of the possibility that our estimates might be sensitive to the level of aggregation, we also examine spending requests and appropriations figures for nondefense appropriations bills for each fiscal year over the same time span. These bills are listed in table 8.1. In contrast to the agency-level sample, the bill-level sample encompasses almost all domestic spending funded by annual appropriations legislation.

Some evidence of the effects we hypothesize can be discerned from the exploratory cut at the data we take in table 8.2, which lists the constant-dollar growth rate for presidential requests and congressional appropriations averaged over the agencies in our sample for each year. The two-chamber majorities won by the Republicans in 1946 and 1952, as well as their taking of the Senate in 1980, appear to have led to sharp decreases in the average change in appropriations in FY1948, FY1954, and FY1982. Ronald Reagan had requested large cuts in his first budget, but the earlier decreases in appropriations occurred even though the president (first Truman and later Eisenhower) had asked for increases in spending. Substantial decreases in domestic spending growth also correspond with the rapid military buildup that occurred at the beginning of the Korean conflict (FY1952) and in the the early stages of U.S. involvement in Viet Nam (FY1967–70).

Before doing the estimation that is required to test our hypotheses, there are several econometric issues we must address. As indicated above,

Table 8.1 Sample of Appropriations Bills, FY1948–85

Bill	Years
Agriculture	1948–85
Independent Offices	1948–67
Independent Offices and Housing and Urban Development	1968–85
Interior	1948–85
Labor–Federal Security	1948–54
Labor–HEW (HHS)	1955–85
State, Commerce, Justice, Judiciary (excluding Commerce, 1956, 1958–62)	1948–85
Commerce	1956, 1958–62
Treasury, Post Office, and General Government (excluding General Government, 1956, 1958–61)	1948–85
General Government	1956, 1958–61
War Department, Civil Functions	1948–55
Public Works	1956–67
Energy and Water Development	1968–85
Atomic Energy Commission	1958, 1960
Military Construction	1959–85
NASA	1968
Transportation	1968–85
Office of Education	1971–72, 1976

the president's ability to veto appropriations bills means that members must accommodate his preferences and anticipate what he will find acceptable. But the president may also anticipate the reaction of Congress to his proposals, and may also be influenced by the same political and economic variables that we hypothesize to affect congressional decisions. It therefore makes sense to treat the president's budget estimates as endogenous and to employ instrumental variables estimation. Second, most accounts of the appropriations process stress that budgetary figures are considered primarily in terms of the changes they represent over the previous fiscal year. Percentage changes in estimates or in appropriations can be expressed in either nominal or constant dollars, which we calculate on the basis of the Implicit Price Deflator for Federal Government Purchases of Goods and Services.

The small number of observations available for each bill or agency presents us with another problem. The full time series is only thirty-eight years long, and for some items there are many fewer observations than that. Pooling data, either across the sixty-three agencies or the dozen

Table 8.2 Average Percentage Change in Requests and Appropriations for Domestic Agencies, FY1948–85

Year	Requests	Appropriations	n
1948	11.7	−12.1	42
1949	16.2	7.0	44
1950	16.1	14.1	43
1951	12.3	5.3	43
1952	−5.2	−11.8	44
1953	10.8	3.6	44
1954	4.9	−9.7	45
1955	4.3	3.7	45
1956	9.0	7.3	45
1957	10.1	8.1	45
1958	16.8	9.1	48
1959	5.0	6.7	48
1960	13.0	11.9	48
1961	11.1	10.3	49
1962	15.9	13.6	50
1963	14.2	10.5	50
1964	12.4	4.6	51
1965	15.1	11.5	51
1966	0.1	−2.4	51
1967	3.0	1.3	50
1968	6.8	1.8	50
1969	−0.3	−4.2	48
1970	−0.3	−0.5	45
1971	6.6	8.4	45
1972	11.5	10.7	45
1973	3.8	4.1	48
1974	−11.8	−9.7	48
1975	6.4	3.4	51
1976	14.4	13.5	49
1977	−0.1	3.5	53
1978	8.1	9.5	54
1979	6.2	5.1	54
1980	−3.4	−5.1	53
1981	−4.6	−4.8	53
1982	−25.6	−17.0	54
1983	−10.9	−0.4	53
1984	−9.3	−0.6	54
1985	−4.5	0.7	54

or so appropriations bills each year, thus becomes an attractive option. We not only gain statistical leverage, but also simplify the analysis, as hypotheses can be tested by estimating a single coefficient. Doing so necessarily assumes that the coefficients of the explanatory variables are equal across each cross-section. Pooling also introduces potential problems of correlated errors in the cross-sections; factors that produce error in predicting appropriations for agency i in year t may produce error in predicting appropriations for agency j in year t. The resulting correlation between error terms for the same year would lead to estimated standard errors that are downwardly biased. Serially correlated errors in the time series on each agency are another potential problem, as are heteroskedastic error variances. Expressing appropriations in percentage change terms substantially reduces the risk of heteroskedasticity, but we took the additional step of calculating standard errors with the heteroskedasticity-consistent covariance matrix procedure developed by White (1980).

With these considerations in mind, the equation we estimate to test our hypotheses is specified as follows:

$$\Delta APP_{it} = \alpha + \beta_1 DEM_t + \beta_2 DIV_t + \beta_3 DPCT_{it} + \beta_4 \Delta EST_{it}^{\dagger}$$
$$+ \beta_5 E_t^c + \beta_6 U_{t-1}^c + \beta_7 I_{t-1}^c + \beta_8 DEF_t + \beta_9 K_t$$
$$+ \beta_{10} V_t + \epsilon_{it}$$

where

$\Delta APP_{it} =$ the percentage change in appropriations awarded to item i in fiscal year t;

$\alpha =$ a constant term;

$DEM_t =$ 1 when the Democrats had a majority of the seats in both houses of Congress, zero otherwise;

$DIV_t =$ 1 when Congress was divided between the Republican Senate and Democratic House (FY1982–85), zero otherwise. Congresses composed of two-chamber Republican majorities thus form the excluded category;

$DPCT_t =$ the Democratic percentage of seats, averaged across the House and Senate, in the years in which they had a majority in both houses;

$\Delta EST_{it}^{\dagger} =$ an instrumental variables estimate for the percentage change in appropriations requested by the president for item i in fiscal year t. It is derived by regressing

ΔEST on all exogenous variables in this equation and in the companion equation decribed in the next section of this chapter;

$E_t^c =$ 1 during congressional election years, zero otherwise. Appropriations decisions concern the upcoming fiscal year, so this variable corresponds to odd-numbered fiscal years;

$U_{t-1}^c =$ the average rate of unemployment during the second half of the preceding fiscal year;

$I_{t-1}^c =$ the (annualized) percentage change in the Consumer Price Index during the second half of the preceding fiscal year;

$DEF_{t-1} =$ the deficit as percent of total federal spending in the previous fiscal year;

$K_t =$ 1 for fiscal years in which the U.S. was engaged in armed conflict in Korea (FY1952–53), zero otherwise;

$V_t =$ 1 for fiscal years during the buildup of U.S. troops in Viet Nam (FY1967–70), zero otherwise; and

$\epsilon_{it} =$ an error term.

Values of the time series variables—unemployment, inflation, the deficit, and percentage Democrats—are entered as deviations from the mean. The Democratic percentage measure is confined to the thirty-one years in which they held a majority in both Houses. Ideally, we could specify analogous percentage measures for years of Republican majorities and perhaps even for the years in which the Democrats held the House and the Republicans the Senate. The fact that these configurations were present for only two Congresses each, however, precludes doing so.

Our hypotheses predict the coefficients of the Democratic Congress and Democratic percentage terms to be positive, as well as those of the endogenous presidential estimate term, the election year dummy, and unemployment term. We expect coefficients of the deficit term and of the war dummies to be negative. What coefficents of the inflation term mean depend upon whether the data are in constant or in nominal dollars. In the constant dollar equations we expect the coefficient to be negative, impying that higher inflation leads to less spending in real terms. In the nominal-dollar equations, however, coefficents need only be significantly less than one to be in keeping with our expectations. A coefficent between zero and one, in other words, would imply that higher inflation leads to higher appropriations figures, but not by enough to maintain real spending at the previous year's level. (The price deflator we use is virtually identical to the Consumer Price Index). It should be kept in mind that the estimated coeffficients of the exogenous variables in this equation are premised upon the president's preferences also being taken into account. Thus, these variables can also affect spending decisions by influencing the budget estimates submitted by the president. As indicated above, we estimate this equation using both agency-level and bill-level data, in nominal dollars as well as in constant (1972) dollars. Standard errors appear in parentheses below each coefficient. Results are reported in table 8.3.

The results obtained in all four equations confirm that appropriations decisions depend dramatically upon the party holding the majority in the House and in the Senate. Clustered in a tight range, coefficients of the Democratic Congress term indicate that when the Democrats hold a majority in both chambers, appropriations awarded to domestic programs and agencies increase by about 8 percent a year more than during Republican Congresses. This is a very large effect and most likely reflects the fact that what we are observing in our data is the initial shock to domestic spending administered by the short-lived Republicans majorities of the 80th and 83d Congresses. We never observe spending decisions the Republicans might have made after several years of majority status, but it seems probable that they would not have continued to enact cuts of this magnitude. Remarkably, coefficients of the Democratic Congress dummy are somewhat larger in the equations estimated with constant-dollar figures than in the ones that used nominal dollars. We attribute this to the fact that during the years of Republican majorities—which the effects of Democratic Congresses are measured against—the government price deflator was either stable or actually falling.

Coefficients of the divided Congress term are also in keeping with our expectations that under such conditions spending should grow slower than when both chambers are Democratic but faster than when they are both Republican. In all four equations they are between the coefficients for the Democratic Congress dummy and zero (the implied effect associated with a Republican Congress). In contrast to the party dummies, the size of the Democratic majority appears not to reliably affect spending decisions. The negative signs of this variable's coefficients are actually in the wrong direction, though they are all statistically indistinguishable from zero. In reporting a positive association between the percentage of Democrats in Congress and spending growth for domestic agencies, previous studies (including those by ourselves) have presented a misleading picture of congressional appropriations decisions. The possession of a majority, at least for appropriations decisions, is crucial. Whether or not that majority is large or small is not.

Table 8.3   Final Appropriations Decisions, FY1948–85

Independent Variables	Agencies		Bills	
	Current Dollars	Constant Dollars	Current Dollars	Constant Dollars
c	−3.21 (2.06)	−5.94* (1.90)	−7.12* (2.61)	−8.76* (2.59)
Democratic Congress	7.67* (1.59)	8.49* (1.80)	7.50* (2.51)	7.80* (2.58)
Divided Congress	2.41 (3.38)	1.35 (3.80)	4.22 (3.28)	5.02* (3.36)
Democratic Percentage	−0.13 (0.09)	−0.10 (0.10)	−0.18 (0.11)	−0.17 (0.11)
President's[†] Request	0.45* (0.11)	0.28* (0.17)	0.76* (0.08)	0.76* (0.08)
Congressional Election	2.03* (0.69)	2.48* (0.83)	−0.34 (0.87)	−0.25 (0.90)
Unemployment	1.86* (0.45)	1.89* (0.50)	2.17* (0.59)	2.10* (0.59)
Inflation	−0.18 (0.11)	−0.86* (0.26)	0.02 (0.13)	−0.18 (0.15)
Deficit	−0.09 (0.07)	−0.07 (0.08)	−0.09 (0.09)	−0.07 (0.09)
Korea	−4.07* (2.30)	−6.14* (2.97)	−7.23* (2.44)	−7.76* (2.47)
Viet Nam	−0.24 (1.26)	−1.28 (1.56)	0.87 (1.88)	0.66 (1.89)
n	1849	1849	320	320

[†] = endogenous variable

* = $p < .05$

Congressional appropriations decisions also accommodate the preferences of the president. In all four equations the sign of the endogenous $\Delta EST_{it}^{\dagger}$ term is in the predicted positive direction and statistically significant. In both bill-level equations the coefficient is .76, which is considerably larger than the coefficients derived from the agency-level equations. We think this is due not to the higher level of aggregation per se, but to the fact that many appropriations bills contain large programs funded through annual appropriations but that have all the other attributes of entitlement programs, such as social security, funded through permanent appropriations. In the last several years, for example, a large majority of the funding made available by Department of Agriculture appropriations bills has gone to cover the Food Stamp program, subsidy payments made by the Commodity Credit Corporation, and cash infusions into loan programs run by the Farmers Home Administration. Much of the Labor, Health and Human Services, and Education bill pays for grants to states for Medicaid benefits and payments to the various trust funds administered by the Health Care Financing Administration. In these areas the president's estimates are precisely that. They are forecasts of what must be spent, and not, barring a change in law, declarations of what the president wants to spend. Congress in turn must largely go along with these estimates (again, assuming no change in law, and that the forecasts are reasonably accurate), and thus appears to afford the president's budget figures much more weight than in the case of the programs and agencies in our sample.

Turning to the economic variables, we see that during this period a 1-percent increase in the unemployment rate *ceteris paribus*, implies a roughly 2-percent increase in appropriations, whether measured in nominal or in constant dollars. The results in table 8.3 also provide some evidence in favor of our hypotheses regarding inflation. The coefficients in the agency-level equations (-0.18 and -0.86) imply that a 1-percent increase in the price level has little or no effect on appropriations in nominal dollars but leads to a nearly 1-percent decline in real dollars. The coefficients in the bill-level equations show a depressive effect in nominal terms, in that the .02 coefficent implies higher inflation does not increase nominal spending. The small, insignificant coefficient in the constant-dollar equation, however, fails to exhibit what should be a resultant decline in real terms. The evidence for a congressional appropriations electoral cycle also varies between levels of aggregation. The coefficients are significant in both of the agency-level equations, but small, insignificant (and actually in the wrong direction) in the bill-level equations.

As for the rest of the variables, coefficients of the size of deficit measure are in the predicted negative direction in all four equations, but never come close to statistical significance. It appears that domestic spending was reduced dramatically in response to the mobilization required by the Korean War, with the estimated effects varying from cuts of around 4 percent in the nominal-dollar, agency-level data to nearly 8 percent when constant-dollar, bill-level data are used. That the results in table 8.3 evince no similar decline in spending during the period in which the U.S. rapidly increased its forces in Viet Nam is somewhat surprising, given that the data displayed in table 8.2 reveal little or no growth in the budgets of the agencies in our sample during this period. Even though the Viet Nam dummy registered no effect upon spending, however, the status of the economic variables in a wartime economy, that is, extremely low rates of unemployment and accelerating price inflation, did point to lower domestic spending. Some of the effect of the Viet Nam War could also have been incorporated into the budget estimates submitted by the president.

Analysis of residuals indicates that serious levels of cross-sectional correlation and serial correlation are not present. The correlation between the residuals of pairs of items (agencies or bills) tend to be positive, but barely so. Most of the Pearson rs lay between .00 and .20, and the number of associations that are statistically significant is only slightly larger than what would be expected by chance. To check for serial correlation, we estimated the equation separately for each agency in our sample and calculated the Durbin-Watson statistic for each equation. In only eight of the resulting sixty-three equations is the Durbin-Watson less than 1.5 or greater than 2.5.

Presidential Requests

The results reported in table 8.3 reveal that final appropriations figures for domestic programs and agencies are heavily influenced by the budget estimates that the president submits to Congress. To measure the full impact that competing partisan policy priorities have upon appropriations decisions it is thus necessary to determine the extent to which Democratic presidents request more for domestic programs than do Republican presidents. Referring back to table 8.2, which reports the average percentage change in requests over previous fiscal year appropriations, we see that there does tend to be a marked difference between presidents of different parties. In the first budget he submitted to Congress, Ronald Reagan asked that appropriations for the agencies in our sample be cut by over 25 percent in real terms, and he requested additional reductions in the following three years as well. Conversely, Harry Truman asked for larger increases in domestic spending than any other president since World War II. Kennedy also requested large increases. The records of other presidents, though, are more mixed. Eisenhower, despite his diatribes against the big-spending ways of congressional liberals, appears to have been more supportive of domestic spending than subsequent Republicans. But even Nixon and Ford requested large average increases

in some years, while Jimmy Carter followed requests for large increases
in his first two years in office with requests for large (constant dollar)
decreases in his last two years.

These data, of course, are more suggestive than definitive. Although
we think that the president's requests strongly reflect his actual policy preferences, the many exogenous variables that affect congressional
appropriations decisions should affect the president's decisions as well.
Also, a president may submit estimates that are higher or lower than
his actual preferences in the hopes of obtaining a better final outcome.
There are some results in bargaining theory that suggest that the president should initially stake out a position that exaggerates the difference
between himself and Congress. In other words, he should shade his budget request downward if he wants lower spending than Congress and
shade it upward if he wants higher spending. To the extent Congress
is unable to discern what his true preferences are and the two sides
end up splitting the difference, this strategy moves outcomes closer to
the president's ideal point. Most observers of national politics, however,
would probably recommend the opposite strategy of formulating budget
requests that accommodate congressional preferences. Ronald Reagan
and his Secretary of Defense, Caspar Weinberger, were often criticized for
not pursuing an accommodative strategy vis-à-vis Congress with respect
to the defense budget. According to their critics, the "wish lists" they
submitted were so far out of step with congressional opinion that they
were virtually ignored. By this line of reasoning they would have fared
better if their spending proposals had been accommodating enough of
congressional preferences to at least be taken seriously.[4]

In an earlier analysis of budget requests we modeled expectations
about congressional action by specifying an instrumental variables estimate of the final appropriations decision (as a percentage change over
the previous year's appropriations) and interpreted this term's large
positive coefficient as evidence that presidential requests accommodate
congressional preferences (Kiewiet and McCubbins 1985b). This would
be accomplished here by simply reversing the positions of the endogenous
variables in the preceding equation. The problem with this approach is
that the final appropriations figure is something that Congress and the
president both agreed to. In the extreme case of the president asking
for exactly what he wanted and getting exactly what he asked for, this
would be tantamount to regressing a variable onto itself. A better way
to gauge the extent to which the president's budget requests anticipate
congressional reaction is to specify measures of key congressional characteristics. For this purpose we can simply incorporate the variables used
previously: a dummy indicating that the Democrats hold a majority in
both chambers; the size of the Democratic margin in percentage terms;

a dummy indicating that the Democrats have a majority in the House but the Republicans control the Senate; and a dummy indicating that it is a congressional election year.

In order to test our battery of hypotheses concerning presidential requests we estimate the following equation:

$$\Delta EST_{it} = \alpha + \beta_1 HST_t + \beta_2 JFK_t + \beta_3 LBJ_t + \beta_4 RMN_t + \beta_5 \beta GRF_t$$
$$+ \beta_6 JEC_t + \beta_7 RWR_t + \beta_8 DEM_t + \beta_9 DPCT_t + \beta_{10} E_t^c$$
$$+ \beta_{11} U_{t-1}^p + \beta_{12} I_{t-1}^p + \beta_{13} E_t^p + \beta_{14} DEF_{t-1} + \beta_{15} K_t$$
$$+ \beta_{16} V_t + \epsilon_{it}$$

The presidential administration terms (indicated by their initials) correspond to the following fiscal years: Truman (1948–53); Kennedy (1962–64); Johnson (1965–69); Nixon (1970–75); Ford (1976–77); Carter (1978–81); and Reagan (1982–85). Effects associated with these dummy variables are thus relative to the excluded category of the Eisenhower years (1954–61). Other variables not defined previously are as follows:

I_{t-1}^p = the (annualized) percentage change in the Consumer Price Index during the six months prior to the president's submission of appropriations requests to Congress in January;

U_{t-1}^p = the average unemployment rate during the six months prior to the president's submission of appropriations requests to Congress;

E_t^p = 1 for budgets considered during presidential election years, zero otherwise;

As in the previous analysis, values of the unemployment, inflation, and deficit variables are expressed as deviations from their means. We expect coefficients of the terms representing Democratic presidents, relative to those associated with Republican presidents, to be positive. If presidential budget requests do accommodate congressional preferences, coefficients of the Democratic Congress, Democratic percentage, and congressional election terms should also be positive. (The Divided Congress dummy that was specified in the first equation is not included here because the fiscal years that it indexes in our series, FY1982–85, are identical to the period spanned by the Reagan administration.) As in the previous equation we estimated, our hypotheses imply negative coefficients for the deficit measure and for the two war dummies, but positive coefficients for the unemployment and election-year terms. Also as before, we estimate this equation using both agency-level and bill-level data, in nominal dollars and in constant dollars.

The results, reported in table 8.4, coincide closely with those in table 8.3 and thus provide strong support for our hypothesis concerning party differences. The presidents requesting the largest increases in spending for the agencies in our sample were Truman and Kennedy, while Reagan requested significantly less for these programs than any other president. Eisenhower is the suppressed reference category, so the coefficients of the Nixon and Ford terms indicate that they requested less for domestic programs, holding all else constant, than he did. These results do not break entirely in our favor, however. The small, insignificant coefficients of the Johnson term mean that his behavior was indistinguishable from Eisenhower's, and the large negative coefficients associated with Carter's budget requests were the opposite of what we would expect from a Democrat. The relative positions of the presidents change somewhat at the bill level. This is especially true of Eisenhower. The coefficients associated with the other presidential administration terms show him to be far less supportive of domestic spending, relative to other presidents, than in the agency-level equations.

Contrary to our expectations, presidents appear not to condition their budget estimates upon expectations of congressional reaction. Coefficients of the Democratic Congress terms are large and positive in all four equations, but the standard errors are so large that none of them approach conventional levels of statistical significance. Effects associated with the Democratic percentage and congressional election year term are also indistinguishable from zero. What would account for this apparent absence of strategizing? One possibility is that our indicators of congressional characteristics are too crude to pick it up. But there are also good reasons why presidents might choose to behave sincerely in submitting their budget requests. One is to keep from sending out confusing signals. As Denzau, Riker, and Shepsle (1985) argue in their analysis of the Powell Amendment, "Although helpful in producing a final result desired by constituents, a strategic vote, for example on some particular amendment, may nevertheless entail behaving in a manner that directly conflicts with the wishes of constituents on the amendment in question. Such actions will need to be explained" (p. 1118).

With enough time, effort, and money, a member might be able to explain to his constituents that a vote for an amendment that would ostensibly strengthen a bill was actually a strategic ploy to kill it. A president might similarly be able to explain to his supporters that he actually preferred higher spending in an area than indicated by his budget estimates, but felt that he would do better pursuing an accommodative strategy with Congress. Explanation is costly, however, and explanations

Table 8.4 Presidential Budget Requests, FY1948–85

Independent Variables	Agencies		Bills	
	Current Dollars	Constant Dollars	Current Dollars	Constant Dollars
c	11.19*	6.52*	5.16	0.70
	(2.96)	(2.96)	(5.60)	(5.62)
Truman	7.43*	7.55*	22.63*	22.80*
	(2.27)	(2.28)	(6.30)	(6.44)
JFK	4.14*	3.85	8.33*	7.99*
	(2.40)	(2.40)	(4.32)	(4.31)
LBJ	−1.84	−4.29	2.25	−0.30
	(3.24)	(3.27)	(4.76)	(4.75)
Nixon	−4.44*	−7.20*	−0.77	−3.64
	(2.39)	(2.39)	(4.76)	(4.76)
Ford	−6.03	−6.34	5.44	4.91
	(4.77)	(4.77)	(9.74)	(9.77)
Carter	−6.70*	−9.99*	2.69	3.32
	(3.29)	(3.29)	(6.82)	(10.49)
Reagan	−23.63*	−21.32*	1.20	3.32
	(6.15)	(6.16)	(10.38)	(10.48)
Democratic Congress	3.58	3.46	6.68	6.56
	(3.01)	(3.01)	(6.40)	(6.40)
Democratic Percentage	0.16	0.08	−0.13	0.12
	(0.22)	(0.22)	(0.41)	(0.41)
Congressional Election Year	0.82	0.74	0.34	0.19
	(1.63)	(1.64)	(2.60)	(2.62)
Unemployment	0.95	−0.32	−3.32*	−4.57*
	(0.94)	(0.95)	(1.80)	(1.82)
Inflation	0.60*	0.03	0.59	0.01
	(0.25)	(0.25)	(0.63)	(0.63)
Presidential Election Year	0.47	1.03	−2.83	−2.32
	(1.96)	(1.96)	(3.70)	(3.71)
Deficit	0.06	0.18	0.53	0.66*
	(0.14)	(0.14)	(0.35)	(0.35)
Korea	−12.33*	−13.34	−27.02*	−28.01*
	(4.48)	(4.50)	(7.45)	(7.61)
Viet Nam	−2.58	−4.08*	−5.05	−6.51
	(2.48)	(2.50)	(4.57)	(4.58)
n	1849	1849	320	320

$* = p < .05$

are not always persuasive. A president may also decide that such strategizing is ineffective in influencing Congress in the first place. As Ronald
Reagan complained in 1982, "It's called the President's Budget, and yet
there is nothing binding in it. It is submitted to the Congress and they
don't even have to consider it" (quoted in Schick 1986, p. 14).

Turning to the rest of the variables in the equation, we see that coefficients of the Korean War term, as in the estimation of the previous equation, are negative and significant in all four equations. Those registering
the period of rapid U.S. military buildup in Viet Nam, however, are
considerably larger than the corresponding coefficients in table 8.3, and
the coefficient in the constant-dollar agency-level equation is statistically
significant at the conventional .05 level. There is at least some evidence,
then, of Presidents Johnson and Nixon trimming their requests for domestic spending in response to the rapidly mounting costs of the U.S.
buildup. Support for our other hypotheses, however, is hard to come by.
Coefficients of the presidential election year dummy are indistinguishable
from zero in all four equations. Those for unemployment and for the size
of the deficit are large and often significant in the bill-level equations,
but their signs are in the opposite direction of what we had predicted.
In the agency-level equations they are both small and insignificant. As
before, the results concerning inflation are inconsistent. Coefficients in
the constant-dollar equations both approximate zero, even though the
coefficients in the other equations indicate increases in nominal appropriations that should have been too modest to maintain real spending
levels.

The responsiveness of Congress to economic conditions, at least as
indicated by the results in table 8.3, thus compares favorably to that
of the president. This is somewhat surprising, given that the president
is almost always seen as the prime mover in stabilization policy. One
possibility is that our findings are a function of the different time frames
specified for the economic variables. Because the president submits his
budget requests several months in advance of congressional action (as
well as several months prior to the beginning of the relevant fiscal year),
the case could be biased in favor of Congress. Perhaps, though, the
president bases his budget requests on forecasts of economic conditions
in the near future and not on recent inflation and unemployment rates.
To investigate this possibility we specified the same economic variables
in the presidential equation as in the congressional equation, effectively
advancing the time frame on these variables by six months. Doing so,
however, had virtually no effect on the results, nor did specifying instead
the average rates of unemployment and inflation during the previous full
year.

Time Dependence, Supplementals, and Entitlements

Our findings so far cover almost the entire postwar period. But is it possible, as many scholars assert, that congressional parties have only recently reasserted their policy-making role after long decades of somnolence? As indicated earlier, we give little credence to such claims; although the structure of party leadership has indeed changed since the days of the Textbook Congress, the incentives to pursue partisan budgetary priorties have persisted over our entire time period. In any case, this raises the issue of time dependence in our results. To examine the possibility that partisan influence over spending policy has increased over the past few decades, we split our time series into two parts: FY1948–62 (the same time period covered in Fenno's study) and FY1963–85. We then reestimated our first equation, allowing the parameters for the Democratic Congress and Democratic percentage terms to vary across the two periods. The results show that effects associated with the partisan balance in Congress during the first period are virtually identical to the effects in the latter period. In neither period does the size of the Democrats' margin appear to matter, but coefficients of the dummies representing the presence of a Democratic majority in both chambers—7.48 in the earlier period and 8.79 in the latter—are virtually identical.

Another potential problem for our analyses is that the data on appropriations and presidential estimates are taken only from regular annual appropriations bills and continuing resolutions. They do not include additional amounts appropriated to various programs and agencies in supplementary and deficiency acts. Wlezian's (1989) comprehensive analysis of this "second round" of the appropriations process indicates that this omission probably has some consequences for our findings, but none that are very large or important. He reports that supplemental appropriations for domestic programs increase during recessions and fall during recoveries, which implies that our findings might understate somewhat the responsiveness of the president and Congress to economic conditions. As for political variables, his finding that Democratic Congresses both receive larger requests and approve larger amounts of supplemental appropriations for domestic programs is entirely in keeping with our results. His finding that Republican presidents tend to request slightly more in nondefense supplementals is not.

Finally, the generality of our results is limited by the fact that annual appropriations for domestic programs has long been declining as a proportion of the total federal budget. Growing steadily over several decades, social welfare entitlement programs are now the largest component of the federal budget. Although some of the appropriations bills in our sample contain large amounts of money for these programs, most of them are funded through trust funds and other forms of permanent appropriations. It is also the case that once these programs are instituted, spending levels are largely determined by the state of the economy and by the demographic profile of the nation's population. Thus the crucial political decisions that are made regarding these programs are not over their annual funding levels, but rather over whether or not to start them up in the first place.

Table 8.5, taken from Browning's (1986) analysis, shows that the data on these programs strongly reinforces the results obtained from the annual appropriations data. Democratic presidents and Democratic Congresses have initiated almost all federal programs related to nutrition, social services, education, and health. New program initiatives occurred nearly twice as frequently when a Democratic Congress paired up with a Democratic president than when a Democratic Congress faced a Republican president (these two configurations were each present for sixteen years between 1947 and 1982). There were virtually no attempts to create new social welfare programs in the United States during periods in which the Republicans controlled Congress.

In sum, federal spending patterns clearly and consistently reflect the preferences of the majority parties in Congress as well as the party of the president. Spending on domestic programs increases faster under Democratic administrations and Congresses than under Republicans. Democratic presidents submit requests for domestic programs and agencies that are larger than those submitted by Republican presidents. Data

Table 8.5   Social Welfare Program Initiatives, 1947–82

Conditions of Party Control	Initiated by President	Initiated by Congress	Total
Democratic President and Democratic Congress	75	41	116
Democratic President and Republican Congress	0	1	1
Republican President and Democratic Congress	16	41	57
Republican President and Republican Congress	2	1	3
Total	93	84	177

Source: Calculated by Browning (1986, p. 80) from data reported in the *Catalog of Federal Domestic Assistance.*

on budget resolutions tell the same story. The balance of party forces in Washington determines the pace of innovation in social welfare entitlement programs as well. We take this evidence to be strong refutation of the abdication hypothesis. Federal spending decisions cannot be understood without understanding congressional party politics.

Data Sources

Presidential requests and final appropriations figures are reported in the Annual Senate Document, *Appropriations, Budget Estimates, Etc.*, in the section entitled "Itemized Comparisons of Budget Estimates and Appropriations Arranged by Senate Acts."

Unemployment and Consumer Price Index figures were taken from issues of the *Monthly Labor Review*, Bureau of Labor Statistics, U.S. Department of Labor. Values of the federal budget deficit were taken from *Historical Statistics of the United States* and from summary tables in *The Budget of the United States Government*.

Values of the Implicit Price Deflator for Federal Government Purchases of Goods and Services were taken primarily from *The National Income and Product Accounts of the United States, 1929–1974*. Data for 1974 through 1985 were taken from issues of the *Survey of Current Business*. Both sources are published by the Bureau of Economic Analysis, U.S. Department of Commerce.

CHAPTER NINE

Turning Appropriations into Expenditures

Congressional Oversight of Expenditures

Economic models of principal/agent relationships proceed from the assumption that agents are averse to effort. In the federal bureaucracy, as in the private sector, "shirking," or withholding effort, undoubtedly is a significant source of agency losses.[1] In delegating to executive branch officials the authority to make expenditures, however, the paramount concern of the founders of the Republic was that these officials would be reckless or corrupt in handling money that was not their own. Recurrent scandals, from Teapot Dome to the exploits of "Robin HUD," indicate that this concern was not misplaced. But by far the most troublesome problem that Congress confronts in delegating the authority to disburse funds from the federal Treasury is that executive branch officials have policy preferences that do not necessarily coincide with those embodied in the legislation granting them "obligational authority," as appropriations are technically (and correctly) defined. This is especially likely to occur when these officials owe their appointment to a president who does not belong to the party that holds a majority of seats in Congress.

In the 1789 legislation that established the Department of the Treasury, Congress sought to prevent the misuse of appropriated funds by creating an elaborate monitoring mechanism which, like the government that had just been established, incorporated a sequence of insitutional checks. Every single commitment of money made by an executive branch official was to be independently scrutinized by a series of officers in the Treasury before the funds would be disbursed. Mosher (1984) provides a good description of the system of financial control that was envisioned:

> On the basis of appropriations ... the treasury secretary issued
> warrants to the agencies and the treasurer to spend and re-
> ceive moneys. The warrants had to be countersigned by the
> comptroller, recorded by the register, and passed on to the trea-
> surer for payments. On the basis of the warrants, officers in the
> agencies would authorize expenditures (and receipts) and would
> transmit to the auditor in the Treasury Department statements
> of their accounts. The auditor would examine them, make ad-
> justments or disllowances as appropriate, and certify the bal-
> ances to the comptroller for settlement. The treasurer would
> then disburse the funds. (pp. 16–17)[2]

A similar system had been adopted under the Articles of Confederation, but had been replaced by other financial controls. Alexander
Hamilton soon jetisoned this one as well in favor of a less byzantine
set of procedures under which he, as Secretary of the Treasury, would
issue warrants in advance to designated, bonded officials in the executive
departments. The auditor and comptroller would then audit expenditure
vouchers after the fact. But even this system was slow and cumbersome,
and God forbid that a Treasury clerk find an error or irregularity. In
such cases, they would hold up the transaction and write the disbursing
officer for clarification or correction. Personally responsible for shortfalls
in their accounts, disbursing officers naturally resisted attempts by Treasury to disallow transactions that they had made. The ensuing dispute
often generated a long sequence of correspondence until the account was
settled, sometimes many years later (Mosher 1984).

Under the terms of the 1894 Dockery Act, Congress delegated responsibility for voucher audits to six Treasury auditors, each in charge
of a specific department. Their rulings could be appealed to another
officer established by the act, the Comptroller of the Treasury, whose
decisions were final. Congress eventually became dissatisifed with this
arrangement, primarily because it assigned the task of reviewing transactions made by the executive branch to individuals who were themselves
members of that branch. In the Budget and Accounting Act of 1921 (the
same legislation that created the Budget Bureau), Congress reassigned
responsibility for expenditure audits to the General Accounting Office,
headed by the Comptroller General. Originally chartered as an independent agency, in 1945 Congress declared GAO to be part of the legislative
branch.

For the first twenty-five years of its existence, the work of the GAO
consisted almost entirely of the auditing and settlement functions it had
inherited from the Treasury auditors. Budgetary scholars often dismiss
voucher audits as little more than a bookkeeping exercise; rarely con-
sisting of more than a check on the arithmetic and adherence to certain

legal nicieties, they certainly do not in and of themselves prevent the misdirection of funds.[3] Whatever the merit of such audits, the growth of the federal government made the GAO's task of auditing every expenditure increasingly arduous. By the beginning of World War II, the GAO employed over 5,000 clerks to maintain hundreds of thousands of separate account ledgers involving millions of claims and payment vouchers, and hundreds of millions of checks and postal money orders. By the end of the war, the army of clerks had grown to nearly 15,000, but the backlog of unaudited vouchers (much of it stacked up in freight cars at Washington, D.C.'s Union Station) would have taken years to work through.

Comptroller General Lindsay Warren decided it made little sense to continue in this Sisyphean endeavor and that it would be best for Congress to delegate to the GAO a different set of responsibilities. He recommended that the GAO prescribe accounting standards for federal agencies and then subsequently monitor the adequacy of the financial control systems the agencies put into place. Accounting and voucher auditing would be assigned to new agencies, such as the Defense Contract Audit Agency, or would be done in-house by the agencies themselves. Warren's recommendations were endorsed by the Hoover Commission and became part of the Accounting and Auditing Act of 1950 (Havens 1990). In response to this change in its mission, the GAO replaced its auditing clerks with a substantially smaller number of professional accountants. Over the past two decades the GAO has transformed itself once again, devoting its resources less to the management of accounting systems and more to policy analysis and program evaluation (activities they refer to as "program results audits"). At the same time, its activities have become increasingly driven by congressional demand. In 1969, according to Havens, GAO officials made only twenty-four appearances before congressional committees, and less than 10 percent of the GAO's reports were in response to congressional requests. By FY1988, the GAO officials testified on over two hundred occasions, and, depending on the policy area, between 80 and 100 percent of their resources were devoted to inquiries specifically requested by a member or committee of Congress. The GAO, in other words, has largely replaced "police patrol" oversight with "fire alarm" oversight.

In addition to establishing auditing and accounting controls, from the beginning of the Republic Congress has also directed executive agencies to provide regular reports on their expenditures. In 1814 the House created a Committee on Public Expenditures to examine these reports and, two years later, established a separate committee on expenditures for each of the six departments (State, Treasury, War, Navy, Post Office, and Public Buildings). The Senate later followed suit, and additional expenditure committees were established after creation of the Departments of Agriculture, Commerce, and Labor.

In principle, these committees could have served as an effective vehicle by which to monitor executive branch expenditures. In practice, they were nothing of the sort. In Wilmerding's (1943) estimation, "They could elucidate particular malfeasances to which their attention was directed by departmental informers or which were accidentally uncovered by action of the muck rake; but any examination of the detail of accounts was quite beyond their competence" (p. 233). Many years often elapsed between meetings of these committees, and many decades between reports. Although not officially abolished until the reforms of 1920, they had long been moribund.

The ineffectualness of these committees was primarily due to a lack of relevant information. Certainly, members on or off the committees could avail themselves of several different compilations of expenditure reports, including the *Book of Receipts and Expenditures* (1791–1893), *A Combined Statement of Receipts and Disbursements (apparent and actual) of the United States* (1873–1912), which, after 1912, was combined with another document published by the Treasury, *A Statement of Balances, Appropriations, and Expenditures.* Unfortunately, these volumes of financial data were of little utility in gauging the closeness of the fit between expenditures and congressional intent. Lack of timeliness was one liability, as there was usually at least a two-year delay between the time expenditures were made and the time the reports were issued. The expenditure committees were also hampered by a lack of an auditing capability independent of the Treasury Department. This was particularly troublesome when it was the action of the Treasury auditors themselves, or of other officials in the department, that was at issue. In some cases the information was made useless by the fact that expenditures were not filed under the relevant appropriations headings.

But the real problem, according to Wilmerding, was that the various reports on expenditures were essentially lists of the disbursing officers and contractors to whom Treasury warrants had been issued. These reports faithfully accounted who had spent the money, but gave no indication as to what they had spent it on! Congress presumably could have ordered that this information be reported as well, but failed to do so even in the sweeping reforms of 1920 and 1921. That they did not do so led Wilmerding to conclude that "with respect to the scrutiny of expenditures ignorance and apathy prevailed" (p. 248), and that "neither Congress nor its committees were imbued with the spirit of scrutiny" (p. 241). When in 1926 the Treasury Department revised the *Combined Statement of Receipts and Expenditures, Balances, etc. of the United*

States, and for the first time reported the actual object of expenditures under each appropriation, it was upon the department's own initiative and not at the behest of Congress.

According to Aberbach (1990), Congress's apparent lack of concern over the oversight of expenditures is symptomatic of an indifference to oversight in general. His data suggest that only in the past few decades has Congress committed a significant amount of effort and attention to oversight activity.[4] Political scientists have blamed the short shrift Congress has given to this function throughout most of the nation's history on several factors: oversight is a public good and therefore undersupplied; there is no electoral payoff to oversight; oversight is boring, especially compared to writing new legislation. Whether or not there is merit to any of these explanations, we think there are a couple of additional considerations that pertain specifically to the members' lack of concern regarding the congruence between expenditures and appropriations. First, they probably have some confidence that the auditing procedures that have been put in place over the years are reasonably effective in discouraging flagrant and recurring abuses. A second, more fundamental, reason is that the misdirection of funds from appropriations accounts is most likely not the most important source of agency loss entailed in delegating to executive officers the authority to make expenditures. Even if we assume that every single expenditure corresponds precisely to the category of appropriations under which it falls, there remain three major ways in which executive officers making expenditures can blunt or distort legislative intent: (1) by transferring funds from one account to another; (2) by impounding or otherwise failing to spend appropriated funds; and (3) by making expenditures or otherwise taking actions that compel Congress to provide additional appropriations in the future.

These three practices all date back to the earliest years of the Republic, as does recognition of the threat they pose to the achievement of congressional policy goals. None of them, however, are inherently abusive or improper. On the contrary, they are valuable sources of administrative flexibility that permit government officials to make beneficial adjustments in policy. No reasonable person would be willing to lock themselves into a particular pattern of spending for a year or more into the future, and it obviously makes no sense for a government to do so. It is frequently in the best interests of both Congress and of the entire country that appropriations not be spent, or that money appropriated for one activity be spent on another, or that expenditures be made prior to making appropriations. What Congress faces here is a classic case of Madison's dilemma: the authority granted to executive officers to advance the policies Congress has chosen can also be used to frustrate these policies.

Transfers

In the first few years of the Republic, the Jeffersonians in Congress became aware that what the Federalists in the executive branch actually did with money they had been appropriated often did not conform to the intent of the legislation. They reasoned that the best way to minimize the slippage between appropriations and expenditures was to make appropriations line items as specific and detailed as possible—"specific funds to every specific purpose susceptible of definition," as Jefferson put it in his first message to Congress. This prescription follows naturally from the more general Jeffersonian tenet that laws should be as explicit as possible so as to permit a minimum of executive discretion. Hamilton and other Federalists rejected these ideas as preposterous, and the Jeffersonians moderated their stance considerably upon taking charge of the executive branch. After a short time in office, Treasury Secretary Gallatin's view concerning the specificity of appropriations—"if carried too far by too many subdivisions, they become injurious, if not impracticable"— was indistinguishable from that of his Federalist predecessors (quoted in Wilmerding 1943, p. 55).

Backsliding on the doctrine of specificity did not occur in Congress, however. With certain exceptions (particularly during wartime), appropriations legislation has always been, in one way or another, extremely specific. In the early years of the Republic, appropriations bills made only a few lump-sum appropriations, but followed these by "that is to say" clauses that laid out detailed instructions. In the years following the Civil War, Congress established budgetary classifications at very low levels of aggregation and requirements for the presentation of budget estimates that were even more fine-tuned. Typical of these was a statute adopted in 1912:

> There shall be submitted in the annual Book of Estimates, following every estimate for a general or lump-sum appropriation, except public buildings or other public works constructed under contract, a statement showing in parallel columns: First, the number of persons, if any, intended to be employed and the rates of compensation to each, and the amounts contemplated to be expended for each of any other objects or classes of expenditures specified or contemplated in the estimate, including a statement of estimated unit cost of any construction work proposed to be done: and Second, the number of persons, if any, employed and the rates of compensation paid each, and the amounts expended for each other object or class of expenditure, and the actual unit cost of any construction work done out of the appropriation corresponding to the estimate so submitted, during the next fiscal year preceding the period for which the

estimate is submitted. (House Select Committee on the Budget
1921b, p. 16)

Other reporting requirements concerned specific departments or activities. In 1872, for instance, Congress directed that "the head of each
of the executive departments and establishments ... shall include in his
annual estimate for appropriations for the next fiscal year such sum
or sums as may to him seem necessary for printing and binding, to
be executed under the direction of the Public Printer (1921b, p. 18).
By the time of the 1920–21 reforms, there were approximately nine
hundred statutes governing the presentation of estimates and appropriations accounts. Charles Dawes, the first director of the Budget Bureau,
characterized this body of law as an "uncoordinated mass of financial
legislation enacted from time to time to meet particular situations and
conditions" and criticized the arbitrary and haphazard way in which
different agencies were affected: "some bureaus are loaded down with administrative limitations and restrictions, while others are left with only a
few governing regulations ... The whole process is now done ... without
any possibility of intelligent comparison of the financial administration
of one bureau with another (1921b, p. 6).

The 1923 Classification Act cleared away much of this thicket by
imposing uniform payscales and consolidating large numbers of accounts
into standard categories (Studenski and Krooss 1952). Following recommendations of the Hoover Commission, Congress further reduced the
number of line items in appropriations bills in the early 1950s. A reduction in line items, however, should not be confused with a move toward
lumpier, more general appropriations. Appropriations bills continue to
be premised upon the accounts specified in the president's budget and
are accompanied by committee reports that preserve a large measure of
detail and specificity (Kirst 1969).

What is ironic about Congress's commitment to specificity is that
members have long recognized that specificity can generally be trumped
by administrative creativity.[5] They have also been fully aware that specificity accounts for nothing if executive branch officials move money from
one account to another after the appropriations are made. The Jeffersonians, of course, claimed to be appalled upon learning of such tranfers,
which they referred to as "mingling funds." Gallatin, in *A Sketch of the
Finances of the United States*, observes that, "if ... the moneys specifically appropriated to one head of service are applied to another head,
they are not applied and accounted for pursuant, but rather contrary
to the law. Such a mode is undoubtedly liable to great abuses" (quoted
in Wilmerding 1943, p. 37). As with the doctrine of specificity, however, Jeffersonian practice strayed from Jeffersonian theory; Wilmerding

reports that once elected to the White House, they fell into "the old Federalist practice of mingling appropriations by executive interpretation" (p. 77).

In principle, Congress could put an end to any abuses arising from the transfer of funds from one account to another by simply making it illegal to do so. This is in fact what they have ostensibly done—in 1809, 1842, 1852, 1868, and on subsequent occasions as well. The 1809 legislation, however, permitted the president to make transfers when Congress was not in session. The ban on transfer adopted in 1842 was amended only a few years later in 1846 to permit transfers in the Navy Department. The 1868 statute appeared to ban transfers without exception, but the actual financial operations of the Treasury Department, Wilmerding notes, allowed substantial amounts of *sub rosa* transfers to continue.

In each case, then, the ban on transfers either contained significant loopholes itself, was quickly followed by additional legislation that permitted exceptions to be made, or was simply not implemented. The law currently holds that "except as otherwise provided by law, sums appropriated for the various branches of expenditures in the public service shall be applied solely to the objects to which they were respectively made and for no others." The key phrase here is "except as otherwise provided by law." Fisher (1975) identifies several major pieces of legislation adopted over the past several decades that have authorized the executive branch to transfer funds from one appropriations account to another. The Central Intelligence Act of 1949, for example, authorizes other agencies of the federal government to transfer to or receive from the CIA funds "without regard to any provisions of law limiting or prohibiting transfers between appropriations" (p. 215). In fact, the CIA's budget is composed entirely of transfers from other government agencies, as are the budgets of the other agencies in the intelligence community.

Transfers can also be effected temporally by carrying forward funds appropriated in previous years. This area was of recurrent concern to Congress throughout much of the nineteenth century, as agencies often carried over amounts of money that were larger than their current year appropriations; unexpended balances, according to Garfield (1879), constituted "a large and forgotten fund which could be used for a great variety of purposes without the special notice of Congress" (p. 749). As in the case of transfers proper, however, the restrictions Congress imposed on this practice have usually been accompanied by significant exceptions. An 1820 statute, for example, directed the Secretary of the Treasury to place into a surplus fund any moneys that the Departments of Navy and War had left unexpended for over two years, but with the proviso that the department secretary report that "the object for which the appropriation was made had been effected." Failure of the secretary to make this declaration left the funds available for future use. The outright ban on transfers enacted in 1868 also applied to the unexpended balances of old appropriations from different accounts, but continued to permit agencies to carry over unexpended balances of appropriations made in earlier years for the same purpose (Wilmerding 1943, p. 122). A series of statutes adopted in 1870, 1872, and 1874 ostensibly halted same-account carryovers as well, but, as before, the practice was not legislated away entirely. In particular, the manner in which the Department of the Treasury applied these statutes meant that unexpended balances did not revert to the surplus fund until at least three years after they had originally been appropriated (Wilmerding 1943, p. 134).

A third type of transfer is accomplished by shifting funds from one purpose to another within the same budgetary account. This is customarily referred to as "reprogramming." The degree to which funds are reprogrammed rather than transferred from one account to another is naturally a function of how broadly defined the accounts are. Congress has never chosen to restrict reprogramming, but has relied instead on requiring executive branch officials to give advance notice of significant reprogrammings to the Appropriations subcommittee under whose jurisdiction they fall. Notification thresholds vary somewhat from agency to agency, but notice is to be given of any reprogramming, no matter how small, to projects or activities for which Congress has explicitly denied funding (Rubin 1990).

The generally sanguine attitude Congress has adopted toward reprogramming may be a function of the relatively small amounts of money involved. Fisher (1975) reports that the largest practitioner of reprogramming, the Department of Defense, annually moved about $1 to $2 billion in this manner in the early 1970s, and the figure had grown to only $2 to $4 billion by the 1980s (Rubin 1990). Another reason is that the key to the success of delegation here is, as Fisher notes, the creation and maintenance of good faith relationships. This is something that cannot be achieved through statute. Indeed, the specification of precise strictures and guidelines may do more to impede such understandings than to facilitate them; executive branch officials have shown repeatedly that it is always possible to adhere to the precise letter of the law and yet violate trust. This same consideration applies to the transfer of funds in general and explains why Congress has chosen only to regulate rather than to ban potentially abusive practices. The most important reason, however, (which we think also pertains to transfers in general) is that reprogramming does not represent a serious threat to party policy priorities. Money appropriated to the Department of Defense remains there, as does the money appropriated to Health and Human Services or any other department or agency. The authority to tranfer funds has sometimes been abused, but the benefits to Congress of making this delegation continue to exceed the resultant agency losses.

Impoundments

What is probably the most compelling and influential model of bureaucratic behavior, that of Niskanen (1971), postulates bureau chiefs to be budget-maximizers. This assumption has the same quality as the analogous propositions that firms maximize profits, or that politicians maximize their probability of being reelected; it is not strictly true, but it is a close enough approximation to what we experience as the "real world" that no alternative assumptions are as compelling. The prospect of budget-maximizing bureaucrats not spending the money they were appropriated thus seems highly improbable. One would presume that government agencies, if left to their own devices, would surely spend every dime in their budget.

Sometimes, however, events occurring after appropriations have been made completely obviate the need for them. It is therefore beneficial to grant those who have the authority to make expenditures the authority to refrain from making them as well. Presidents and department heads going back to at least the Jefferson administration have impounded funds. For much of the nation's history, the authority to do so was based upon a conventional understanding that appropriations were "permissive rather than mandatory" (Fisher 1975, p. 148). This authority was formalized in the Anti-Deficiency Act of 1906, which called for the apportionment of funds to federal agencies and the establishment of reserves, that is, impoundments. The act assigned these financial management responsibilities to department heads, but Congress approved the transfer of this authority to the Budget Bureau in 1933.[6] From then on, the primary agency problem entailed in delegating the authority to impound did not involve department or agency officials per se, but rather the president.

Most impoundments were made for routine technical and administrative reasons. The most prominent cases of their salutory use, however, are those made to halt spending on domestic programs at the beginning of a war or to block further expenditures on armaments at war's end. In early 1942, for example, President Franklin Roosevelt directed the Budget Bureau to impound funds from the Civilian Conservation Corps, the Surplus Marketing Corporation, and other nondefense projects. After the surrender of Japan in 1945, Truman in turn ordered the impoundment of funds that had been appropriated for weapons procurement.

Although impoundments are technically a way to alter appropriations decisions after they have been made, a number of appropriations bills during the Truman era explicitly called for them in advance. The omnibus appropriations bill for FY1951, for example, ordered Truman to put at least $550 million of the spending provided for in the bill in reserve. Other bills did not directly call for impoundments, but their passage was premised on the expectation that they would be made. In 1950, for example, House and Senate conferees were stalemated over the issue of how many new air groups should be added to the Air Force. The impasse was broken when Senate conferees agreed to accede to the higher number specified in the House bill after Truman assured them that funding for the ten additional groups would be impounded (Bailey and Samuel 1965).

This is not to say that all impoundments were without controversy or that Congress always welcomed them. In reaction to the impoundments Roosevelt made in 1942, the following year the Senate attached a rider to an appropriations bill that would have prohibited any further impoundments of appropriated funds (Pfiffner 1979, p. 34). House Democrats sought a similar stricture after Eisenhower impounded appropriations for highways, military construction, water projects, and other programs. Lyndon Johnson's impoundment of highway trust funds provoked the first anti-impoundment measure to pass both Houses—a "sense of Congress" amendment to the Federal Highway Act of 1968, indicating that such funds should not be impounded.

These were minor squabbles, of course, compared to the full-scale constitutional crisis that erupted during the Nixon administration. His impoundments differed from those of his predecessors in several important ways. First, as Pfiffner (1979) and many others point out, they were of much greater magnitude. Actually, as a percentage of total appropriations they were not unusually large. According to data compiled by Wlezian (1989), impoundments during his six years in office averaged 6.0 percent of total expenditures. During the Johnson, Kennedy, and Eisenhower administrations the figures were 5.7 percent, 4.5 percent, and 8.0 percent, respectively.[7] As a percentage of discretionary spending on domestic programs, however, they dwarfed the impoundments made by previous presidents. It should be recognized, though, that the total amount of funds that were subject to impoundment is not in and of itself an important or informative piece of information. The real issue here is the amount of time that lapses before they are released, if indeed they are released at all. Spokesmen for the Nixon administration repeatedly asserted that they were adhering to conventional procedures and would ultimately release impounded funds. Rarely, however, did they ever give any indication as to exactly when that might be.

In justifying his impoundments, Nixon appealed to the provisions of a 1950 amendment to the Anti-Deficiency Act which stipulated that "reserves may be established to provide for contingencies, or to effect savings whenever savings are made possible by or through changes in requirements, greater efficiency of operations, or other developments subsequent to the date on which such appropriation was made available." He argued for a broad interpretation of the "other developments" clause so as to include inflation and increases in the public debt as legitimate grounds for halting expenditures. Eisenhower and Lyndon Johnson had previously justified impoundments as a way of achieving a less expansionary fiscal policy, so this was not without precedent. What was new, however, was his assertion of a constitutional prerogative to refrain from spending any appropriated funds that were, in his judgment, better left unspent. This view was radical, aggressive, and erroneous.[8] Testifying on behalf of the administration in 1973 before the Separation of Powers Subcommittee of the Senate Judiciary Committee, Deputy Attorney General Joseph Sneed informed the Senators that "decisions to impound inevitably involve policy judgments concerning national needs and highly technical predictions about their effect on the economy ... These trade-offs involve delicate adjustments peculiarly within the competence of the executive branch" (quoted in Glass 1973, p. 237). One supposes that Sam Ervin (D, North Carolina), Chairman of the Subcommittee and soon to be Chairman of the Senate Watergate Committee, was duly impressed by Sneed's line of argument.

Fisher (1975), however, identifies the crucial break Nixon made with the past: unlike those of his predecessors, Nixon's impoundments were made to advance Republican policy objectives at the expense of Democratic ones:

> In contrast, after less than a year in office President Nixon announced plans to reduce research health grants, Model Cities funds, and grants for urban renewal. Critics noted that the cutbacks were made at the same time that the Administration was sponsoring such costly projects as the supersonic transport, a manned landing on Mars, general revenue sharing, a larger Merchant Marine fleet, and the Safeguard ABM system. While the cutbacks were made in the name of fiscal integrity, in actual fact they were part of a redistribution of Federal funds from Democratic programs to those supported by the Nixon Administration. (p. 169)

Nixon's impoundments, in other words, were impoundments "with prejudice" (Fisher 1975, p. 148). Pfiffner (1979) identifies two additional features of Nixon's impoundments that were symptomatic of efforts to substitute his policies for those favored by congressional Democrats. First, impoundments were focused on funds for programs which had not been proposed in the budget he submitted to Congress. Second, they were frequently made in the face of explicit expressions of intent by Congress that the funds be spent.

Reaction against Nixon's assault on the Democratic policy agenda took a variety of forms. In 1971 then Majority Whip Tip O'Neill introduced a joint resolution that directly ordered the immediate release of all impounded funds. Other efforts included proposals to hold up expenditures on defense and foreign assistance programs until Nixon released funds for domestic programs. These turned out to be mere preliminaries to the main event, however, as Democratic opposition eventually culminated in the restrictions on impoundment written into the Congressional Budget and Impoundment Control Act of 1974. The act allows the president to defer expenditures, but for no longer than until the end of the current fiscal year. Even then, the act provided that either chamber of Congress could force the president to release funds for obligation by adopting a resolution to that effect within forty-five days of the president's announcement of the deferral. The president may also ask for appropriations to be eliminated entirely by asking for a rescission, which must be approved by both houses within forty-five days. Such a request is necessarily accompanied by a deferral order, so this action delays spending even if Congress fails to approve the rescission. The legislation also ordered that the OMB report all deferrals to Congress and that the General Accounting Office review them to assure their legality and proper classification. Even though the GAO opted for a narrow definition of deferral that requires evidence of intent on the part of the executive branch, this new reporting requirement is obviously an onerous one. As Schick (1980) observes, Congress evidently decided that "excessive paperwork is preferable to excessive strife" (p. 402).

According to Fisher (1975), Gerald Ford initially tried to make the new procedures work like the old ones, sending back to Congress requests to rescind or to defer almost all the spending they had added to his budget requests. Not surprisingly, Congress, having only recently approved the appropriations, approved few of the rescissions and overturned a large percentage of the deferrals. Schick (1980) reports that Ford and his successors also sought to exploit the tactic of delay. It usually takes weeks before an agency reports a delay in expenditures, and additional time is required for GAO review. The OMB usually waits until it has several deferral orders to send to Congress in a single package, and Congress usually crowds the 45-day deadline before acting on the matter, if then; on a number of occasions during the first Reagan administration, House Democrats sought to overturn deferrals after the deadline for disapproving them had passed. Wlezien (1989) points out that the president could also seek to delay expenditures indefinitely, at least in the case of multiyear appropriations, by issuing a new deferral order as soon as the previous one lapsed at the beginning of the new fiscal year. We suspect, though, that Congress would vote to disapprove any significant deferrals of this nature.

The Congressional Budget and Impoundment Control Act thus did not completely eliminate the possibility of the president frustrating congressional policy objectives by blocking expenditures. Indeed, in 1986 congressional Democrats charged that the Reagan administration's deferrals were designed to do just that (Wehr 1986b). Still, the major effect of the act has been to substantially reduce the amount of federal expenditures subject to impoundment. Wlezian's (1989) analysis reveals that in the ten years following the reforms, presidential deferral orders involved less than 3 percent of total domestic spending, and nearly two-thirds of the deferred funds were released voluntarily before the end of the fiscal year. Given how circumspect presidents have been in issuing them, it is not surprising that Congress has in turn disapproved very few of them (at least after the initial spate of rejections in the Ford administration). Rescissions have been an even rarer commodity. Although Ronald Reagan won approval for nearly $12 billion in rescissions for FY1981, in most years they total only a few hundred million dollars. Subsequent legal and legislative developments have served to depress deferral activity even farther. Congress's position was undercut by the Supreme Court's 1983 ruling in *INS vs. Chadha* that the one-chamber legislative veto was unconstitutional. Four years later, however, in *City of New Haven vs. U.S.* the courts ruled that *Chadha* also implied that it was unconsitutional for the president to order deferrals on the basis of policy objections. Congress codified this restriction in the 1987 Balanced Budget and Emergency Deficit Control Reaffirmation Act (Gramm-Rudman-Hollings II), which amends the Antideficiency Act so as to eliminate the "other developments" provision which Nixon had invoked to justify his impoundments.

Congressional scholars have generally interpreted the restrictions on impoundments included in the Congressional Budget and Impoundment Control Act and in subsequent legislation as indicative of Congress's "resurgence" during the 1970s and 1980s: after having abdicated it for so long to the executive branch, Congress has finally reclaimed the power of the purse. We strongly disagree with this assessment. Prior to the Nixon administration, the ability of the executive branch to make impoundments had been both a source of discretion and flexibility in the timing of expenditures and a convenient way for halting expenditures that had

been made superfluous by intervening events. Rarely were impoundments invoked to subvert or even to stall policies favored by Congress.
Nixon's abuse of authority to impound provoked Congress to codify and
to restrict the terms of this delegation. It is Fisher (1975) who again gets
to the heart of the matter: "Without good-faith efforts and integrity on
the part of administrative officials, the delicate system of nonstatutory
controls, informal understandings, and discretionary authority could not
last. At a time when public programs could have benefitted from flexibility and executive judgment, Congress was forced to pass legislation
with mandatory language and greater rigidities" (p. 201).

Congress has replaced the authority to impound, which was rooted
largely in convention and shared understandings, with an explicit contract that imposes significant costs in terms of both reporting requirements and monitoring effort. In effectively banning impoundments that
could undercut the policies they have chosen, the data strongly suggest
that they have also forgone impoundments that might have allowed them
to achieve their policy goals in a more cost-effective fashion. The 1974
reforms and subsequent restrictions were an acknowledgment that the
looser, more informal delegation of authority to the president could not
necessarily be satisfactorily managed. Congress is the loser here, not the
winner.

Creating Deficiencies

Fisher (1975) notes that presidents going back to at least Jefferson (who
committed the United States to pay France $15 million for the Lousiana
Territories without prior congressional approval) have ordered the expenditure of funds in advance of appropriations. Indeed, since 1799 the
armed forces of the United States have had explicit statutory authority
under the Feed and Forage Act to move, provision, and equip troops
prior to Congress making appropriations. This act was invoked in 1990
to move air, land, and naval forces to Saudi Arabia and the Persian Gulf.
As with impoundments and transfers, it can be extremely advantageous
to allow the president and other officials in the executive branch the
authority to exercise this intitiative.

But members of Congress going back to at least the time of Jefferson
have also recognized the potential abuses that could arise from executive
officers committing to expenditures in advance of appropriations, or from
simply spending money faster than they were supposed to. During debate over the Navy's request for appropriations in 1806, John Randolph,
Chairman of the Ways and Means Committee, observed that it was futile
to closely scrutinize these requests and to search for ways of reducing
them. Even if departments were given all the funds they requested, they

all too frequently returned with a request for additional funds long before their appropriations were supposed to have run out:

> Appropriations have become a matter of form, or less than the shadow of a shade, a mere cobweb of defence against expenditures. You have fixed limits, but the expenditure exceeds the appropriation; and those who disburse the money are like a saucy boy who knows that his grandfather will gratify him and overruns the sum allowed at pleasure. As to appropriations, I have no faith in them. We have seen that so long as there is money in the Treasury, there is no defence against its expenditure. (quoted in Wilmerding 1943, p. 67)

In the classic form of what Wilmerding calls a "coercive deficiency," an agency would spend what it had been appropriated before the year was out and then threaten Congress with the cessation of its services and the breach of contracts it had made if additional funds were not forthcoming. Coercive deficiencies put Congress in the unenviable position, as portrayed in Niskanen's (1971) model, of a legislature confronting a discriminating bureaucratic monopolist. To the extent Congress tolerates such practices, they are engaging in abdication. As Wilmerding puts it, the occurrence of coercive deficiencies implied that "the departments had become the appropriating authorities and that Congress had sunk to be the mere register of their determinations" (p. 140).

In addition to the case involving the Navy that provoked Randolph's grumbling, Wilmerding describes in some detail a coercive deficiency engineered by the Post Office in 1879. What was particularly sobering about the latter episode was that it occurred after Congress had supposedly outlawed coercive deficiencies in 1870 by forbidding departments from spending in any fiscal year more than had been appropriated for that year, or from entering into contracts that would result in obligations in excess of their appropriations. This provision was an amendment to a bill designed primarily to eliminate practices discussed previously, that is, transfers across appropriations accounts and carryovers of unexpended balances. As long as departmental threats to close down their operations remained credible, however, laws forbidding deficiencies were not. This measure was thus no more successful in ending deficiencies than the other provisions were in halting transfers and carryovers.

Wilmerding asserts that coercive deficiencies posed a grave threat to policy-making by party-based majorities in the nineteenth-century Congress. There is, however, a fundamental tension between this assessment and the balance of his account, which indicates that episodes in which departments flagrantly abused their authority were the exception rather than the rule. Deficiencies were commonplace, but it was Congress who was their author. In the first half-century of the Republic, executive agencies really had little choice but to operate on a deficiency basis, making expenditures or committing to expenditures prior to receiving appropriations. Their funding would expire on 31 December, and no new appropriations would be forthcoming until at least February in the short session and April in the long. In the meantime they could either borrow against anticipated appropriations or defer payment on their bills. These gaps in funding also made it prudent to engage in the other two practices discussed above, namely, to carry forward unexpended balances and to transfer funds from one account to another ("borrowing from other appropriations"). The necessity for such financial maneuvers was alleviated somewhat by moving to a fiscal year basis in 1843 and, later, by the practice of adopting stop-gap continuing resolutions.

Wilmerding also acknowledges that in the decades following the Civil War, Congress took an even more active role in the creation of deficiencies by knowingly and purposively appropriating agencies less than they needed to operate for the full fiscal year. Under this budgetary regime it was highly unusual for an agency not to return some months later needing additional appropriations to cover the shortfall. There were a number of reasons for making partial year appropriations—or "appropriating on the installment plan," as Wilmerding (p. 142) calls it. Arguably it kept agencies on a short leash and helped prevent them from accumulating large unexpended balances. By several accounts, however, underappropriating was primarily the product of partisan politics and election-year gimmickry. James Garfield, who, prior to becoming president, had been Chairman of the House Appropriations Committee for a number of years, charged that it had become a common practice "to cut down the annual bills below the actual amount necessary to carry on the Government, announce to the country that a great reduction has been made in the interest of economy, and, after the elections are over, make up the necessary amounts by deficiency bills" (1879, p. 584). Thomas Reed subsequently observed that this was especially likely to happen when the next Congress was to be controlled by the opposition party: "It exalts your own virtue and brings into bolder relief the wickedness of the enemy" (1892, p. 326).

Shortly after the turn of the century, Congress, despite its own complicity in the matter, attempted again to put an end to the practice of agencies routinely creating deficiencies. The Anti-Deficiency Act of 1905 imposed restrictions identical to the 1870 legislation, but added an innovative new clause: based on the reasoning that the best way to prevent agencies from running out of money too soon was to not hand it over all at once, this measure stipulated that all appropriations were to be so apportioned by monthly or other allotments as to prevent undue expenditures in one portion of the year that may require deficiency or additional appropriations to complete the service of the fiscal year. There was, however, a major loophole; department heads could simply waive the apportionment provision, which is precisely what they did. The following year Congress voted to forbid such waivers "except upon the happening of some extraordinary emergency or unusual circumstance which could not be anticipated at the time of making such apportionment" (Wilmerding 1943, p. 147).

Wilmerding and other fiscal historians credit the Anti-Deficiency Acts with bringing about a substantial decline in the size and frequency of deficiency appropriations. This is not to say that deficiencies, coercive or otherwise, were entirely legislated away; as Fisher (1975) notes, the Anti-Deficiency Act is "far from self-executing" (p. 235). It is probably no accident, given the indispensable nature of its operations, that the most flagrant coercive deficiency in modern times involved the Post Office. Just as in 1879, in 1947 the Post Office expended its appropriations at such a rate so as to exhaust them by the end of the third quarter and then threatened to halt delivery of the mail if it were not appropriated additional funds (Fisher 1975, p. 155). Rubin (1990) recounts some recent coercive deficiencies the Defense Department created by reprogramming funds for spare parts and ammunition (items particularly valued by members of the Defense Subcommittee of House Appropriations) to new weapons systems development and then requesting additional funds for spare parts and ammunition. Overall, though, violations of the Anti-Deficiency Acts have been small in both number and size. According to Fisher, between 1963 and 1973 there were 278 violations involving $188 million, and many of these were technical in nature. To be sure, many violations probably go unreported. But even if all violations of the law were coercive deficiencies and only 10 percent of them were reported, the amount of money involved would still be much less money than the sums subject to either reprogramming or to deferral.

In our view, the reduction in deficiencies, coercive or otherwise, that has been achieved through various reforms is due far more to the changes they wrought in the way Congress appropriated than in the way agencies ran their finances. In particular, requiring the periodic apportionment of funds over the course of the fiscal year makes it far more problematic to underappropriate, as the agency runs out of money sooner rather than later.[9] This is true of subsequent reforms as well. As indicated earlier in the discussion of impoundments, a 1950 amendment to the Anti-Deficiency Act—inspired to a large extent by the 1947 Post Office episode—instructs agencies to "establish reserves." By making allowances for such reserves or, similarly, by explicitly providing for contingency funds, Congress is far less likely to underappropriate.

Coercive deficiencies created by either the president or by agency administrators thus do not appear to be a serious threat to the policy-making role of congressional parties and probably never were. Congratulations, however, are not in order. Congress currently confronts a new sort of deficiency that is orders of magnitude greater than anything that has come before. This is the bill for losses resulting from the failure of savings and loans (hereafter S&L's) covered by federal deposit insurance. According to the more conservative of current estimates, the federal government must commit between $120 billion and $150 billion (derived from appropriations or from selling bonds) to close down all insolvent S&L's. The tab is larger if the tax breaks used to induce healthy S&L's to take over failed ones are counted and much larger still if interest payments are included. For congressional parties pursuing their policy objectives, these expenditures represent enormous opportunity costs if nothing else.[10] According to Calmes' (1990c) calculations, $120 billion would purchase any one of the following: housing vouchers for twenty-two million families; three years of funding for Medicaid; seventeen years worth of nutrition programs; one hundred Trident submarines; one hundred forty B-2 Bombers; or Pell grants for fifty-two million college students. The electoral return, though, would seem minimal at best. As one congressional staffer puts it, "You don't get a program, you don't get education, you don't get a bomber, you don't get anything, really. You're just spending the money" (Calmes 1990c, p. 896).

The key question for our analysis is the same as before: is the necessity of bailing out the S&L industry truly a coercive deficiency? Certainly Congress now has little choice but to pick up the tab. It is also the case that the provision of federal deposit insurance is tantamount to delegating to private citizens the authority to commit the federal government, at least probabilistically, to making expenditures. All they have to do is make some bad investments and go broke. In our view, however, this deficiency, like any other, can be considered coercive only if it resulted from abuses of delegated authority that Congress could not have foreseen and could not have prevented. If this turns out to have been the case we must concede a great deal to the abdication hypothesis, for we will have identified a major instance in which delegation did result in Congress leaving itself unable to subsequently influence the course of policy, even while experiencing massive, ongoing agency losses.

In seeking to answer this question we begin with a brief review of the history of deposit insurance. First provided to banks in 1933, federal deposit insurance was extended to S&L's the following year. Besides its obvious function of protecting depositors, deposit insurance was also envisioned as a mechanism for preventing bank runs. Without it, the rumor of trouble at a bank or S&L became a self-fulfilling prophecy, as panicky depositors raced to withdraw their funds. Lenders also face an inherent problem of "maturity mismatch" in making thirty-year mortgages on the basis of demand deposits. Deposit insurance was intended to ameliorate this problem as well by creating depository stability. Congress has periodically increased the extent of coverage, which presently stands at $100,000 per account. The federal government currently insures approximately $4 trillion in deposits in approximately 30,000 banks, S&L's, and credit unions and guarantees over $1.6 trillion in mortgage insurance programs run by the Federal Housing Administration and Veterans' Administration.

An unfortunate side effect of insurance is that it induces the insured to become less vigilant in preventing the bad outcomes they are insured against. To counter this tendency, commonly referred to as "moral hazard," Congress originally bundled deposit insurance with regulations that made it highly unlikely that an S&L would fail for reasons other than criminal fraud or embezzlement. The most important of these were interest rate ceilings and the quarter percent differential in favor of S&L's vis-à-vis banks. These regulations eliminated much of the risk of guaranteeing S&L deposits by virtually guaranteeing S&L profits and nearly made deposit insurance superfluous. Indeed, when *It's a Wonderful Life* first played before the American public in 1946, more S&L's operated without federal deposit insurance than with it (Crawford 1990).

This regime was undermined by the inflation and high nominal interest rates of the late 1970s and by the resultant flight of capital to unregulated money-market accounts. Removing the interest-rate ceiling allowed S&L's to compete for deposits, but they were not able to shed their low fixed-rate mortgages. S&L's suffered huge losses. The Federal Home Loan Bank Board lowered capital reserve requirements from 5 percent to 4 percent and then to 3 percent, yet hundreds of S&L's were still unable to meet even these new lower standards. Worse yet, funds the FSLIC (Federal Savings and Loan Insurance Corporation) had on hand were grossly inadequate to cover liabilities. By 1982 Congress faced a menu of extremely unappealing choices. Closing S&L's and paying off depositors would cost several billion dollars. But where would the money come from? Charging significantly higher premiums for deposit insurance would only nudge many more S&L's into insolvency and push extremely high interest rates even higher. The federal government could increase its borrowing to replenish the FSLIC, but it was already well on its way to running a string of $200 billion deficits. Raising taxes was politically out of the question, given the presence of Ronald Reagan in the White House and the fact that a major tax cut had just been enacted. At any rate, the economy was rapidly sliding into a deep recession.

It was in this context that Congress passed the Garn-St. Germain

Depository Institutions Act, which sought to aid S&L's in a number of ways. It abolished due-on-sale clauses that had allowed buyers to assume low-interest-rate mortgages. It allowed S&L's to offer checking accounts and to invest in areas that were potentially more profitable than home mortgages, such as consumer and commercial loans, nonresidential real estate, and direct construction loans. It also explicitly initiated, through the Net Worth Certificate Program, a policy that has come to be known as forbearance. Instead of closing an S&L that was either insolvent or in danger of becoming so, the FSLIC would instead accept a promissory note payable upon the institution's return to profitability. (Insolvency is usually defined as having zero or negative net worth according to Generally Accepted Accounting Principles.) The Garn-St. Germain solution came at the cost of accepting an unprecedented level of risk in the provision of federal deposit insurance. S&L's were no longer guaranteed profitability. Hundreds of them were broke already. They were now allowed to make much riskier investments than traditional home loans. But if successful, these policies would buy time for the S&L's (and thus for the federal government and ultimately for the taxpayer) until lower interest rates, economic recovery, and the shift into more profitable forms of investment restored their profitability.

Several measures could have been taken to compensate for this additional risk. The logic of delegation, reviewed in chapter 2, points to several things that could have been done. Congress could have required S&L's to supply the Federal Home Loan Bank with more and better information about their investments. They could have invested more resources in monitoring S&L activities by having the FHLBB hire more examiners. They could have required S&L's to set up a variety of internal checks to make sure that their portfolios were reasonably well diversified and that prospective deals had been adequately researched. They could have instituted screening procedures to make sure that S&L owners and managers were not the type of people liable to commit felonies and required them to put substantial sums of their own money at risk.

Garn-St. Germain was accompanied instead by a spate of regulatory and legislative innovations that were precisely the opposite of what was called for. Instead of requiring more accurate and more timely information, Congress instead permitted S&L's to adopt regulatory accounting standards and other bookkeeping practices, such as "loan loss deferral," that disguised huge losses. According to their financial statements, many S&L's seemed fine until days before their collapse into insolvency. In some S&L's over 90 percent of all loans were nonperforming at the time the institutions were seized (Day 1989). Instead of additional institutional checks on S&L managers, existing checks were removed. The

Federal Home Loan Bank Board had long required an S&L to have at least four hundred shareholders all residing close to the institution. In 1981 this number was reduced to one. In 1982 individuals were allowed to put up real estate holdings in acquiring an S&L instead of cash. Instead of insisting on more examiners, Congress went along with the Reagan administration's plans to reduce their numbers. Nothing was done about state-chartered S&L's when several states, most notably California, removed virtually all remaining barriers on S&L investment activities. It was primarily the state-chartered S&L's that went in for the truly exotic investments and that have so far been responsible for about two-thirds of the cost of the S&L bailout.

Despite the fact that S&L financial statements were generally lacking in informational value, GAO analysts were able to determine by late 1985 that things were going badly.[11] S&L's in the Net Worth Certificate Program were getting worse, not better (General Accounting Office 1985). Over 40 percent of the nation's S&L's were in serious financial trouble (General Accounting Office 1986a). Of the 159 S&L's insolvent at the end of 1982, 107 (70 percent) were still insolvent at the end of 1985 despite the appreciation in assets they should have experienced as a result of declining interest rates (General Accounting Office 1986b).

The arguments for reporting requirements, monitoring, institutional checks, screening procedures, and risk-sharing contracts take on a special urgency in the case of insolvent S&L's that are permitted to remain in business. As program auditors from the General Accounting Office (1986b) explain in their customary understated fashion, in this situation moral hazard kicks in with a vengeance:

> Managers of thrift institutions that are permitted to continue operating while insolvent have a different set of incentives than solvent institution managers. Most importantly, in this context, is a propensity among managers of insolvent institutions to gamble by engaging in risky investments. Having no equity to preserve and protected against liability for losses by the FSLIC deposit insurance guarantee, managers may see the potential for high returns from such investments as the best hope for returning to solvency. This suggests that, on average, insolvent thrifts should experience a deterioration in the value of their asset portfolios due to an accumulation of risky investments. (p. 16)

This is precisely what happened at insolvent institutions. Romer and Weingast (1990) refer to this shift toward riskiness as "gambling for resurrection." In her analysis of the S&L crisis, Garcia (1988) sees "forbearance," as the strategy of not intervening came to be called, as the "most important regulatory error" of them all.[12]

Congress did not create the S&L crisis and Garn-St. Germain was not in and of itself a reckless gamble. But they did make things worse by clinging to the strategy of forbearance for so long. In 1986 they failed to approve the Reagan administration's request for a $15 billion infusion into the FSLIC to close down insolvent S&L's. A considerably smaller bill was not approved until nearly two years later, and it came with new restrictions that made it even more difficult for federal regulators to close down insolvent institutions. Lacking sufficient operating capital, the FSLIC could do little except to arrange for mergers and takeovers, using large tax breaks as inducements. Not until 1989 did Congress move decisively to staunch the flow by creating the Resolution Trust Corporation and providing it with the immense borrowing authority required to deal effectively with the crisis.

Many books on the S&L crisis have already appeared, and dozens more are surely on the way. They will doubtlessly offer all sorts of explanations as to why Congress slept: the large campaign contributions made by the S&L's and the corrupt Senators and House members who solicited them; the Reagan administration's blind faith in deregulation; the ineptness of key regulators and the villainy of others. Some will surely argue that the inherent institutional limitations of Congress make it unable to deal effectively with such thorny, complicated problems. We would make only the following observations. First, the owners and operators of high-flying S&L's were by no means the only beneficiaries of loose regulation and forbearance. A large collection of interests drawn from both parties' major constituencies must also be included: homeowners who obtained mortgages they would otherwise not have qualified for; individuals who received higher interest rates on their federally insured deposits than would have otherwise have been the case; developers who built projects that would otherwise never have been undertaken, as well as the construction workers whom they employed. Who was complaining? A few lonely voices at the GAO, perhaps, but there is rarely any shortage of doom-and-gloom predictions when any serious problem develops.

Another reason why most members of Congress and their leaders were less than anxious to intervene is that they perceived that the many tens of billions that the bailout would add to the federal deficit would put severe new pressure on their parties' spending priorities. The Democrats were struggling to maintain domestic spending in the face of the Reagan administration's opposition, while Republicans were striving to minimize the cuts congressional Democrats were making in the defense budget. Romer and Weingast (1990) put it this way:

> In times of budgetary restraint, nearly all congressmen had
> to face constituents who wanted funds for existing programs

increased, without the political wherewithal for added revenues. To the extent that the new resources for the FSLIC or the FHLBB were to come in the form of newly-funded budget authority, these resources would probably have to come at the expense of competing programs. To refuse valued, long-term constituents while creating a large new program would be politically difficult. (p. 23)

Finally, despite the highly publicized exploits of several S&L executives, we must conclude that to a large extent the S&L crisis, as in the case of the "coercive" deficiencies described by Wilmerding, is of Congress's own making. This is not to say that Congress, or even any one member of Congress, desired the collapse of a thousand S&L's and deliberately set out to achieve that outcome. They were, however, willing to take the risk.

Summary

Making appropriations is nothing more and nothing less than delegating to agency administrators the authority to spend a certain sum of money in a certain period of time. Specific and detailed instructions as to how that money is to be spent provide no real protection against agency losses, because it is never in the interest of Congress or of the nation to lock into a particular pattern of expenditures a year or more in advance. It is instead beneficial for those making expenditures to be able to transfer funds from one account to another, to refrain from making expenditures, and to commit to expenditures in advance of appropriations. As is always the case, though, authority granted to others for the purpose of advancing policies Congress has chosen can be used to frustrate these policies as well.

In the case of transfers, Congress has periodically reacted to administrative abuses by enacting legislation that would seem to outlaw them, but has always preserved enough loopholes and escape clauses to allow them to continue. This is not because of legislative carelessness or poor draftsmanship, but because they desired to regulate the practice rather than to ban it. A major reason for this approach is that transfers (now accomplished primarily through reprogramming) do not pose a particularly dire threat to party policy priorities. Money appropriated to one department, except in certain cases explicitly permitted by law, is not reprogrammed or transferred to another.

For most of this nation's history, Congress also tolerated occasional abuses associated with impoundments, and rightly so, given the benefits derived from granting discretion to time expenditures or to halt them entirely. Nixon's wholesale violations of this trust convinced Congress to impose a number of important restrictions on impoundments that have largely discouraged presidents from invoking them. Most congressional scholars hail the anti-impoundment reforms as signifying that Congress has at last reclaimed the power of the purse. This is erroneous. Withdrawing a beneficial delegation of authority because it could not be effectively managed is not a success story.

Finally, Congress has also moved on several occasions to prevent departments and agencies from presenting them with the budgetary fait accompli known as coercive deficiencies. For the most part, however, deficiencies occurred because the way Congress appropriated made them inevitable. That measures to curtail deficiencies came to bear some success is primarily because they reformed the way Congress made appropriations. The massive deficiency that Congress faces today—the bill for losses resulting from the failure of S&L's covered by federal deposit insurance—does more to undercut the policy agenda of congressional parties than any previous deficiency in history. Congress did not create the S&L crisis, but by not taking reasonable measures to manage the delegation that is entailed in providing deposit insurance they did allow a bad situation to grow much worse.

CHAPTER TEN

Conclusion

National policy-making, at least as seen through the lens of the abdication hypothesis, would seem to be have little to do with how many Democrats or Republicans are elected to Congress. By this view congressional parties have forefeited any role they might play in the legislative process to their members serving on committees. Members' claims to their committee positions are so overriding of any other considerations that congressional scholars have described them as property rights. Thus it is in the committees that the locus of policy-making in Congress is to be found: "Committees are more than just a part of the policymaking process ... Since World War II they have effectively made policy" (Brady 1989, p. 115). Observers of Congress often characterize the policy that emerges from the committee nexus as haphazard and inconsistent, depending, as it does, "on the composition of committees and thus, by indirection, on patterns of seniority within the House and within committees" (Dodd and Oppenheimer 1977, p. 22). Policy-making by committee also appears to allow small minorities of strategically placed members to prevent legislation that they oppose from even being considered. Hopelessly deadlocked, Congress all too often decides to let somebody else—either the president or unelected officials in the federal bureaucracy—decide what to do.

The facts of delegation are indisputable. A great deal of legislative authority has been delegated within Congress to committees and subcommittees. Congress has in turn chosen to delegate major policy tasks to the president and to department and agency administrators. There is, however, a serious flaw in the simple, compelling account of national politics that the abdication hypothesis provides: congressional parties exert a strong and systematic influence upon national policy-making! The partisan composition of the U.S. Congress is a key determinant of how funds are allocated to the myriad programs and agencies of the federal government. Congressional Democrats have successfully put their stamp on major spending decisions. When confronting a Republican in the White House, they have adopted budget resolutions that pare tens of billions of dollars from requests for military spending and add tens of billions to requests for domestic programs. The balance of party forces in Congress also determines the pace of innovation in social welfare programs, which have come to constitute the largest component of the federal budget.

How is it that congressional parties are able to exert so much influence over national policy? The proposition advanced in this book is that they have done so by successfully managing the delegation of authority both inside of Congress and to the outside. Indeed, congressional parties are themselves the product of individual members of the caucus delegating agenda-setting authority to their leaders. Such delegation is needed to overcome collective action, coordination, and social choice instability problems and derives from the strong incentives individual Democrats and Republicans in Congress have to organize the institution along party lines. We do not wish to dismiss the importance to members of narrowly defined, constituency-oriented concerns. But it should also be recognized that for the vast majority of them, the party label, which conveys a simple, low-cost signal to voters about policy preferences, is not a liability. It is instead their most important electoral asset. Put another way, let us consider what most members would do if forced to choose between the following three undesirable choices: (1) be reassigned to a different committee; (2) reduce the amount of franked mail they can send by 50 percent; (3) run under the other party label. We submit that few would choose the third alternative.

Contrary to the facile analogy that is often made between them, committee positions that members hold lack and have always lacked certain characteristics that adhere in property rights. Committee positions are not alienable; members may not bilaterally trade their positions, but must instead go through party channels to obtain both their original assignments and subsequent transfers. During the past several years the Democratic caucus has removed several chairmen and threatened others. Such actions are infrequent, but of great exemplary value. Mostly, however, the majority party advances the collective policy interests of its members primarily by conditioning the institutional environment in which committees operate. The data on assignments to the House Appropriations Committee show that the Democrats, who have held a majority in that chamber for all but four years since World War II, have sought and largely succeeded in keeping their contingent on the House Appropriations Committee ideologically representative of the caucus as a whole. Most of the time they have also succeeded in keeping other major committees, including Ways and Means and the Budget Committee, from becoming unrepresentative of the caucus. The majority party leadership provides the proposals made by Appropriations and other committees with key parliamentary advantages when they move to the floor, but at the same time prevents committees from using the conference process to advance their policy preferences at the expense of the party's. The majority party in Congress has undertaken major procedural reforms—in 1885, 1921, and 1974—to signal a standing commitment to a particular set of policies. As in all such relationships, it is the agents (committees) that play the game, but the principal (the party caucus) that makes the rules.

Our claim that congressional parties have successfully managed the delegation of policy-making authority to their members serving on committees should not be construed as an assertion about the amount of power parties have relative to committees. Political science has often been defined as the analysis of power. The key words here are "power" and "control." Those who possess power exercise it to control the actions of others. Thus the party caucus exerts power over committees when it deposes committee chairmen. The floor exerts power over a committee when it amends its bills. The president exerts power over Congress when he casts a veto. More recently, studies by Shepsle and Weingast (1987a) and a number of others have posited that particular institutional arrangements, such as the ex post veto discussed in chapter 6, confer power to a particular actor, such as the committee, the Speaker, or the president. Power on Capitol Hill is seen to ebb and flow; prior to 1974 or so committees were "more powerful," but since then congressional parties and their leaders have "reasserted control." With rare exception, the delegation of authority is equated with the transfer of power.

To be sure, controversies over how to define and measure power have been around for a long time.[1] Even if we were able to agree upon a useful definition of power, the actual patterns of behavior we observe in Congress reveal very little about it. This is primarily due to the problem of anticipated reactions; most decisions and actions in which we are interested are rationally conditioned upon how they will affect the subsequent decisions and actions of other actors in the policy-making process. Ultimately, constitutions, governments, legislative organizations, and all other institutional arrangements are themselves objects of choice.

What may be the most important departure this book makes from the existing literature on Congress is its rejection of the "power" approach— because of the intractable problems in applying it to empirical analysis, and, more important, because we do not find it theoretically useful. Thinking in terms of power and control is very seductive, but it is entirely counter to the way in which we seek to analyze policy-making. Our aim has not been to demonstrate that congressional parties control their many agents or are more powerful than other institutional entities. What we have sought to show is that congressional parties can use delegation to effectively pursue their policy objectives. What is generally taken as the exercise of power—floor amendments, presidential vetoes, or dumping committee chairmen—tells us nothing about the success of delegation.

Consider, for instance, a hypothetical situation in which a particular committee in Congress possesses so many informational and strategic advantages that floor consideration of its proposals amounts to nothing more than a rubber stamp. Vacancies on the committee attract a swarm of applicants, but the party caucuses are only able to select new members by choosing randomly from their respective applicant pools. They possess no other mechanism through which they might influence the behavior of the committee. We would seem to have here the classic combination of strong committee and weak party. To members assigned to the committee, it would appear that their policy preferences had nothing to do with their selection. Yet this passive process of random selection would yield party contingents on the committee that mirrored the distribution of preferences in each caucus. As an ideological microcosm of the floor, the committee produces proposals that are identical to what the majority party would have achieved had its delegation of authority to the committee never taken place. In this case the majority party would have benefited greatly from delegating to this committee. To the extent assignments to the Appropriations Committee approximate this stylized account, the majority party will be successful in its delegation.

Are parties more powerful than committees? Are committees less powerful than they used to be? Is Thomas Foley a less powerful Speaker than Jim Wright or Sam Rayburn? Did the Congressional Budget and Impoundment Control Act allow Congress to reassert power that had gradually been accumulated by the president? Is the General Accounting Office more powerful doing policy analysis instead of auditing vouchers? Knowledgeable observers of American politics continually debate these and similar questions. To all these questions we would answer that it is impossible to tell, and that it is the wrong question to ask in the first place. Do the policies that emerge from Congress reflect the preferences of the majority party? Do the expenditures that agencies make from the appropriations they receive follow from the intent of the legislation? These are questions that we can answer, and the answer is yes.

We have so far discussed only our claims about the success of delegation within Congress. What about our claim that Congress has also successfully delegated authority to the president and other officials? How do we reconcile this claim with the rather more negative assessment of delegation reached by Lowi (1979)? Lowi recognizes that the choice Congress must make is not whether to delegate but rather *how* to delegate: "It is of course impossible to imagine a modern state in which central authorities do not delegate functions, responsibilities, and powers to administrators. Thus the practice of delegation itself can hardly be criticized. The practice becomes pathological, and criticizable, at the point where it comes to be considered a good thing in itself, flowing to administrators without guides, checks, and safeguards" (pp. 93–94).

Delegation "without guides, checks, and safeguards" is a good working definition of abdication, and in his view this is exactly the course Congress has chosen in the chartering of one regulatory agency after another. He singles out two agencies for special disapprobation—the Occupational Safety and Health Administration and the Consumer Product Safety Commission. In characterizing the legislation that created OSHA and CPSC, Lowi asserts, "In neither piece of public policy did Congress attempt by law to identify a single specific evil that the regulatory agency was to seek to minimize or eliminate ... Congress provided no standards whatsoever ... nor did Congress provide any standards for the conduct of these two regulatory agencies. All Congress did was to assume that the agencies in their wisdom would be able to provide such standards" (116–17).

Lowi sees these unbridled grants of authority as having very different consequences. OSHA's actions have been confined primarily to rubberstamping safety standards already adopted by trade associations, thus providing, perhaps, a small push toward industry cartelization. The CPSC, in contrast, is "a monster of unadulterated administrative power," proceeding on its Naderesque vendettas "with a vigor that is matched only by its unpredictability" (pp. 118–19). Both policy-making debacles, however, are the unpalatable fruit of abdication.

There is no logical reason why Lowi's jeremiad on delegation to regulatory agencies cannot coexist with our favorable assessment of how Congress has managed delegation in the context of the appropriations process. Yet it is obviously difficult to keep such disparate views of the world in one's head at the same time. Why would the same legislature, composed of the same members, belonging to the same parties, elected by the same constituents, confronting the same economic and political environment, delegate so carefully and effectively in one context and so recklessly in another?

In our view Congress and the parties that organize it do not exhibit this sort of schizophrenia and employ the same principles of delegation in regulatory affairs as they do in the appropriations process. OSHA and the CPSC are both subject to the standard monitoring and over-sight by their authorizing committees and Appropriations subcommittees in both chambers. Non-committee members can challenge both agencies' actions on the floor and have done so on dozens of occasions. Indeed, Idaho's Republican Senators Symms and McClure have repeatedly sought to block the CPSC's reauthorization legislation because of the agency's attempts to ban sales of the Worm Gett'r.[2] There are institutional checks on unilateral action. OSHA, which is housed in the Labor Department, can promulgate regulations only for health hazards identified by the National Institute of Occupational Safety and Health (NIOSH), a separate agency located in the Department of Health and Human Services. NIOSH has proven to be only partially cooperative with OSHA and has thus constrained OSHA's ability to set its own regulatory agenda.

The 1970 Occupational Safety and Health Act and 1972 Consumer Products Safety Act also impose a substantial number of reporting requirements that supplement the more general provisions of the Administrative Procedures Act and the National Environmental Policy Act. Among other things, the APA requires agencies to give public notice of its rule proposals and other impending actions, to hold public hearings, and to invite public comment on proposed rules. The agency's 1981 reauthorization legislation also stipulated that the CPSC give prompt notice of proposed new standards to its authorizing committees (the Senate Commerce, Science, and Transportation Committee and the House Energy and Commerce Committee). Lowi and other critics of regulatory agencies often point to the burgeoning size of the *Federal Register* as symptomatic of runaway regulation resulting from abdication. The *Register* is in fact a multivolume document that is currently about fifty thousand pages long.[3] But its size is testament only of the extent to which Congress has employed reporting requirements as a mechanism for managing delegation.

The most important feature of the delegation made to both agencies, however, is the tightly circumscribed nature of it. Lowi is correct in observing that OSHA is instructed to adopt voluntary industry standards whenever it deems them adequate, but that requirement was subsequently applied to the CPSC as well in its 1981 reauthorization legislation. This measure also shifted the burden of proof against independent CPSC action by imposing tougher evidentiary standards and the performance of cost-benefit analyses. Any gains that consumer advocates have made in recent years have come through state and federal legislation and through favorable innovations in product liability law—not through the administrative fiat of the CPSC. Indeed, the CPSC has frequently sought to impose standards by referring "imminent hazard" cases to the

Justice Department or by going to court directly, rather than follow its own rule-making procedures (McCubbins, Noll, and Weingast 1989).

The existence of these contractual limitations and checks on the agencies' authority is no accident. Consumer product and workplace safety regulation have long been and continue to be subjects of intense partisan controversy. Those who favor such regulation are predominately Democrats, those who oppose it are predominately Republicans. Both agencies were created by Democratic Congresses during the Nixon administration, and both reflect the best deal they could get at the time. The size of their budgets and staffs peaked at the end of the Carter administration. House Democrats thwarted the Reagan administration's attempts to either neutralize or eliminate OSHA and CPSC, but had to accept additional restrictions and sizable cutbacks in the agencies' staffing and funding levels. The delegation of authority to OSHA, CPSC, and other regulatory agencies has not halted congressional involvement in these policy areas nor has it put an end to partisan controversy. Congressional policy-making through regulation differs from policy-making through the appropriations process in several important ways. What we see in both arenas, however, is the continuing struggle between the major parties' competing policy agendas. What we do not see is abdication.

Notes

Chapter One

1. The Jeffersonians initially favored the appointment of temporary select committees. Prior to the official establishment of permanent standing committees, however, many select committees enjoyed such continuity of existence and membership that they were standing in all but name (Skladony 1985).

2. This legislative doctrine also had the advantage of submerging an inherent tension in Jeffersonian thought as to whether executive branch officials were ultimately responsible to the president, the chief executive officer of the United States, or to Congress, the ultimate source of law (see Cooper 1970, p. 76).

3. Fiorina (1977) offers the truly cynical observation that after delegating all difficult policy problems to federal agencies, congressional members then bolster their reelection prospects by intervening on behalf of their constituents in struggles against an unresponsive officialdom and by regularly castigating the bureaucratic mess in Washington.

4. The main reason why such a vast body of rules and precedents has grown up over the distinction between appropriations and substantive policy is not out of concern for parliamentary niceties. It instead reflects ongoing efforts to demarcate where the jurisdiction of the Appropriations Committee in each chamber ends and where that of the authorizing committees begins.

5. Not all budget estimates are screened by the Bureau of the Budget (now Office of Management and Budget). The 1921 legislation ordered the Budget Bureau to include spending figures for the legislative and judicial branches in the president's budget without review or revision. In the 1970s Congress instructed several agencies (primarily regulatory commissions) to either submit their budget estimates directly to Congress or to submit them to Congress and to OMB concurrently.

Chapter Two

1. In most of the economics literature, a principal is defined as the person who offers a binding contract to another person—the agent—for the performance of specified services. A key element of this definition is that the principal moves first, and by so doing can commit to a certain compensation scheme governing the outcomes of the agent's actions. The agent then takes action that is optimal in light of his or her own goals and the incentives offered by the principal. Our definition is more general. We posit that an agency relationship

is established when an agent is delegated, implicitly or explicitly, the authority to take action on behalf of another, that is, the principal. For our purposes, it is not important who offers the contract that governs the relationship; the principal may seek to employ an agent for a particular task, or the agent may offer to serve and define his or her own terms. Nor does our definition require the principal to be able to commit to a schedule of rewards or punishments in advance. The agent may take action in anticipation of reward from the principal. Or the principal may hire the agent "to do good things," leaving for later the specification of what constitutes good things as well as the nature of the reward for doing them.

2. This is called adverse selection because the principal, in making a wage offer, receives applications only from agents whose opportunity costs are less than or equal to the wage rate offered. The principal would prefer to select from agents with opportunity costs greater than the wage offered or, failing that, to at least choose randomly from the distribution of potential agents.

3. For a thorough analysis of the economics of DRG reimbursement see Dranove (1987).

4. There are more provisions in actual sharecropping arrangements, for example, than simply the specification of output shares. If the contract provides the tenant with only a fixed portion of the crop, he lacks incentive, at least in the short-run, to conserve the tilth and fertility of the soil. That is why most such contracts typically enjoin the tenant and landlord to share the costs of fertilizer and other inputs as well (Stiglitz 1974, 1986).

5. Hamilton County (Cincinnati) hired the Morgenthaler brothers as tax inquisitors in the early 1880s. Over a twelve-year period the pair netted the County only about $840,000, but, according to Keller (1977), "engaged in bribery and self-enrichment on a scale that made them and the inquisitor system objects of intense public hostility" (p. 325).

6. The effectiveness of this policy depends upon the degree of correlation between the agent's performance in the current position and the one to which he or she would be promoted. According to proponents of the well-known Peter Principle, of course, this correlation is not high enough to prevent people in hierarchical organizations from eventually rising to a level at which they perform incompetently (Hull and Peter 1969).

7. About the only thing the principal can do about adverse selection via contract design is to offer an agent a variety of possible contracts. This can be done through what Baiman and Evans (1983) call "participative standard-setting," that is, when the principal and agent bargain over performance standards and compensation level. Allowing students to contract for grades is an example of this practice. The contract chosen by the agent will likely reveal some of his or her hidden information, thus ameliorating the adverse selection problem.

8. The signal Spence analyzes most thoroughly is formal education. In medicine, engineering, and certain other fields, an advanced degree is indicative of a certain level of job-relevant knowledge and expertise. In many other fields it is not. In these cases educational attainment does not certify that a person

knows anything in particular, but is rather a signal as to what type of person he or she is. Someone who earns an MBA, for example, is likely to be ambitious, at least moderately intelligent, and able to tolerate a substantial amount of pettiness and boredom—all reliable indicators of successful performance in the corporate world.

9. According to those in charge of the SEC program, many anonymous tips reporting insider trading are actually groundless charges made by those seeking revenge against someone (Paltrow 1989). Fraudulent use of a fraud hotline can be discouraged by not guaranteeing tipsters' anonymity, but this necessarily discourages reports of actual wrongdoing as well.

10. Consumers—a vast, diffuse group—face serious collective action problems; as individuals they have small stakes in the outcomes of most policy decisions. Their interests thus tend to be underrepresented relative to those of affected producer groups in the decisions of regulatory agencies and other administrative bodies (Noll and Owen 1983). According to McCubbins, Noll, and Weingast (1987), however, in recent years Congress has sought to change the balance of representation through "public intervenor" programs that subsidize the participation of consumers and other relatively underrepresented groups.

11. The most sweeping, unchecked delegation of authority we have come across was the product of a truly untenable status quo. The following commission was granted to Baron de Breteuil in 1789 by Louis XVI, at that time pinned down at the Tuileries by troops of the revolutionary National Guard and in grave danger:

> M. de Bretueil, conscious of all your devotion and fidelity, and wishing to give you fresh proof of my confidence, I have chosen to entrust you with the interests of my crown. Since circumstances do not permit me to give you my instructions on particular topics, nor to maintain a steady correspondence with you, I am sending you this letter giving you full power and authorization vis-à-vis the various powers with whom you may have to deal on my behalf. You know my wishes, and I trust your wisdom to use this power as you think necessary for the good of my service. I approve all that you may do to attain my objectives, namely to reinstate my legitimate authority and the happiness of my people. (Cobb and Jones 1988, p. 108)

12. The standing committee system in the U.S. Congress is hardly a distinguishing characteristic. A recent compendium reported that only two of the 110 parliamentary chambers in the world for which data are available were devoid of permanent committees (Inter-Parliamentary Union 1986, p. 626).

13. A Ponzi scheme is a swindle in which new investors are promised very high rates of return and given a list of earlier investors who have in fact received these returns. Even at the point people realize they have been duped and that their investment simply went to pay earlier investors, they have every incentive to keep the scheme going and to suck in new victims. A chain letter is a form of Ponzi scheme. So too, many allege, is social security.

Chapter Three

1. In response to this transformation of party politics in the South, many incumbent officeholders switched over to the Republican party. In the 1980s there were a number of highly visible defections by members of Congress, including Phil Gramm of Texas in 1983, Andy Ireland of Florida in 1984, and Bill Grant, also of Florida, in 1989. It is hard to understand why politicians would do this if party labels were not of major electoral significance. Perhaps more remarkably, other southern politicians, George Wallace being the most prominent example, continued to be elected as Democrats after making the necessary radical changes in their public position on civil rights.

2. Most analyses of survey data indicate that more partisan individuals are also politically better informed, but a decline in the average strength of party attachments by no means implies that party labels provide less information. Indeed, a decline in partisanship could reflect an increase in the amount of information provided by party labels. According to Poole and Rosenthal (1984), over the past few decades congressional Democrats and Republicans have become ideologically more polarized. If so, party labels would imply bigger differences in policy and hence more information. On average, though, individual citizens would perceive more distance between their own preferences and those of the parties and consequently "identify" less strongly with a party.

3. In delegating, principals frequently specify a schedule of sanctions that the agent will incur for undesirable actions or outcomes. But it is also possible to assign agents the task of imposing sanctions on the principal for certain failures and deficiencies, as in the case of someone who hires a fitness coach. In such situations, however, the principal may not be able to credibly commit to accepting the regimen imposed by his or her agent.

4. Endowing leaders with the authority to sanction defectors is not the only way a legislative party might seek to impose discipline on roll call votes. In principle, members of the same party could contract with each other to all vote the same way. In the early part of this century the Democratic caucus in the House adopted a version of this approach by allowing for binding caucus votes. A vote to bind the caucus, however, required a two-thirds majority and was therefore difficult to obtain. The rules also provided that even when the caucus did vote to bind its members on roll call vote, a member was not bound if he had made "contrary pledges to his constituents prior to his election or received contrary instructions by resolutions or platform from his nominating authority" (Hasbrouck 1927, p. 29).

5. Leaders can spare members a tough vote by referring a bill to a graveyard committee only if they can also block a vote challenging the referral decision. John Kennedy, for example, alienated many black leaders in 1958 when he voted to send a civil rights bill over the bridge of sighs to the Senate Judiciary Committee (Stern 1989).

6. Black's theorem, i.e., the ideal point of the median voter is unbeatable in a majority vote and is thus a stable outcome, requires the assumptions that preferences lie along a single dimension, are single-peaked, that there are no restrictions on the manner in which proposals are made or paired against each other, and that there is no probabilistic component in voters' choices.

7. Although the head of the majority party in the House is the Speaker, we examine the voting record of the majority floor leader because the Speaker does not generally cast roll call votes.

8. In running the NOMINATE procedure, Poole and Rosenthal exclude roll calls in which fewer than 2.5 percent of the membership supported the minority position. It is necessary to exclude such votes because they consume so many degrees of freedom while revealing virtually no information about members' relative positions. Poole and Rosenthal also combine votes from both sessions of some Congresses because of the relatively small number of roll call votes that were recorded. This is done for the Senate through 1958, except for sessions of the 89th Congress (1949–50), which are scaled separately, and for the House for all sessions through 1964. In all subsequent years, separate NOMINATE scores are estimated for each session. The correlation between members' percentile rankings in the first and second session of the same Congress averaged .97 (Pearson r for the Democrats and .94 for the Republicans). For that reason we base this and all subsequent analyses upon members' percentile rankings for the first session only when sessions of the same Congress were scaled separately.

Chapter Four

1. It is not a logical necessity that representative assemblies enact expenditure logrolls that are too large; if members are unable to make the requisite vote trades, too *little* spending will be approved (Buchanan and Tullock 1962, p. 135). Furthermore, parties to any vote trading agreement subsequently have an incentive to defect: As Ferejohn (1985) points out, "Logrolling relationships are inherently unstable: if a logroll is required to enact some set of bills, then there can be no package of bills that could win a majority against any other package . . . A logroll is inherently vulnerable to tactical counter-offers by those who are excluded from it" (pp. 2–3). It would appear, however, that members of Congress are routinely able to overcome whatever obstacles stand in the way of expenditure logrolls.

2. Bipartisan commitment to guardianship is not the only interpretation that is consistent with a lack of overt partisan conflict emanating from Appropriations. Republicans on the floor sometimes suspect that their contingent on the committee has fallen sway to the free-spending ways of the Democrats. Robert Walker (R, Pennsylvania), latest in the H. R. Gross line of GOP "watchdogs," asserts this to be the case: "It is not good enough to just rely on the minority members of particular committee[s] to keep an eye on things.

Committee members are, by the very nature of their role, captives of the wheeling and dealing within the committee and may not be the best judge of the interests of the whole committee membership"(quoted in Smith 1989, p. 157). In general, though, insiders' depictions strongly uphold the Guardian of the Treasury model; according to most of Fenno's interviewees, the minimal partisanship of the committee resulted from them and their colleagues putting aside ideological predilections in a bipartisan pursuit of economy and efficiency.

3. See Stewart (1989) and Schick (1980) respectively for comprehensive accounts of the 1885 divestiture and the 1974 Budget Act.

4. These trends were mirrored by a drop in the wholesale price level (190.7 in 1866 to 99.2 in 1884) that wiped out the Civil War inflation (1860 = 100).

5. The House established several new committees in the 1880s and 1890s, including Education, Labor, and Rivers and Harbors (1883), Merchant Marine and Fisheries (1887), Expenditures in the Department of Agriculture (1889), Immigration and Naturalization, Civil Service, Alcoholic and Liquor Traffic (1893), and Insular Affairs (1899). The divestiture of Appropriations was thus part of a general trend toward the specialization and division of labor that is the hallmark of the modern committee system (Keller 1977, p. 304).

6. Rates on the $1.8 billion in long-term debt issued in accordance with the Refunding Acts of 1870 and 1871 (ten-year bonds at 5 percent, fifteen-year bonds at 4.5 percent, and thirty-year bonds at 4 percent) were considerably higher than the interest rates that prevailed in the following decades. Because the bonds were not callable, the Treasury was forced to buy them on the open market at premiums that ran as high as 29 percent in 1888 (Studenski and Krooss 1952, p. 204).

7. Some federal pension expenditures went to the South, in that veterans of the Revolutionary War, the War of 1812, Indian Wars, and the War with Mexico received pensions. Some state governments also provided aid to those who had fought for the South; pensions for Confederate veterans and their widows accounted for over 20 percent of the state of Georgia's expenditures in 1911 (Wallenstein 1987). The amount spent by the federal government on Civil War pensions, however, was several times larger than that spent on pensions for all previous wars. Per capita pension expenditures in 1885 were therefore over four times higher in New England than in the South (Legler 1967).

8. Republicans in the 45th House supported the Pension Arrears Act 122–1, as did non-southern Democrats by a margin of 62–12. Democrats from the former Confederacy voted against it, 3–55.

9. Pensions were not the only form of veterans' benefits. During this period the federal government also spent millions of dollars annually on the Home for Disabled Volunteer Soldiers, on various state and territorial Old Soldiers' Homes, and on the provision of artificial limbs. Appropriations for these items were contained in the sundry civil bill, which, like the pensions bill, was not divested from House Appropriations in 1885.

10. There are a couple of reasons why we choose to report expenditures in table 4.1 instead of appropriations, even though the two series display the same overall trends. First, Wilmerding (1943) reports that during this period many federal agencies maintained large unexpended balances and that they often derived as much of their budget from the deficiency bill as from the regular appropriations bill. Second, during this period Congress sometimes chose to adjourn without appropriating money for pension funds and other mandatory expenditures, thus leaving it to the next Congress to make the necessary infusions.

11. In reasoning that preceded the Laffer Curve by nearly a century, protectionist Republicans proposed to cut tariff revenue by *increasing* tariff rates and thus stifling imports. The McKinley Tariff enacted in 1890 incorporated this logic, but the reduction in revenue it effected was in large part due to the $60 million or so lost annually to the Treasury by replacing the duty on sugar with a two-cent-per-pound subsidy to domestic producers.

12. Because budget resolutions break down spending totals into only twenty or so broad functional categories while appropriations bills contain hundreds of specific line items, one might assume that the Budget Committee looks at the "big picture" while Appropriations concentrates on the details. From the very beginning, however, budget resolutions, to the chagrin of Appropriations members, have been based upon a line-item-level consideration of program spending. As Havemann (1978) observes:

> The Budget Committee was guilty of the cardinal sin—it threatened the Appropriations Committee's jurisdiction over budget line items. ... The Appropriations Committee understood that the Budget Committee could not pick the budget's functional spending totals from thin air. It knew the Budget Committee could not recommend total defense spending without judging whether the B-1 bomber should be built or set a total for veterans' benefits without considering whether GI Bill benefits should be increased. (pp. 146–47)

13. There are members, including Jamie Whitten, Chairman of the House Appropriations Committee, who do reject the notion that Congress can impose binding constraints on itself: "Let us not kid ourselves that some artificial gimmick will ever substitute for the real will of Congress. Congress by its very nature is unlikely to lock itself into a room without keeping a key. And when the confinement begins to pain us, we tend to be all too willing to use the key" (quoted in Rubin 1990, p. 163).

14. In late 1981 the House and Senate Budget Committees reported second, "binding" budget resolutions that were identical to the first, even though a rapidly declining economy made previous revenue projections bankrupt, and legislation already enacted that year had pushed spending levels far over the ceiling figures! In fairness to the Budget Committees, they were hardly trying

to fool anybody; in "sense of Congress" clauses appended to the resolutions, they admitted that the spending, revenue, and deficit projections were no longer operative and called upon the president to submit as soon as possible a plan to lower interest rates, decrease unemployment, reduce inflation, and balance the budget by 1984. Then ranking minority member Ernest Hollings and other Senate Budget Committee members described the resolution their committee had reported as a "sham," a "travesty," and the "height of irresponsibility" (Tate 1981).

15. The original target for balancing the budget was FY1991, but the Supreme Court subsequently ruled that the sequestering provision of Gramm-Rudman-Hollings had made an unconstitutional delegation of authority to the Comptroller General, who is an agent of Congress. Such delegations can be made only to officials in the executive branch who are thereby subject to presidential removal. This constitutional defect was repaired by granting sole authority over sequestering to the Director of the Office of Management and Budget, but when Congress enacted the new version of Gramm-Rudman-Hollings in 1987 they rolled the original deficit targets back by two years. See White and Wildavsky (1989) for a comprehensive account of the budget battles leading up to the adoption of Gramm-Rudman-Hollings.

16. According to Fisher (1982, 1984), Democratic leaders have generally acceded to the demands of party liberals for more spending because their votes are indispensable to the passage of a budget resolution. Republican intransigence, by this line of reasoning, has only served to produce higher spending than would otherwise occur in the absence of the budget process.

Chapter Five

1. Upon losing control of the House, the Democrats in 1947 and 1953 and the Republicans in 1949 and 1955 were forced to trim several positions from their contingents on Appropriations. Upon regaining control of the House they regained these positions, and frequently assigned them to the same members who had held the positions when they were lost two years earlier or to another member from the same state. In these cases, we deemed the parties to have made "same state" appointments. Had we decided otherwise, the percentage of times we reported the parties to have adhered to this strategy would be slightly lower.

2. In 1974 the House Democrats transferred the task of making committee assignments from their contingent on the Ways and Means Committee to the Policy and Steering Committee. The Republican Committee on Committees in the House is comprised of one member from every state having at least one Republican, but their votes are weighted by the number of Republicans in the state delegation. As a consequence, an executive committee comprised of members from states with the largest Republican delegations (New York,

California, Ohio, Pennsylvania, Michigan, and Illinois) dominates the process (see Masters 1961).

 In the Senate, Democrats made assignments via a steering committee appointed by the floor leader. Members of this committee are typically the senior Democrats who are almost always committee chairmen. Since the 1950s the decisions of this committee have adhered to the "Johnson Rule" (named after Lyndon Johnson), which calls for all Democrats to be given a choice of one committee assignment before anyone is given a choice for a second assignment. The Senate Republicans' Committee on Committees adheres to a similar rule, adopted in 1965, that no Republican can hold seats on more than one of the four most-desired committees (Appropriations, Armed Services, Finance, and Foreign Relations) until every Republican has been given a chance to pass up an assignment to one of these committees.

3. In referring to percentile rankings derived from NOMINATE scores as measures of "ideology," we mean to imply nothing about the extent to which they are a function of members' true policy preferences versus a product of party pressures, constituency interests, or whatever. We use this term only as a synonym for the relative degree of liberalism or conservatism revealed by a member's voting record.

4. After the 1980 election, Speaker Tip O'Neill mollified conservative Democrats who were threatening to join with Republicans to oust him by naming several of their number to the House Budget Committee and to the Steering and Policy Committee (Arieff 1981).

5. Our assumption that the size of committees, party ratios, and the seniority system are fixed is based on our view of these arrangements as the equilibria to other games and that upsetting these equilibria in order to affect assignments, though possible, is expensive because of the renegotiation involved. But these equilibria certainly are upset from time to time. The commonly accepted rationale for committee expansion is to satisfy excess demand for positions, even though this necessarily lowers their value. But changes in the size of committees are made when it is important for the caucus to get its way on legislation and when the common means of ensuring committee compliance are not effective. The Rules Committee and the Ways and Means Committee, for example, were enlarged in 1961 and in 1975 respectively in order to enable passage of legislation desired by the Democratic caucus (Cummings and Peabody 1963; Shepsle 1978).

6. Distinguishing the effects of generational replacement (where generations are defined as electoral cohorts) from those due to socialization or to aging is usually referred to as cohort analysis. With most cohort data one must also specify "period" effects, that is, exogenous shocks to the entire distribution of the dependent variable up or down at the time of a particular observation. Unfortunately, each one of the three effects—age, cohort, and period—make the classic cohort analysis underidentified and impossible to estimate without

some prior restrictions on the parameters (Mason et al., 1973). According to Glenn (1976), this estimation strategy is, in turn, invalidated by the presence of interaction effects, for example, between age and period. Two features of our research design allow us to avoid these classic identification problems. First, the socialization effects we seek to detect are confined to the small subset of members in our sample who served on the Appropriations Committee. Second, because our dependent variable is the individual congressman's percentile rank along a liberal–conservative dimension, it is not perturbed by "period" effects. We have no way of telling whether particular events, such as, the Soviet invasion of Afghanistan or the demise of the Berlin Wall, make all members of a particular Congress more liberal or more conservative. It is only the members' relative positions to each other that matters for this analysis, however, so this is something we are willing to accept.

7. Upon assuming the chairmanship, Mahon adopted a version of the "Johnson Rule" that his fellow Texan had instituted in the Senate; specifically, every Democrat on Appropriations was guaranteed at least one "good" subcommittee assignment (personal communication from Joe White, 11 September 1988).

Chapter Six

1. Late in the session, printing of the *Congressional Record* often lags several days behind schedule, which means that members have little choice but to accept the floor manager's word for what is in a bill and what is not. In October 1986, for example, the House approved the conference agreement on the FY1987 omnibus continuing resolution even though only one copy of the bill was in existence—a two-foot-high stack of papers setting on a desk near Chairman Whitten (Wehr 1986).

2. In September 1983, Appropriations reported the FY1984 omnibus continuing resolution, which stipulated that funding to keep the Marines in Lebanon would be cut off on 1 December if Reagan failed to invoke the War Powers Resolution. This undercut an agreement to extend funding for eighteen months that Speaker Tip O'Neill and other House leaders had reached with the Reagan White House. O'Neill responded by referring the bill to the Foreign Affairs Committee. Knowing that Foreign Affairs would not report the bill back to the floor (and also that Reagan would veto the bill if it ever passed), Appropriations Chairman Jamie Whitten immediately introduced a "clean" bill that omitted this and several other legislative riders. O'Neill then bypassed Appropriations again and instead referred Whitten's bill to the Rules Committee, which in turn sent the bill directly to the floor (Granat 1983b).

3. See Krehbiel (1988) for a survey of research in this area.

4. The three agencies we omitted were two divisions in the Labor Department (the Wage and Hours Division and the Women's Bureau) and the

Social Security Administration. The first two were dropped because of their extremely small size, the third because of the frequent incomparability of figures reported from one year to the next.

5. The data in figures 6.3 and 6.4 do not reflect the impact of limitations amendments, as they do not alter the amounts of new budgetary authority that are obligated. As Bach and Sachs (1989) note, however, limitations amendments are often coupled with reductions in funding, which of course are reflected in these figures.

6. When reporting continuing resolutions, the House Appropriations Committee has generally returned legislation to the floor in the form in which it had previously passed the House. The Senate committee has usually followed the same practice vis-à-vis its parent chamber. There have been notable exceptions, however. In late 1982 the House committee increased appropriations for many agencies over previously adopted figures by appending a $5.4 billion emergency jobs bill to the FY1983 continuing resolution, along with suggestions ("for illustrative purposes only") as to where these funds might be most effectively committed.

7. In 1983 Subcommittee Chairman Neal Smith (D, Iowa), tired of negotiating with Rules and unwilling to wait any longer for the authorizing legislation his bill required, brought the FY1984 Commerce, State, Justice, and Judiciary bill to the floor without a rule. Points of order lodged against programs that lacked authorization reduced funding in the bill from $10.7 billion to $6.7 billion. As Smith promised, however, appropriations for these programs reappeared in the subsequent continuing resolution and were duly approved.

8. Steiner's (1951) analysis of conference agreements involving substantive legislation found a high level of adherence to the scope of legislation restriction.

9. The House Appropriations Committee had recommended $315 million for the Economic Development Administration, but this figure had been stricken on a point of order because the agency lacked authorizing legislation. Upholding this objection effectively converted the appropriations recommended for the EDA in the House bill to zero. The Senate subsequently voted to appropriate $200 million, and the conferees decided upon $240 million—a clear violation of the interval rule. Robert Walker (R, Pennslvania) noticed the transgression and moved to strike $40 million from the $240 million in order to bring it back within the proper scope of the conference.

Neal Smith, Chairman of the subcommittee and floor manager, was unapologetic. Acknowledging that the EDA had not been authorized, he countered with the following:

> ... unfortunately about half of this bill has not been authorized. We on the subcommittee do not like it. We would much rather work with authorized programs. As a matter of fact, the programs that we

are appropriating for today should have been authorized a year ago in September. But, on the other hand, you cannot stop the whole government, especially when the majority wants these programs to continue. ... In the continuing resolution that expires tonight they are authorized to spend at the rate of $250 million. Upon looking at the whole program and upon talking to Members of the House on both sides of the aisle, we felt that under all the constraints we had, $240 million would be a proper level for this program in this bill. Personally I would rather have had more money than that. But that is what we arrived at. (*Congressional Record*, 9 November 1983, pp. H9569)

The House turned back Walker's amendment by a 305–107 vote (*Congressional Record*, 9 November 1983, pp. H9570–2). As in all other cases, the ultimate rule of the House is that a majority can always vote to break the rules.

10. One possible rationale for misrepresentation by the committee is offered by Weingast (1989). In the agenda game he models, committees report initial proposals whose win sets constrain possible floor amendments, which the committee may in turn seek to amend, so as to minimize the amount by which the final bill departs from their ideal point. But limiting the agenda process to two stages (an amendment and an amendment to the amendment) violates our earlier assumption of an open agenda process. Weingast's analysis raises an interesting question, however, in that under general conditions a committee whose proposal has been amended can make itself better off by offering an amendment to the floor amendment. Yet we only came across one instance in which an Appropriations Committee sought to amend a floor amendment. This occurred in 1978, when the Senate Appropriations Committee sought to replace several amendments that had cut particular agency budgets with an across-the-board cut in the entire bill.

11. This assumes that appropriations for each agency are negotiated separately. Technically speaking, the restrictions we impose should hold across the hundreds of line items in an entire bill, but a restriction of this magnitude would rule out any possibility of subjecting the model to empirical scrutiny.

12. Republicans believed their cause would be aided by passage of Rule X, clause 6(f) in 1974, which formally replaced the practice of sending members of the originating subcommittee to conference with the following: "The Speaker shall appoint no less than a majority of members who generally supported the House position as determined by the Speaker. The Speaker shall name Members who are primarily reponsible for the legislation and shall, to the fullest extent feasible, include the principal proponents of the major provisions of the bill as it passed the House." In this they were badly disappointed. As Nagler notes, the key phrase here is "as determined by the Speaker." Even after the rules change, Speaker Tip O'Neill persisted in sending the conferees

suggested by Education and Labor Committee Chairman Carl Perkins (D, Kentucky), even though a majority of them clearly opposed the weakening Erlenborn amendment. The Speaker's decisions regarding the appointment of House conferees, by the way, are not subject to a point of order.

Chapter Seven

1. Actually, if either members of Congress or scholarly observers are to be believed, Congress's role in the formulation of public policy has been on the wane relative to the president from the very beginning of the Republic. In 1793, many in Congress, including James Madison, saw Washington's proclamation of neutrality in the conflict between England and France as a usurpation of legislative authority. Jefferson, Madison, and "King Andrew" Jackson were all seen by their contemporaries as dominating a disorganized Congress. Executive leadership during the Civil War and Reconstruction led J. M. Ashley (R, Ohio) to charge in 1869 that "the experience of the past quarter of a century demonstrates the fact that the whole power of the national Government is gradually but surely passing under the complete control of our Presidents" (quoted in Sundquist 1981, p. 15). During Wilson's second term, Black (1919) observed, "The President of the United States has grown into a position of overwhelming influence over the legislative department of government. He presents and procures the enactment of such measures as he desires, and prevents the passage of those which he disapproves. Congress is subservient to his will; its independence is in eclipse" (p. v).

2. There is a strong statutory basis for Dawes's views; the Budget and Accounting Act requires all agencies within the exective branch to designate a budget officer to serve as a liaison with the Budget Bureau and to provide the bureau with whatever "books, documents, papers, or records" it requested (Marx 1945, p. 669).

3. Congress adopted the original version of the Budget and Accounting Act in 1920—prior to approving the return of all annual appropriations legislation to the jurisdiction of the House Appropriations Committee. As Stewart (1989) notes, James Good (R, Iowa) and other proponents of the reforms had sought consideration of the two measures in this order, reasoning that passage of the noncontroversial Budget Act (it passed 285–3) would facilitate adoption of the more controversial measure to reconsolidate House Appropriations (the special order allowing floor consideration of the measure passed 158–154). What they had not anticipated was Wilson's veto of the bill on the grounds that the provision for the removal of the Comptroller General infringed upon the president's constitutional prerogatives. The bill was changed to provide for the removal of the Comptroller General by joint resolution, and it was in this form that Harding signed it in 1921.

4. James Good, Chairman of the Select Committee on the Budget as well

as of the House Appropriations Committee, charged that in the absence of an
executive budget:

> ... expenditures are not considered in connection with revenues; that
> Congress does not require of the President any carefully thought-out
> financial and work program representing what provision in his opinion
> should be made for meeting the financial needs of the Government;
> that the estimates of expenditure needs now submitted to Congress
> represent only the desires of the individual departments, establish-
> ments, and bureaus; and that these requests have been subjected to
> no superior revision with a view to bringing them into harmony with
> each other, to eliminating duplication of organization or activities,
> or of making them, as a whole, conform to the needs of the Nation
> as represented by the condition of the Treasury and prospective rev-
> enues ... The various bureau chiefs act independently of each other.
> Bureaus of executive departments doing similar work are thus stimu-
> lated in a rivalry, and so far as the estimates go, very little effort has
> been made to coordinate the activities of the several departments and
> bureaus, and in practice this method has resulted in extravagance,
> inefficiency, and duplication of service.
>
> The waste and extravagance resulting from the operation of this
> plan must be apparent to anyone who has a study of it. Practically
> every one familiar with its workings agrees that its failure lies in the
> fact that no one is made responsible for the extravagance. The esti-
> mates are a patchwork and not a structure. As a result, a great deal
> of the time of the committees of Congress is taken up in exploding
> the visionary schemes of bureau chiefs for which no administration
> would be willing to stand responsible. (House Select Committee on
> the Budget 1919, p. 4)

5. During the Civil War the federal government had levied a tax of 3 percent on incomes in the $600–$10,000 bracket and 5 percent on incomes over
$10,000. The tax was discontinued in 1872, however, and subsequent attempts
to reinstate—primarily by the Democrats—had been ruled unconstitutional.
In 1912, the Taft administration, in need of more revenues, reached a compromise with Democrats and Progressive Republicans. In return for their dropping
demands for an income tax, Taft agreed to a one-percent tax on corporate net
incomes (defined as an excise tax on "the privilege of doing busines") and to
not oppose introduction of a constitutional amendment that would permit
direct taxation of income. Taft and congressional Republican leaders believed
such an amendment would never be ratified, but they obviously miscalculated
(Studenski and Krooss, 1952 p. 272).

6. Upon regaining the Congress and the presidency, the Republicans took
major steps toward reversing Democratic tax policy. In 1922, the Republican
67th Congress passed the Fordney-McCumber Act, which replaced the relatively low rates of the Underwood Tariff with the highest average tariff rates

in U.S. history. Only seven of the 131 Democrats in the House supported the bill, while only seven of 301 Republicans voted against it. Revenues from the tariff rose from $308 million in FY1921 to over $600 million by FY1929. Successive rate reductions in 1921, 1924, 1926, and 1928 lowered the amount of revenue produced by individual and corporate income taxes from $3.2 billion in FY1921 to $2.3 billion in FY1929. During the same period, receipts from manufacturers' excise taxes dropped from $229 million to $6 million.

7. Bureaucrats apparently have a strong hoarding instinct, as caches of fugitive furniture were still being uncovered in government facilities as recently as a decade ago. In its 1980 Annual Report, the General Services Administration reports finding a pile of discarded chairs in the attic of the Pension Building, which, in their view, "should have been re-used, donated, or sold" (p. 14). Operation Clean Sweep, undertaken by GSA in response to this discovery, netted nearly 50,000 pieces of furniture valued at roughly $50 million.

8. Nixon vetoed an initial version of the legislation that would have abolished the offices of director and deputy director and then recreated them, thereby making the current Director Roy Ash and Deputy Director Fred Malek subject to Senate confirmation. He signed the bill after Ash and Malek were exempted.

Chapter Eight

1. The corollary hypothesis is that defense spending contracts (or at least expands more slowly) when the Democrats control Congress. The reason we choose not to examine defense spending in this chapter is primarily due to the limitations of the appropriations data; although there are about a dozen appropriations bills funding domestic programs, each containing dozens of programs and agencies, throughout most of our time series there is only one appropriations bill for the Department of Defense, broken down into only a small number of broad titles. We think that available data on appropriations and on budget resolutions (refer back to table 3.3) strongly support the hypothesis that Republicans are more supportive of defense spending. There is just not enough of it to justify a regression analysis of the kind undertaken in this chapter.

2. The limitations of this particular measure are shared by other indicators of a collectivity's characteristics. Many economists, such as Inman (1978), have taken as evidence for the median voter model the presence of a strong positive relationship between median measures (for example, income, tax share, and housing price) and the level of public goods supplied by various jurisdictions. As Romer and Rosenthal (1979) convincingly demonstrate, however, such inferences are subject to the "fractile fallacy." Replacing median values of these variables with values taken anywhere between their 20th and 80th percentile yields virtually identical R^2s, though dramatically different coefficients.

3. Some standard assumptions are required to properly characterize the

objective function defining spending choice in our model. First, we assume that in order to maximize their reelection prospects, members of Congress (and the president) prefer appropriation levels that equate marginal returns in electoral support across federal agencies. We also assume that voters' evaluations of candidates are a nondecreasing function of the appropriations awarded to agencies, but that members and the president experience declining marginal returns in electoral support from the appropriations awarded to each agency. It follows from these assumptions that unique vote-maximizing spending levels exist for each agency, for every member and for the president.

4. For the president's estimates to anticipate congressional reaction does not require that the president sit down, perhaps with his budget director, and calculate through backward induction the optimal request to submit to Congress for each agency and program. No doubt some such strategizing does occur at a fairly global level. As Fenno (1966) points out, however, anticipation of congressional reaction can also take place in a very decentralized fashion. In bargaining with program reviewers in the Budget Bureau, agency officials often argue that they cannot credibly defend budget estimates that are unrealistically low, but promise to loyally support estimates that are in line with the support the program enjoys in Congress.

Chapter Nine

1. Fiorina (1977), among others, suggests that incumbents are able to assure themselves of a virtual lock on reelection by intervening on behalf of constituents who, after having been caught up in some bureaucratic snafu, are unable to obtain remedy on their own. This scenario is in accord with popular images of lazy, erratic, and irresponsible bureaucrats, but actual research on the subject generates little evidence to support these common stereotypes. According to Katz et al. (1975), most respondents in their survey reported that in their encounters with government bureacracies they had been treated fairly, that their problem had been addressed with a reasonable degree of efficiency, and that the "people at the office" had worked hard to help them. This is not to say that public employees do not shirk, but rather that there is no compelling evidence that they are more prone to do so than private-sector workers.

2. Congressional concern that the power of the purse not slip away from them and to the executive was plainly evident in the special attention they gave to the design of the Treasury Department. The legislation of 1789 that established War and State characterized them as "executive departments," headed by "principal officers." Heads of these departments were directed to "perform and execute such duties as shall from time to time be enjoined on or entrusted to him by the President of the United States." The act creating Treasury, in contrast, referred to it only as a "department," made no mention of the

president, specifically directed it to prepare a variety of reports pertaining to government finances, and established below the Secretary several subordinate officers—a comptroller, auditor, treasurer, and register—all subject to Senate confirmation.

3. Wilmerding (1943) cites Wilson's (1956) description of an 1882 Senate Appropriations Committee investigation of the Treasury Department, which found that monies from the contingency fund ... "had been spent in repairs on the Secretary's private residence, for expensive suppers spread before the Secretary's political friends, for lemonade for the delectation of the Secretary's private palate, for bouquets for the gratification of the Secretary's busiest allies, for carpets never delivered, ice never used, and services never rendered; although these were secrets of which the honest faces of the vouchers submitted with the accounts gave not a hint (p. 237)." He is certainly correct that voucher audits cannot, in and of themselves, uncover fraud. But vouchers form the paper trails that enable subsequent investigations to take place and therefore surely discourage wrongdoing. Wilmerding's view is analogous to saying that it is not worthwhile for the Internal Revenue Service to audit 1040s because these forms do not reveal that individuals have failed to report income or have taken a deduction to which they were not entitled. In any case, filing phony expenditure vouchers or tax returns are in themselves criminal offenses.

4. Wilmerding documents occasional surges in congressional "oversight" activity in the nineteenth century. Most notably, in the 44th Congress, House Democrats went on an investigatory binge following the revelations of official corruption in the Credit Mobilier, Sanborn Contracts, and Whiskey Ring scandals. Their primary aim, however, was to press the electoral advantage gained from embarrassing the Republican Grant administration and not to establish an effective system of oversight.

5. Wilmerding (1943) quotes Henry Clay, who in 1819 regaled his colleagues in the House with the following anecdote:

> Some years ago it had been the custom, now abolished, to use in this House a beverage in lieu of water for those members who preferred it. A member of the House said he was not in the habit of using this sort of substitute for one of nature's greatest and purest bounties, but would prefer something stronger. The officers of the House said they should be glad to gratify him, but did not know how they could with propriety pay for it out of the contingent fund. Why, said the member, under what head of appropriation do you pay for this syrup for the use of the members? Under the head of stationery, the officer said. Well, replied the member, put down a little grog under the head of fuel, and let me have it. (p. 82)

6. In reality, the Budget Bureau had taken over management of the apportionment process soon after its inception (Pfiffner 1979).

7. In 1973, OMB Director Roy Ash testified before the House Rules Committee that Nixon's impoundments amounted to only 3.5 percent of expenditures and were therefore less than the 6.0 percent of the Kennedy administration. The discrepancy between Ash's figure and ours for the Nixon years (6.0 percent) is due to the fact that Ash did not include in his figures several billion dollars for water pollution control, housing, and several other programs. See Fisher (1975, pp. 172–73) for a discussion of the dissembling rationale Ash invoked to justify these omissions. Ash's 6.0 percent figure for impoundments during the Kennedy administration is also higher than our 4.5 percent figure, but we do not know the reason for this discrepancy.

8. At least it was according to Chief Justice William H. Rehnquist. While deputy attorney general in charge of the Office of Legal Counsel, he informed the Nixon White House in 1969 that "with respect to the suggestion that the President has a constitutional power to decline to spend appropriated funds, we must conclude that existence of such broad power is supported by neither reason nor precedent" (quoted in Glass 1973, p. 237).

9. As reported in chapter 4, the practice of underappropriating reappeared during the Reagan administration, when congressional Democrats frequently chose to fund crop subsidy payments, food stamps, and other entitlement programs for less than the entire fiscal year. The purpose here, of course, was to appear to meet budget resolution spending ceilings.

10. Although journalistic accounts of the S&L crisis suggest that the $120–150 billion simply vanished or that the crooks got most of it, the major beneficiaries of S&L failures were actually homeowners with pre-1980 mortgages, the legitimate real estate industry, and holders of brokered deposits (Thomas and Ricks 1990).

11. In 1981 Congress voted to extend GAO auditing authority to the Federal Home Loan Bank Board and the Federal Deposit Insurance Corporation. However, the legislation prohibited them from conducting on-site examinations of banks and bank holding companies without written consent of the relevant regulatory agency.

12. Forbearance for insolvent S&L's also injures healthy, well-run institutions that must compete with them, as the former are willing to pay higher rates of interest to attract depositors so as to make even more high risk loans. Across-the-board increases in deposit insurance premiums only increase further the subsidies healthy S&L's pay to the bad ones (Garcia 1988).

Chapter Ten

1. Riker (1964) argues that competing definitions of power are derived from different conceptions of causality, which are themselves inherently ambiguous and contradictory.

2. The Worm Gett'r, which retails for under $10, consists of two metal

probes that send an electrical shock into the ground, thereby inducing earthworms to move to the surface. It is an important labor-saving technology in Idaho's $5 million worm-harvesting industry. The CPSC alleges that such devices have caused twenty-eight deaths by electrocution over the past several years. Defenders of the Worm Gett'r argue that almost all of these deaths have actually resulted from the use of inferior homemade tools, for example, wired-together coat hangers (Pytte 1990).

3. This actually represents a considerable downsizing of the *Federal Register* from the peak of 87,000 pages reached in 1980. The Paperwork Reduction Act, subsequent restrictions on agency requests for information, and the central clearance of regulatory proposals by OIRA (see chapter 7) are primarily responsible for this decline.

References

Aberbach, Joel. 1990. *Keeping a Watchful Eye*. Washington, D.C.: The Brookings Institution.

Ainsworth, Scott, and Marcus Flathman. 1990. "Leadership in a Sparse Environment: A Formal Model of UCAs in the U.S. Senate." Paper presented at the Annual Meeting of the Midwest Political Science Association, Chicago, IL.

Alchian, Armen. 1950. "Uncertainty, Evolution, and Economic Theory." *Journal of Political Economy* 58:211–21.

Aldrich, John. 1988. "Modeling the Party-in-the-Legislature." Unpublished manuscript, Duke University.

American Political Science Association, Committee on Political Parties. 1950. "Toward a More Responsible Two-Party System." Supplement, *American Political Science Review* 44:1–99.

Arieff, Irwin. 1981. "Budget Fight Shows O'Neill's Fragile Grasp." *Congressional Quarterly Weekly Report* 39:786.

Arrow, Kenneth. 1951. *Social Choice and Individual Values*. New Haven, CT: Yale University Press.

Auten, Gerald, Barry Bozeman, and Robert Cline. 1984. "A Sequential Model of Congressional Appropriations." *American Journal of Political Science* 28:503–23.

Axelrod, Robert. 1984. *The Evolution of Cooperation*. New York, NY: Basic Books.

Bach, Stanley. 1986a. "Procedures for Reaching Legislative Agreement: A Case Study of H.R. 3128." Congressional Research Service Report.

————. 1986b. "Representatives and Committees on the Floor: Amendments to Appropriations Bills in the House of Representatives, 1963–82." *Congress and the Presidency* 13:40–58.

————, and Richard Sachs. 1989. "Legislation, Appropriations, and Limitations: The Effect of Procedural Change on Policy Choice." Paper presented at the Annual Meeting of the American Political Science Association, Atlanta, GA.

Bailey, Stephen, and Howard Samuel. 1965. *Congress at Work*. Hamden, CT: Archon Books.

Baiman, Stanley, and John Evans. 1983. "Pre-Decision Information and Participative Management Control Systems." *Journal of Accounting Research* 21:371–95.

Barton, Weldon. 1976. "Coalition Building in the U.S. House of Representatives: Agricultural Legislation." In James Anderson, ed., *Cases in Public Policy-Making*, pp. 100–115. New York, NY: Praeger Publishers.

Beloff, Max, and Gillian Peele. 1980. *The Government of the United Kingdom: Political Authority in a Changing Society*. New York, NY: W. W. Norton and Company.

Berman, Larry. 1979. *The Office of Management and Budget and the Presidency*. Princeton, NJ: Princeton University Press.

Black, Duncan. 1958. *Theory of Committees and Elections*. New York, NY: Cambridge University Press.

Black, Henry. 1919. *The Relation of the Executive Power to Legislation*. Princeton, NJ: Princeton University Press.

Brady, David. 1973. *Congressional Voting in a Partisan Era*. Lawrence, KS: University of Kansas Press.

——. 1988. *Critical Elections and Congressional Policymaking*. Stanford, CA: Stanford University Press.

——, and John Alford. 1988. "Personal and Partisan Advantage in U.S. House Elections, 1846–1986." Paper presented at the Southern California Political Behavior Seminar, La Jolla, CA.

——, and Mark Morgan. 1987. "Reforming the Structure of the House Appropriations Process: The Effects of the 1885 and 1919–1920 Reforms on Money Decisions." In Mathew McCubbins and Terry Sullivan, eds., *Congress: Structure and Policy*, pp. 207–34. New York, NY: Cambridge University Press.

——, and Barbara Sinclair. 1984. "Building Majorities for Policy Changes in the House of Representatives." *The Journal of Politics* 46:1033–60.

Browning, Robert. 1986. *Politics and Social Welfare Policy in the United States*. Knoxville: University of Tennessee Press.

Buchanan, James M. 1977. "Why Does Government Grow?" In Thomas E. Borcherding, ed., *Budgets and Bureaucrats: The Sources of Government Growth*, pp. 3–18. Durham, NC: Duke University Press.

——, and Gordon Tullock. 1962. *The Calculus of Consent: Logical Foundations of Constitutional Democracy*. Ann Arbor, MI: University of Michigan Press.

Bullock, Charles, and John Sprague. 1969. "A Research Note on the Committee Reassignments of Southern Democratic Congressmen." *Journal of Politics* 31:483–512.

Cain, Bruce. 1984. *The Reapportionment Puzzle*. Berkeley, CA: University of California Press.

Calmes, Jacqueline. 1985. "The Basis for Budget Options: Forecasts Are Rarely Reliable." *Congressional Quarterly Weekly Report* 43:1054.

——. 1990a. "Democrats Face Pitfalls in Drafting Own Plan." *Congressional Quarterly Weekly Report* 48:375–76.

——. 1990b. "OMB's Hard-Hitting Darman Leaves Scars on the Hill." *Congressional Quarterly Weekly Report* 48:91–94.

————. 1990c. "How Lasting Is the Legacy of the Reagan Era?" *Congressional Quarterly Weekly Report* 48:894–97.

Calvert, Randall. 1987. "Coordination and Power: The Foundation of Leadership among Rational Legislators." Paper presented at the Annual Meeting of the American Political Science Association, Chicago, IL.

Cameron, David. 1978. "The Expansion of the Public Economy: A Comparative Analysis." *American Political Science Review* 72:1243–61.

Campos, Jose Edgardo. 1988. "Committee Power: The Role of Jurisdictions." Unpublished manuscript, The Wharton School, University of Pennsylvania.

Cannon, Joseph. 1919. "The National Budget." *Harper's Magazine* 139:123–28.

Cater, Douglass. 1964. *Power in Washington.* New York, NY: Random House.

Chappell, Henry, and William R. Keech. 1985. "A New View of Political Accountability for Economic Performance." *American Political Science Review* 79:10–27.

Cobb, Richard, and Colin Jones, eds. 1988. *Voices of the French Revolution.* Topsfield, MA: Salem House Publishers.

Cogan, John F. 1988. "The Evolution of Congressional Budget Decision-making and the Emergence of Federal Deficits." Working Paper E-88-33, Domestic Studies Program, Hoover Institution.

Cohodas, Nadine. 1982. "House Judiciary Committee Bottles Up the Tough Ones." *Congressional Quarterly Weekly Report* 40:863–64.

Collie, Melissa. 1988. "Universalism and the Parties in the U.S. House of Representatives, 1921–80." *American Journal of Political Science* 32:865–83.

Cooper, Joseph. 1970. *The Origins of the Standing Committees and the Development of the Modern House.* Houston, TX: Rice University.

Cooper, Joseph, and Cheryl Young. 1989. "Bill Introduction in the Nineteenth Century: A Study of Institutional Change." *Legislative Studies Quarterly* 14:67–106.

Cox, Gary. 1987. *The Efficient Secret.* New York, NY: Cambridge University Press.

————, and Richard McKelvey. 1984. "Ham Sandwich Theorems for General Measures." *Social Choice and Welfare* 1:75–83.

Crawford, John. 1990. "Deposit-Insurance System Under Close Scrutiny." *Congressional Quarterly Weekly Report* 48:520–25.

Crawford, Vincent, and Hans Haller. 1988. "Learning How to Cooperate: Optimal Play in Repeated Coordination Games." Unpublished manuscript, University of California, San Diego.

Cummings, Milton, and Robert Peabody. 1963. "The Decision to Enlarge the Committee on Rules: An Analysis of the 1961 Vote." In Robert Peabody and Nelson Polsby, eds., *New Perspectives on the House of Representatives,* pp. 167–94. Chicago, IL: Rand McNally.

Davidson, Roger. 1985. "Senate Leaders: Janitors for an Untidy Chamber?" In Lawrence Dodd and Bruce Oppenheimer, eds., *Congress Reconsidered,* 3d ed., pp. 225–52. Washington, D.C.: Congressional Quarterly Press.

Davis, Joseph. 1985. "Reagan Gave OMB a Regulatory Veto . . . But Decision is Being Tested in Court." *Congressional Quarterly Weekly Report* 43:1816–17.

Davis, Kenneth. 1958. *Administrative Law Treatise.* St. Paul, MN: West Publishing.

———. 1969. *Discretionary Justice.* Baton Rouge, LA: Louisiana State University Press.

Davis, Lance, and Douglass North. 1971. *Institutional Change and American Economic Growth.* New York, NY: Cambridge University Press.

Davis, Otto, M. A. H. Dempster, and Aaron Wildavsky. 1966. "A Theory of the Budgetary Process." *American Political Science Review* 60:529–47.

———. 1974. "Toward a Predictive Theory of Government Expenditures: U.S. Domestic Appropriations." *British Journal of Political Science* 4:419–52.

Dawes, Charles. 1923. *The First Year of the Budget of the United States.* New York, NY: Harper and Brothers Publishers.

Day, Kathleen. 1989. "When Hell Sleazes Over: Judgement Day for S&L Slimeballs." *The New Republic* 200:26–30.

Demsetz, Harold. 1967. "Toward a Theory of Property Rights." *American Economic Review Papers and Proceedings* 57:347–59.

Demski, Joel, and David Kreps. 1982. "Models in Managerial Accounting." *Journal of Accounting Research* 20:117–48.

——— and D. Sappington. 1987. "Delegated Expertise." *Journal of Accounting Research* 25:68–89.

Denzau, Arthur, William Riker, and Kenneth Shepsle. 1985. "Farquarson and Fenno: Sophisticated Voting and Home Style." *American Political Science Review* 79:1117–34.

Deschler, Lewis. 1977. *Deschler's Precedents of the United States House of Representatives* (House Document 94–661). Washington, D.C.: GPO.

Dodd, Lawrence, and Bruce Oppenheimer. 1977. "The House in Transition." In Lawrence Dodd and Bruce Oppenheimer, eds., *Congress Reconsidered,* 1st ed., pp. 21–53. New York, NY: Praeger Publishers.

———, and Richard Schott. 1979. *Congress and the Administrative State.* New York, NY: John Wiley and Sons.

Donnelly, Harrison. 1981a. "House Approves 1981 Funding Measure." *Congressional Quarterly Weekly Report* 39:844–45.

———. 1981b. "Fiscal 1982 Funding Crisis Goes Down to the Wire." *Congressional Quarterly Weekly Report* 39:2272–74.

Downs, Anthony. 1957. *An Economic Theory of Democracy.* New York, NY: Harper and Row.

Dranove, David. 1987. "Rate-Setting by Diagnosis Related Groups and Hospital Specialization." *RAND Journal of Economics* 18:417–27.

Driscoll, Gerald. 1988. "Deposit Insurance in Theory and Practice." *Cato Journal* 7:661–74.

Drucker, Peter F. 1973. *Management: Tasks, Responsibilities, Practices.* New York, NY: Harper and Row.

Enelow, James, and Melvin Hinich. 1984. *The Spatial Theory of Voting: An Introduction.* New York, NY: Cambridge University Press.

Erikson, Robert, Norman Luttbeg, and Kent Tedin. 1991. *American Public Opinion: Its Origins, Content, and Impact.* New York, NY: Macmillan and Company.

————, and Gerald Wright. 1985. "Voters, Candidates, and Issues in Congressional Elections." In Lawrence Dodd and Bruce Oppenheimer, eds., *Congress Reconsidered*, 3d ed., pp. 87–108. Washington, D.C.: Congressional Quarterly Press.

Fair, Ray. 1978. "The Effect of Economic Events on Votes for President." *Review of Economics and Statistics* 60:159–73.

Fama, Eugene. 1980. "Agency Problems and the Theory of the Firm." *Journal of Political Economy* 88:288–307.

Farrell, Joseph, and Garth Saloner. 1985. "Standardization, Compatibility, and Innovation." *Rand Journal of Economics* 16:70–83.

————. 1987. "Coordination through Committees and Markets." Unpublished manuscript. Hoover Institution, Stanford University.

Fenno, Richard F. 1966. *The Power of the Purse: Appropriations Politics in Congress.* Boston, MA: Little, Brown, and Co.

————. 1973. *Congressmen in Committees.* Boston, MA: Little, Brown, and Co.

————. 1975. "If, as Ralph Nader says, Congress is the 'Broken Branch,' Why Do We Love Our Congressman So Much?" In Norman Ornstein, ed., *Congress in Change*, pp. 227–87. New York, NY: Praeger.

————. 1978. *Homestyle: House Members in Their Districts.* Boston, MA: Little, Brown, and Co.

Ferejohn, John. 1985. "Logrolling in an Institutional Context: A Case Study of Food Stamps Legislation." Working Paper P-85-5, Domestic Studies Program, Hoover Institution, Stanford University.

————, and Keith Krehbiel. 1987. "The Budget Process and the Size of the Budget." *American Journal of Political Science* 31:296–320.

Fiorina, Morris P. 1974. *Representatives, Roll Calls, and Constituencies.* Boston, MA: Lexington.

————. 1977. *Congress: Keystone of the Washington Establishment.* New Haven, CT: Yale University Press.

————. 1981a. "Congressional Control of the Bureaucracy: A Mismatch of Incentives and Capabilities." In Lawrence Dodd and Bruce Oppenheimer, eds., *Congress Reconsidered*, 2d ed., pp. 332–48. Washington, D.C.: Congressional Quarterly Press.

————. 1981b. *Retrospective Voting in American National Elections.* New Haven, CT: Yale University Press.

————. 1982. "Group Concentration and the Delegation of Legislative Authority." Social Science Working Paper 112, California Institute of Technology.

Fisher, Louis. 1975. *Presidential Spending Power.* Princeton, NJ: Princeton University Press.

———. 1982. "The Congressional Budget Act: Does It Have a Spending Bias?" Paper delivered at the Conference on the Congressional Budget Process, Carl Albert Congressional Research and Studies Center, University of Oklahoma.

———. 1984. "The Budget Act: A Further Loss of Spending Control." In Thomas Wander, Ted F. Hebert, and Gary Copeland, eds., *Congressional Budgeting: Politics, Process, and Power*, pp. 170–89. Baltimore, MD: Johns Hopkins University Press.

———. 1985. *Constitutional Conflicts Between Congress and the President*. Princeton, NJ: Princeton University Press.

Fowler, Linda. 1982. "How Interest Groups Select Issues for Rating Voting Records of Members of the U.S. Congress." *Legislative Studies Quarterly* 3:401–14.

Friedman, James. 1986. *Game Theory with Applications to Economics*. Oxford, UK: Oxford University Press.

Garcia, Gillian. 1988. "The FSLIC Is 'Broke' in More Ways than One." *Cato Journal* 7:727–41.

Garfield, James A. 1879. "National Appropriations and Misappropriations." *North American Review* 128:572–86.

General Accounting Office. 1986a. *Thrift Industry Problems: Potential Demands on the FSLIC Insurance Fund*. Washington, D.C.:GPO

———. 1986b. *Cost to FSLIC of Delaying Action on Insolvent Savings Institutions*. Briefing Report to the Chairman, Subcommittee on Commerce, Consumer, and Monetary Affairs, Government Operations Committee, House of Representatives. Washington, D.C.: GPO.

———. 1987. *Thrift Industry: Forbearance for Troubled Institutions 1982–1986*. Briefing Report to the Chairman, Subcommittee on Commerce, Consumer, and Monetary Affairs, Government Operations Committee, House of Representatives. Washington, D.C.: GPO.

———. 1989a. *Thrift Failures: Costly Failures Resulted from Regulatory Violations and Unsafe Practices*. Washington, D.C.: GPO.

———. 1989b. *CPA Audit Quality: Costly Failures Resulted from Regulatory Violations and Unsafe Practices*. Washington, D.C.: GPO.

General Services Administration. 1980. *Annual Report*. Washington, D.C.: GPO.

Gettinger, Stephen. 1984. "Conservative Strength Still High for Fourth Reagan Year." *Congressional Quarterly Weekly Report* 42:2820–25.

Gilligan, Thomas, and Keith Krehbiel. 1987. "Collective Decision-Making and Standing Committees: An Informational Rationale for Restrictive Amendment Procedures." *Journal of Law, Economics, and Organization* 3:287–335.

Gilmour, Robert. 1971. "Central Legislative Clearance: A Revised Perspective." *Public Administration Review* 31:150–58.

Glass, Andrew, 1973. "Congress Weighs Novel Procedures to Overturn Nixon Impoundment Policy." *National Journal* 5:236–42.

Glenn, Norval D. 1976. "Cohort Analysts' Futile Quest: Statistical Attempts to Separate Age, Period, and Cohort Effects." *American Sociological Review* 41:900–904.

Goodwin, George. 1970. *The Little Legislatures.* Amherst, MA: University of Massachusetts Press.

Granat, Diane. 1983a. "House Appropriations Panel Doles Out Cold Federal Cash, Chafes at Budget Procedures." *Congressional Quarterly Weekly Report* 41:1209–15.

———. 1983b. "Congress Clears Clean FY1984 Continuing Appropriations Bill." *Congressional Quarterly Weekly Report* 41:2023–25.

———. 1985. "House Committee Seats Filled: Assignments Delayed in the Senate." *Congressional Quarterly Weekly Report* 43:141–43.

Gregg, Gail. 1981. "Beleagured Budget Process Faces New Pressures in 1981." *Congressional Quarterly Weekly Report* 39:62–65.

Grossman, S., and O. Hart. 1983. "An Analysis of the Principal-Agent Problem." *Econometrica* 51:7–46.

Hager, George. 1989. "OMB Tampering of Testimony Hurts Bush's Credibility." *Congressional Quarterly Weekly Report* 47:1112.

Halberstam, David. 1986. *The Reckoning.* New York, NY: William Morrow and Company.

Hardin, Garrett. 1968. "The Tragedy of the Commons." *Science* 162:1243–48.

Hardin, Russell. 1982. *Collective Action.* Baltimore, MD: Johns Hopkins University Press.

Harlow, Ralph V. 1917. *The History of Legislative Methods in the Period Prior to 1825.* New Haven, CT: Yale University Press.

Harris, Joseph. 1964. *Congressional Control of Administration.* Washington, D.C.: The Brookings Institution.

Hasbrouck, Paul. 1927. *Party Government in the House of Representatives.* New York, NY: Macmillan Co.

Havemann, Joel. 1973. "OMB's Legislative Role Is Growing More Powerful and More Political." *National Journal* 5:1589–98.

———. 1978. *Congress and the Budget.* Bloomington, IN: Indiana University Press.

Havens, Harry. 1990. "The Evolution of the General Accounting Office: From Voucher Audits to Program Evaluations." Washington, D.C.: General Accounting Office.

Heclo, Hugh. 1975. "OMB and the Presidency: The Problem of Neutral Competence." *Public Interest* 38:80–98.

———. 1977. *A Government of Strangers: Executive Politics in Washington.* Washington, D.C.: The Brookings Institution.

———. 1984. "Executive Budget Making." In Gregory Mills and John Palmer, eds., *Federal Budget Policy in the 1980s*, pp. 255–91. Washington, D.C.: Urban Institute Press.

Hibbs, Douglas. 1977. "Political Parties and Macroeconomic Policy." *American Political Science Review* 71:467–87.

————, and Christopher Dennis. 1988. "Income Distribution in the United States." *American Political Science Review* 82:467–90.

Hirschman, Albert. 1970. *Exit, Voice, and Loyalty*. Cambridge, MA: Harvard University Press.

Hogg, Robert, and Allen Craig. 1978. *Introduction to Mathematical Statistics*, 4th ed. New York, NY: Macmillan and Company.

Holmström, Bengt. 1979. "Moral Hazard and Observability." *Bell Journal of Economics* 4:74–91.

Hook, Janet. 1986. "Congress Approves Increases in Treasury-Postal Funding." *Congressional Quarterly Weekly Report* 44:2744–45.

————. 1987. "Speaker Jim Wright Takes Charge in the House." *Congressional Quarterly Weekly Report* 45:1483–88.

House Budget Committee. 1983. *First Concurrent Resolution in the Budget, FY1984* (House Report 98:41). Washington, D.C.: GPO.

House Committee on Appropriations. 1948. *Report to Accompany H. R. 5214, Independent Offices Appropriations Bill, 1949* (House Report 80:1288). Washington, D.C.: GPO.

————. 1949. *Report to Accompany H. R. 4177, Independent Offices Appropriations Bill, 1950* (House Report 81:425). Washington, D.C.: GPO.

————. 1958. *Report on Independent Offices Appropriations Bill, 1959* (House Report 85:1543). Washington, D.C.: GPO.

House Committee on Government Operations. 1957. *Providing for Improved Methods of Stating Budget Estimates for Deficiency and Supplemental Appropriations: Report to Accompany H. R. 8002* (House Report 85:572). Washington, D.C.: GPO.

House Select Committee on the Budget. 1919. *To Provide National Budget System and Independent Audit of Government Accounts: Report to Accompany H. R. 83* (House Report 66:362). Washington, D.C.: GPO.

————. 1921a. *National Budget System: Report to Accompany H.R. 30* (House Report 67:14). Washington, D.C.: GPO.

————. 1921b. *Communication from the President of the United States Transmitting Laws Relating to the Estimates of Appropriations, the Appropriations, and Reports of Receipts and Expenditures* (House Report 67:129). Washington, D.C.: GPO.

Huitt, Ralph K. 1961. "Democratic Party Leadership in the Senate." *American Political Science Review* 55:331–44.

Hull, S. and L. Peter. 1969. *The Peter Principle*. New York, NY: Bantam Books.

Huntington, Samuel. 1965. "Congressional Responses to the Twentieth Century." In David B. Truman, ed., *The Congress and America's Future*, pp. 5–31. New York, NY: Prentice-Hall.

Inman, Robert. 1978. "Testing Political Economy's 'As-If' Proposition: Is the Median Voter Really Decisive?" *Public Choice* 33:45–66.

Inter-Parliamentary Union. 1986. *Parliaments of the World: A Comparative Reference Compendium*. Aldershot, UK: Gower Publishing Company, Ltd.

Jacobson, Gary. 1987. *The Politics of Congressional Elections*. Boston, MA: Little, Brown, and Co.

—— and Samuel Kernell. 1981. *Strategy and Choice in Congressional Elections*. New Haven, CT: Yale University Press.

Joint Study Committee on Budgetary Control. 1973. *Recommendations for Improving Congressional Control over Budgetary Outlay and Receipt Totals* (House Report 93-147). Washington, D.C.: GPO.

Jones, Charles. 1968. "Joseph G. Cannon and Howard W. Smith: An Essay on the Limits of Leadership in the House of Representatives." *Journal of Politics* 30:617–46.

Kamlet, Mark, and David Mowery. 1987. "Influences on Executive and Congressional Budgetary Priorities, 1955–1981." *American Political Science Review* 81:155–78.

Kanodia, Chandra. 1987. "Stochastic Monitoring and Moral Hazard." *Journal of Accounting Research* 23:175–93.

Katz, Daniel, Barbara Gutek, Robert Kahn, and Eugenia Barton. 1975. *Bureaucratic Encounters: A Pilot Study in the Evaluation of Government Services*. Ann Arbor, MI: Institute for Social Research, University of Michigan.

Keller, Morton. 1977. *Affairs of State*. Cambridge, MA: The Belknap Press of Harvard University Press.

Kennedy, David. 1980. *Over Here: The First World War and American Society*. New York, NY: Oxford University Press.

Kiewiet, D. Roderick. 1983. *Macroeconomics and Micropolitics*. Chicago, IL: University of Chicago Press.

Kiewiet, D. Roderick, and Mathew McCubbins. 1985a. "Congressional Appropriations and the Electoral Connection." *Journal of Politics* 47 (1985):59–82.

——. 1985b. "Appropriations Decisions as a Bilateral Bargaining Game between President and Congress." *Legislative Studies Quarterly* 9:181–202.

——. 1988. "Presidential Influence on Congressional Appropriations Decisions." *American Journal of Political Science* 32:713–36.

Kintner, Earl. 1978. *A Primer on the Law of Deceptive Practices*. New York, NY: Macmillan and Company.

Kirst, Michael. 1969. *Government Without Passing Laws: Congress' Nonstatutory Techniques for Appropriations Control*. Chapel Hill, NC: The University of North Carolina Press.

Kramer, Gerald. 1971. "Short-term Fluctuations in U.S. Voting Behavior, 1896–1964." *American Political Science Review* 65:131–43.

Krehbiel, Keith. 1987. "Institutional Erosion of Committee Power." *American Political Science Review* 81:929–35.

——. 1988. "Spatial Models of Legislative Choice." *Legislative Studies Quarterly* 13:259–320.

Legler, John. 1967. "Regional Distribution of Federal Receipts and Expenditures in the Nineteenth Century: A Quantitative Study." Ph.D. dissertation, Purdue University.

LeLoup, Lance. 1980. *The Fiscal Congress: Legislative Control of the Budget.* Westport, CT: Greenwood Press.

Lester, Robert. 1969. "Developments in Presidential-Congressional Relations: F.D.R.-J.F.K." Ph.D. dissertation, University of Virginia.

Levine, Michael, and Charles Plott. 1981. "Agenda Influence and Its Implications." *Virginia Law Review* 63:561-604.

Livermore, Seward. 1966. *Woodrow Wilson and the War Congress, 1916-18.* Seattle, WA: University of Washington Press.

Longley, Lawrence, and Walter Oleszek. 1989. *Bicameral Politics: Conference Committees in Congress.* New Haven, CT: Yale University Press.

Lowery, David, Samuel Bookheimer, and James Malachowski. 1985. "Partisanship in the Appropriations Process: Fenno Revisited." *American Politics Quarterly* 13:188-99.

Lowi, Theodore J. 1979. *The End of Liberalism: The Second Republic of the United States.* New York, NY: W. W. Norton and Co.

Maass, Arthur. 1983. *Congress and the Common Good.* New York, NY: Basic Books.

McCubbins, Mathew, Roger Noll, and Barry Weingast. 1989. "Structure and Process, Politics and Policy: Administrative Arrangements and the Political Control of Agencies." *Virginia Law Review* 75:431-82.

———, Roger Noll, and Barry Weingast. 1987. "Administrative Procedures as an Instrument of Political Control." *Journal of Law, Economics, and Organization* 3:243-77.

———, and Thomas Schwartz. 1984. "Congressional Oversight Overlooked: Police Patrols versus Fire Alarms." *American Journal of Political Science* 28:165-79.

———, and Terry Sullivan, eds. 1987. *Congress: Structure and Policy.* New York, NY: Cambridge University Press.

McCurdy, Karen. 1989. "New Constituency Integration: The House Interior Committee and Environmental Policy." Paper presented at the Annual Meeting of the Midwest Political Science Association, Chicago, IL.

Maddala, G. S. 1977. *Econometrics.* New York, NY: McGraw-Hill.

Manley, John. 1970. *The Politics of Finance.* Boston, MA: Little, Brown, and Company.

———. 1977. "The Conservative Coalition in Congress." In Lawrence Dodd and Bruce Oppenheimer, eds., *Congress Reconsidered,* 1st ed. pp. 75-95. New York, NY: Praeger Press.

Marvick, Duane. 1952. "Congressional Appropriations Politics." Ph.D. dissertation, Columbia University.

Marx, Fritz Morstein. 1945. "The Bureau of the Budget: Its Evolution and Present Role." *American Political Science Review* 39:653-84.

Mason, Karen, William Mason, H. H. Winsborough, and Kenneth W. Poole. 1973. "Some Methodological Issues in the Cohort Analysis of Archival Data." *American Sociological Review* 38:242-58.

Masters, Nicholas. 1961. "Committee Assignments in the House of Representatives." *American Political Science Review* 55:33-58.

Mayhew, David. 1974. *Congress: The Electoral Connection.* New Haven, CT: Yale University Press.

Melnick, R. Shep. 1983. *Regulation and the Courts: The Case of the Clean Air Act.* Washington, D.C.: The Brookings Institution.

Mirrlees, James. 1976. "The Optimal Structure of Incentives and Authority within an Organization." *The Bell Journal of Economics* 7:105–31.

Moe, Terry. 1984. "The New Economics of Organization." *American Journal of Political Science* 28:739–77.

———. 1985. "The Politicized Presidency." In John Chubb and Paul Peterson, eds., *The New Direction in American Politics*, pp. 235–72. Washington, D.C.: The Brookings Institution.

Morehouse, Macon. 1989. "Darman Reassures, but Panel Wary." *Congressional Quarterly Weekly Report* 47:1253.

Morgan, H. Wayne. 1969. *From Hayes to McKinley: National Party Politics, 1877–1896.* Syracuse, NY: Syracuse University Press.

Mosher, Frederick. 1984. *A Tale of Two Agencies: A Comparative Analysis of the GAO and OMB.* Baton Rouge, LA: Louisiana State University Press.

Munger, Michael. 1988. "Allocation of Desirable Committee Assignments: Extended Queues versus Committee Expansion." *American Journal of Political Science* 32:317–44.

Nagler, Jonathan. 1989. "Strategic Implications of Conferee Selection in the House of Representatives: It Ain't Over 'Til It's Over." *American Politics Quarterly* 17:54–79.

Neustadt, Richard. 1954. "Presidency and Legislation: The Growth of Central Clearance." *American Political Science Review* 48:641–71.

———. 1955. "Presidency and Legislation: Planning the President's Program." *American Political Science Review* 49:980–1021.

Niskanen, William A. 1971. *Bureaucracy and Representative Government.* Chicago, IL: Aldine-Atherton.

Noll, Roger, and Bruce Owen. 1983. *The Political Economy of Deregulation.* Washington, D.C.: American Enterprise Institute.

Norris, George. 1945. *Fighting Liberal.* New York, NY: Macmillan and Co.

Ogul, Morris. 1976. *Congress Oversees the Bureaucracy.* Pittsburgh, PA: University of Pittsburgh Press.

Oleszek, Walter. 1984. *Congressional Procedures and the Policy Process*, 2d ed. Washington, D.C.: Congressional Quarterly Press.

Olson, Mancur. 1965. *The Logic of Collective Action.* Cambridge, MA: Harvard University Press.

Oppenheimer, Bruce. 1977. "The Rules Committee: New Arm of Leadership in a Decentralized House." In Lawrence Dodd and Bruce Oppenheimer, eds., *Congress Reconsidered*, 1st ed. New York, NY: Praeger Press.

Ordeshook, Peter, and Thomas Schwartz. 1987. "Agendas and the Control of Political Outcomes." *American Political Science Review* 81:179–99.

Palazzolo, Dan. 1988. "The Speaker's Relationship with the House Budget Committee: Assessing the Effect of Contextual Change and Individual

Leader Discretion on a Leadership Committee." Paper presented at the Annual Meeting of the Midwest Political Science Association, Chicago, IL.

Paletz, David. 1970. "Influence in Congress: An Analysis of the Nature and Effects of Conference Committees." Ph.D. dissertation, University of California at Los Angeles.

Paltrow, Scot. 1989. "Insider Trading Tipsters: SEC Lets Your Fingers Do the Finking." *Los Angeles Times*, 29 July, part IV, p. 1.

Petrocik, John. 1987, "Realignment: New Party Coalitiions and the Nationalization of the South." *Journal of Politics*, 49:347–375.

Pertschuk, Michael. 1982. *Revolt Against Regulation*. Berkeley, CA: University of California Press.

Peterson, Paul. 1985. "The New Politics of Deficits." In John Chubb and Paul Peterson, eds., *The New Direction in American Politics*, pp. 365–98. Washington, D.C.: The Brookings Institution.

Pfiffner, James. 1979. *The President, the Budget, and Congress: Impoundment and the 1974 Budget Act*. New York, NY: Westview Press.

Plott, Charles. 1967. "A Notion of Equilibrium and Its Possibility Under Majority Rule." *American Economic Review* 57:787–806.

———. 1982. "Committee Karate." Unpublished manuscript, California Institute of Technology.

Poole, Keith. 1988. "Recent Developments in Analytical Models of Voting in the U.S. Congress." *Legislative Studies Quarterly* 13:117–134.

———, and Howard Rosenthal. 1984. "The Polarization of American Politics." *Journal of Politics* 46:1061–79.

———. 1985. "A Spatial Model for Legislative Roll Call Analysis." *American Journal of Political Science* 29:357–84.

———. 1987. "The Regional Realignment of Congress, 1919–84." In Peter Calderisi et. al., eds., *The Politics of Realignment: Party Change in the Mountain West*, pp. 101–28. Boulder, CO: Westview Press.

Poole, Keith, and Stephen Spear. 1989. "Statistical Properties of Metric Unidimensional Scaling." GSIA Working Paper 88-89-94, Carnegie-Mellon University, Pittsburgh, PA.

Pytte, Alyson. 1990. "Consumer Panel Goes Adrift Under Constant Meddling." *Congressional Quarterly Weekly Report* 48:659–63.

Raff, George W. 1866. *The War Claimant's Guide: A Manual of Laws, Regulations, Instructions, Forms, and Official Decisions, Relating to Pensions, Bounty, Pay, Prize Money, Salvage, Applications for Artificial Limbs, Compensation for Steamboats, Cars, Horses, Clothing, Slaves, and Other Property Lost or Damaged, Commutation of Rations, Travel, etc., and the Prosecution of All Claims Against the Government Growing Out of the War of 1861–1865*. Cincinnati, OH.

Redburn, Tom. 1989. "Lawmakers Become Masters of Illusion When It Comes to Gramm-Rudman Law." *Los Angeles Times*, 16 October, p. A12.

Redman, Eric. 1973. *The Dance of Legislation*. New York, NY: Simon and Schuster.

Reed, Thomas B. 1892. "Appropriations for the Nation." *North American Review* 154:319–28.

Reid, T. R. 1980. *Congressional Odyssey: The Saga of a Senate Bill.* San Francisco, CA: W. H. Freeman and Company.

Riker, William. 1964. "Some Ambiguities in the Notion of Power." *American Political Science Review* 58 (1964): 341–49.

———. 1980. "Implications from the Disequilibrium of Majority Rule for the Study of Institutions." *American Political Science Review* 74:432–47.

———. 1986. *The Art of Political Manipulation.* New Haven, CT: Yale University Press.

Ripley, Randall. 1967. *Party Leaders in the House of Representatives.* Washington, D.C.: The Brookings Institution.

———. 1969. *Majority Party Leadership in Congress.* Boston, MA: Little, Brown, and Company.

———, and Grace Franklin. 1980. *Congress, the Bureaucracy, and Public Policy.* Homewood, IL: Dorsey Press.

Roberts, Steven, and Gary Cohen. 1990. "Villains of the S&L Crisis." *U.S. News and World Report* 109:53–59.

Rohde, David. 1986. "Something's Happening Here; What It Is Ain't Exactly Clear: Southern Democrats in the House of Representatives." Paper presented at the Conference in Honor of Richard Fenno in Rochester, NY.

———. 1988. "Variations in Partisanship in the House of Representatives, 1953–1988: Southern Democrats, Realignment, and Agenda Change." Paper presented at the Annual Meeting of the American Political Science Association, Washington, D.C.

Romer, Thomas, and Howard Rosenthal. 1979. "The Elusive Median Voter." *Journal of Public Economics* 12:143–70.

Romer, Thomas, and Barry Weingast. 1990. "Political Foundations of the Thrift Debacle." Working Paper P-90-8, Domestic Studies Program, Hoover Institution.

Rosen, Bernard. 1989. *Holding Government Bureaucracies Accountable.* New York, NY: Praeger Press.

Rovner, Julie. 1986. "OMB's Regulatory Activities Draw Fire in Congress, Courts." *Congressional Quarterly Weekly Report* 44:1339–41.

Rubin, Irene. 1990. *The Politics of Federal Budgeting: Getting and Spending, Borrowing and Balancing.* Chatham, NJ: Chatham House Publishers.

Salmore, Barbara, and Stephen Salmore. 1987. "Back to Basics: Party as Legislative Caucus." Paper presented at the Annual Meeting of the Midwest Political Science Association, Chicago, IL.

Sarasohn, Judy. 1983. "House OKs Money Bill with West Front Funds." *Congressional Quarterly Weekly Report* 41:1086–87.

Satterthwaite, Mark. 1975. "Strategy-Proofness and Arrow's Conditions: Existence and Correspondence Theorems for Voting Procedures and Social Welfare Functions." *Journal of Economic Theory* 10:187–217.

Schick, Allen. 1976. "Congress and the 'Details' of Administration." *Public Administration Review* 36:516–28.

————. 1980. *Congress and Money.* Washington, D.C.: The Urban Institute.

————. 1984. "The Budget as an Instrument of Presidential Policy." In Lester Salamon and Michael Lund, eds., *The Reagan Presidency and the Governing of America*, pp. 91–125. Washington, D.C.: The Urban Institute.

————. 1986. *Crisis in the Budget Process: Exercising Political Choice.* Washington, D.C.: American Enterprise Institute.

Schneider, Jerrold E. 1979. *Ideological Coalitions in Congress.* Westport, CT: Greenwood Press.

Selko, Daniel. 1940. *The Federal Financial System.* Washington, D.C.: The Brookings Institution.

Selten, Reinhard. 1975. "Reexamination of the Perfectness Concept for Equilibrium Points in Extensive Games." *International Journal of Game Theory* 4:25–55.

Senate Committee on Appropriations. 1958. *Providing for Improved Methods of Stating Budget Estimates: Report to Accompany H.R. 8002* (Senate Report 85:1866). Washington, D.C.: GPO.

————. 1989. *Report to Accompany H. R. 4775, Treasury, Postal Service, and General Government Appropriations Bill, 1990* (Senate Report 100:387). Washington, D.C.: GPO.

Senate Committee on Government Operations. 1956. *Improving Governmental Budgeting and Accounting Methods and Procedures: Report to Accompany S. R. 3897* (Senate Report 84:2265). Washington, D.C.: GPO.

Shaffer, William R. 1980. *Party and Ideology in the United States Congress.* Washington, D.C.: University Press of America.

Shelley, Mack C. 1983. *The Permanent Majority: The Conservative Coalition in the United States Congress.* Birmingham, AL: The University of Alabama Press.

Shepsle, Kenneth. 1978. *The Giant Jigsaw Puzzle.* Chicago: The University of Chicago Press.

————. 1979. "Institutional Arrangements and Equilibrium in Multidimensional Voting Models." *American Journal of Political Science* 57:27–59.

————. 1988. "The Changing Textbook Congress: Equilibrium Congressional Institutions and Behavior." Center for American Political Studies Occasional Paper 88-3, Harvard University.

————, and Brian Humes. 1984. "Legislative Leadership: Organizational Entrepreneurs as Agents." Paper presented at the Conference on Adaptive Institutions, Stanford University, Palo Alto, CA.

————, and Barry Weingast. 1987a. "The Institutional Foundations of Committee Power." *American Political Science Review* 81:86–108.

————. 1987b. "Reflections on Committee Power." *American Political Science Review* 81:935–45.

Sinclair, Barbara. 1983. *Majority Leadership in the U.S. House.* Baltimore, MD: The Johns Hopkins University Press.

Skladony, Thomas. 1985. "The House at Work: Select and Standing Committees in the U.S. House of Representatives, 1789–1818." Paper presented at the Annual Meeting of the Midwest Political Science Association, Chicago, IL.

Skowronek, Stephen. 1982. *Building the New American State: The Expansion of National Administrative Capacities, 1877–1920.* New York, NY: Cambridge University Press.

Smith, Steven. 1989. *Call to Order: Floor Politics in the House and Senate.* Washington, D.C.: Brookings Institution.

———, and Stanley Bach. 1988. "Craftsmanship on Capitol Hill: The Pattern of Diversity in Special Rules." Paper presented at the Annual Meeting of the Midwest Political Science Association, Chicago, IL.

———, and Christopher Deering. 1984. *Committees in Congress.* Washington, D.C.: Congressional Quarterly Press.

Sorauf, Frank. 1976. *Party Politics in America.* Boston, MA: Little, Brown, and Co.

Spence, A. Michael. 1974. *Market Signalling: Informational Transfer in Hiring and Related Screening Processes.* Cambridge, MA: Harvard University Press.

Stanga, John, and James Sheffield. 1987. "The Myth of Zero Partisanship: Attitudes toward American Political Parties, 1964–84." *American Journal of Political Science* 31:829–55.

Steiner, Gil. 1951. *The Congressional Conference Committee: Seventieth to Eightieth Congresses.* Urbana, IL: University of Illinois Press.

Stern, Mark. 1989. "John F. Kennedy and Civil Rights: From Congress to the Presidency." *Presidential Studies Quarterly* 4:797–823.

Stewart, Charles. 1988. "Changes in Latitude, Changes in Magnitude: Spending Decisions and Institutions in the House after the Civil War." Paper presented at the Conference on Legislative Institutions, Practices, and Behavior, Stanford, CA.

———. 1989. *Budget Reform Politics.* New York, NY: Cambridge University Press.

Stewart, Richard. 1975. "The Reformation of American Administrative Law." *Harvard Law Review* 88:1669–1813.

Stiglitz, Joseph. 1974. "Incentives and Risk-Sharing in Sharecropping." *Review of Economic Studies* 41:219–55.

———. 1986. "The New Developmental Economics." *World Development* 14:257–65.

Stockman, David. 1986. *The Triumph of Politics: How the Reagan Revolution Failed.* New York, NY: Harper and Row.

Strom, Kaare. 1984. "Minority Governments in Parliamentary Democracies: The Rationality of Nonwinning Cabinet Solutions." *Comparative Political Studies* 17:199–227.

Studenski, Paul, and Herman Krooss. 1952. *Financial History of the United States.* New York, NY: McGraw-Hill.

Sundquist, James L. 1968. *Politics and Policy: The Eisenhower, Kennedy, and Johnson Years.* Washington, D.C.: The Brookings Institution.

———. 1981. *The Decline and Resurgence of Congress.* Washington, D.C.: Brookings Institution.

Tate, Dale. 1981. "'Pro Forma' Budget Resolution Reported." *Congressional Quarterly Weekly Report* 39:2271.

———. 1982. "'Constitutional Debate Prompts Interest in Reform of Congress' Budget Process." *Congressional Quarterly Weekly Report* 40:1890–91.

Taylor, Edward. 1941. *A History of the Committee on Appropriations.* Washington, D.C.: GPO.

Thomas, Paulette, and Thomas Ricks. 1990. "Tracing the Billions: Just What Happened to All That Money Savings & Loans Lost?" *Wall Street Journal,* 5 November, pp. A1–A6.

Tirole, Jean. 1986. "Hierarchies and Bureaucracies: On the Role of Coercion in Organizations. *Journal of Law, Economics, and Organization* 2:181–214.

Truman, David. 1959. *The Congressional Party.* New York, NY: John Wiley & Sons.

Tufte, Edward. 1978. *Political Control of the Economy.* Princeton, NJ: Princeton University Press.

Wattenberg, Martin. 1984. *The Decline of American Political Parties, 1952–80.* Cambridge, MA: Harvard University Press.

Wallenstein, Peter. 1987. *From Slave South to New South: Public Policy in Nineteenth-Century Georgia.* Chapel Hill, NC: University of North Carolina Press.

Wayne, Stephen. 1978. *The Legislative Presidency.* New York, NY: Harper & Row.

Wehr, Elizabeth. 1985. "Trouble Brewing as Congress Moves to Reduce Spending." *Congressional Quarterly Weekly Report* 43:1863.

———. 1986a. "Congress Clears $576 Billion Spending Measure." *Congressional Quarterly Weekly Report* 44:2584–87.

———. 1986b. "Fight Brewing Over Spending 'Deferrals."' *Congressional Quarterly Weekly Report* 44:491–92.

———. 1987. "Loyalty Test: Party First, Committee Second?" *Congressional Quarterly Weekly Report* 45:1720.

Weingast, Barry. 1988. "Floor Behavior in Congress: Committee Power Under the Open Rule." Paper presented at the Hoover Institution Conference on Legislative Institutions, Practices, and Behavior, Stanford, CA.

———. 1989. "Floor Behavior in Congress: Committee Power Under the Open Rule." *American Political Science Review* 83:795–815.

———, and William Marshall. 1988. "The Industrial Organization of Congress; or, Why Legislatures, Like Firms, Are Not Organized as Markets." *Journal of Political Economy* 96:132–63.

Weinstein, Henry. 1989. "Lawsuit Alleges $20 Billion in Stealth Fraud." *Los Angeles Times,* 7 November, D2.

White, Halbert. 1980. "A Heteroskedasticity-Consistent Covariance Matrix Estimator and a Direct Test for Heteroskedasticity." *Econometrica* 48: 817–38.

White, Joseph. 1988. "The Continuing Resolution: A Crazy Way to Govern?" *The Brookings Review* 6:28–35.

——. 1989. "The Power and Function of the House Appropriations Committee." Ph.D. dissertation, University of California, Berkeley, CA.

——. 1990. "The Presidential Budget." Unpublished manuscript, Brookings Institution, Washington, D.C.

——, and Wildavsky, Aaron. 1989. *The Deficit and the Public Interest.* Berkeley, CA: University of California Press.

Wildavsky, Aaron. 1974. *The Politics of the Budgetary Process*, 2d ed. Boston, MA: Little, Brown, and Company.

Williamson, Oliver. 1975. *Markets and Hierarchies: Analysis and Antitrust Implications.* New York, NY: The Free Press.

Willoughby, William. 1936. *The Government of Modern States.* New York, NY: Appleton Century Co.

Wilmerding, Lucius. 1943. *The Spending Power: A History of the Efforts of Congress to Control Expenditures.* New Haven, CT: Yale University Press.

Wilson, Woodrow. 1956. *Congressional Government.* Baltimore, MD: The Johns Hopkins University Press. Originally published in 1885 in Boston, MA, by Houghton-Mifflin.

Wlezian, Christopher. 1989. "The Political Economy of the Budgetary System." Ph.D. dissertation, University of Iowa.

Index